The History of the Jews i
Early Modern Italy

MW00789522

Challenging traditional historiographical approaches, this book offers a new history of Italian Jews in the early modern age. The fortunes of the Jewish communities of Italy in their various aspects – demographic, social, economic, cultural, and religious – can only be understood if these communities are integrated into the picture of a broader European, or better still, global system of Jewish communities and populations; and, that this history should be analyzed from within the dense web of relationships with the non-Jewish surroundings that enveloped the Italian communities. The book presents new approaches on such essential issues as ghettoization, antisemitism, the Inquisition, the history of conversion, and Jewish-Christian relations. It sheds light on the autonomous culture of the Jews in Italy, focusing on case studies of intellectual and cultural life using a micro-historical perspective. This book was first published in Italy in 2014 by one of the leading scholars on Italian Jewish history.

This book will appeal to students and scholars alike studying and researching Jewish history, early modern Italy, early modern Jewish and Italian culture, and early modern society.

Marina Caffiero is honorary professor of History at the University of Rome La Sapienza. A scholar of the social and cultural history of early modern and modern Europe, her research focuses on religious history and the relationship between politics and religion in Italy and Europe between the 16th and 19th centuries, the history of minorities, particularly Jewish minorities, gender history, and women's writings. She has published numerous monographs and edited collections as well as articles in Italian and other languages.

Routledge Studies in Early Modern Religious Dissents and Radicalism

Series editors: Federico Barbierato, Hannah Marcus, Stefano Villani and Xenia von Tippelskirch

Titles in this series address the discursive constructions of religious dissent and the practices of radical movements in the early modern world. The series transcends traditional national and confessional historiographies to examine early modern religious culture as a dynamic system that was essential in forging complex identities and encouraging dialogue among them. The editors seek manuscripts that consider questions of dissent, radicalism, dissidence, libertinism, heresy, and heterodoxy, and that examine these themes historically as socio-cultural constructions.

British Protestant Missions and the Conversion of Europe, 1600–1900
Edited By Simone Maghenzani, Stefano Villani

Bodies in Early Modern Religious Dissent
Naked, Veiled, Vilified, Worshiped
Edited By Elisabeth Fischer, Xenia von Tippelskirch

Early Modern Diasporas
A European History
Mathilde Monge and Natalia Muchnik

The History of the Jews in Early Modern Italy
From the Renaissance to the Restoration
Marina Caffiero

For more information about this series, please visit: https://www.routledge.com/

The History of the Jews in Early Modern Italy

From the Renaissance to the Restoration

Marina Caffiero

**Translated by
Paul M. Rosenberg**

Routledge
Taylor & Francis Group

LONDON AND NEW YORK

First published in English 2022
by Routledge
4 Park Square, Milton Park, Abingdon, Oxon OX14 4RN

and by Routledge
605 Third Avenue, New York, NY 10158

Routledge is an imprint of the Taylor & Francis Group, an informa business

Translated by Paul M. Rosenberg

Published in Italian by Carocci 2014

British Library Cataloguing-in-Publication Data
A catalogue record for this book is available from the British Library

Library of Congress Cataloging-in-Publication Data
Names: Caffiero, Marina, author. | Rosenberg, Paul M., translator.
Title: The history of the Jews in early modern Italy : from the
renaissance to the restoration / Marina Caffiero ; translated by
Paul M. Rosenberg.
Other titles: Storia degli ebrei nell'Italia moderna. English | From
the renaissance to the restoration
Description: Abingdon, Oxon ; New York : Routledge, 2022. |
Series: Routledge studies in early modern religious dissents and
radicalism | Includes bibliographical references and index.
Identifiers: LCCN 2021057800 (print) | LCCN 2021057801 (ebook) |
ISBN 9781032036687 (hardback) | ISBN 9781032036694 (paperback) |
ISBN 9781003188445 (ebook)
Subjects: LCSH: Jews—Italy—History—16th century. | Jews—
Italy—History—17th century. | Italy—Ethnic relations—History.
Classification: LCC DS135.I8 C33513 2022 (print) |
LCC DS135.I8 (ebook) | DDC 305.892/4045—dc23/eng/20220105
LC record available at https://lccn.loc.gov/2021057800
LC ebook record available at https://lccn.loc.gov/2021057801

ISBN: 978-1-032-03668-7 (hbk)
ISBN: 978-1-032-03669-4 (pbk)
ISBN: 978-1-003-18844-5 (ebk)

DOI: 10.4324/9781003188445

Typeset in Times New Roman
by codeMantra

Contents

Figures

Foreword

The publication in English of Marina Caffiero's last important contribution to the history of Italian Judaism is intended as a respectful homage to the conclusion of her academic career. It was therefore with great pleasure that the Foundation for the Museo Ebraico di Roma accepted the proposal to contribute to the translation of the text, as an act of gratitude not only to a scholar of rare worth but also to a friend. The relations of mutual esteem that bind us date back to the early years of the much needed renovation of the Museo Ebraico di Roma, given its current appearance in 2005. This was achieved thanks to the determination of the then director, my sister Daniela Di Castro z.l., who until 2010, the year of her untimely death, kept up a continuous and fruitful dialogue with Marina Caffiero.

The scenic presentation in 2008 of Caffiero's volume *Rubare le annime. Diario di Anna del Monte, ebrea romana*, a text in which the scholar tells a compelling story of resistance and pride in identity with passion and clarity, was unforgettable. On that occasion, and to accentuate its singularity, we put on display for the first time a ceremonial fabric that celebrated the return of the young Jewish woman to the ghetto, an event recounted years later by her brother, the man of letters Tranquillo Del Monte.

The publication of the English translation of *Storia degli ebrei in Italia* – The History of the Jews in Early Modern Italy – thus aims to fill a still existing gap in the circulation of Marina Caffiero's studies on the history of Italian Jews, and those on Rome in particular, among a wider public.

We are also very pleased with our collaboration with Carocci, the publishers of the Italian edition (who generously granted the rights for the translation free of charge), and with Routledge, the publisher of this volume. Finally, the agreement of the EMoDiR group, which accepted this proposal to be published as part of its series, was fundamental. Thanks to these collaborations, we are finally able to discuss Italian Judaism in an international context.

—Alessandra di Castro
—Olga Melasecchi

Acknowledgments

The English translation of my book, *Storia degli ebrei nell'Italia moderna*, originally published in Italy by Carocci (2014, 2017), is indebted to many people and institutions. First and foremost, I want to thank the Foundation for the Museo Ebraico di Rome for its contribution, and in particular Foundation President Alessandra di Castro, who together with Museum Director Olga Melasecchi wrote an affectionate Foreword to this volume which I found quite moving. I also want to thank my Italian publisher, Carocci, and the English publisher of this edition, Routledge. I am grateful to the international research group EMoDiR, which accepted this publication in its series, and in particular to my friend Stefano Villani, who has followed all the editorial work step by step. Last but not least, my warmest thanks go to Paul M. Rosenberg, who has brilliantly and patiently taken on a very demanding translation project that was certainly not easy, and which merits great appreciation.

—Marina Caffiero

Introduction
Global Contexts and Transcultural Networks

Most contemporary historians agree that two things must be taken into account in order to understand the demographic, social, economic, and cultural fortunes of the Jewish communities in Italy. First of all, these communities must be seen within the broader European – or better still, global – networks of Jewish communities. The history of the Jewish presence in Italy is often rooted in the histories of Jews from other countries. Thus, as Sergio Della Pergola has pointed out, it is important to "understand the global Jewish context to which Jews organically belonged".[1] Second, the history of the Italian Jews must be analyzed as part of a dense network of relationships with the surrounding non-Jewish society.[2]

The global networks of Italian Jewish communities have a long history that can be traced back to immigration which began in classical antiquity. After more than twenty centuries of migration, mobility had become a key trait of Italian Jewry. The centrality of migration created a community with diverse origins and complex relationships within the group and within the Jewish world more broadly, as well as with other external social and cultural groups. Migration also meant that Jews occupied a very wide geographical space, well beyond the geopolitical borders of the Italian Peninsula and extending beyond the undeniably unique characteristics of Italian Judaism.

Jewish immigration to Italy brought together several distinct Jewish identities: Italian Jews, Ponentine/Sephardic Jews from Iberia, Levantine Jews from the Ottoman Orient, and Ashkenazic Jews from Germanic lands. Immigration also brought Jews who had been forced to convert to Christianity, referred to as *conversos* and *marranos*, to the Italian Peninsula from Spain and Portugal. This mobility was defined by participation in cultural and religious systems, and also in a vast national and international economic, banking, mercantile, and financial system that extended across Europe and beyond. Strongly cohesive groups operated within this economic-financial system and within a complex apparatus of international social and economic networks (networks built on family and social relations) that were able to manage information, guarantee reciprocity and trust, and establish genuine "social capital".

DOI: 10.4324/9781003188445-1

It may, therefore, be most accurate to discuss Italian *Judaisms* in the plural. Italian Judaism was far from homogeneous and monolithic, and despite the bonds of trust guaranteed by their shared Jewish membership, these identities and ethnicities were sufficiently distinct from each other that a plurality of identities and paths developed, often creating conflict between groups. The most original historical scholarship has thus situated the experience of the Italian Jews in a transregional and transnational context, emphasizing the complex and often conflictual relationships, bonds, and interests that characterized life in the diaspora from the 16th to the 20th century. Jewish history – and not only its Italian subset – is now treated as an immense web of connections with mobility as a central component.

The second condition – that Italian Jews were deeply interconnected with Christian society – derives from the same lived experience as a vast network of relations. It also stands in stark contrast to a long dominant, but substantially false historiographical and interpretive paradigm that assumes that Jewish communities and the majority Christian society remained separate and unable to communicate with each other. In this antiquated, schematic narrative, the harsh reality of inequality and persecution has obscured a complicated system of encounters, clashes, and even mundane daily interactions. This simplistic schema of impenetrable borders between the two worlds has been challenged by contemporary scholarship that draws on copious archival documentation, especially from the Counter-Reformation period. This recent historiography rejects the traditional "us and them" model, and instead highlights an ongoing oscillation between the foreign and the familiar, which characterized relations between the two societies and cultures.

This shift in emphasis uncovered a complex system of exchanges and interactions in everyday life as well as in cultural affairs. Relationships were constantly negotiated and renegotiated. Acquaintances and collaborations formed and disintegrated. Jewish and Christian histories intertwined. Of course, there were also misunderstandings, and stereotypes formed with varying degrees of hostility. Dialogue took place not only among elites and governing authorities but also among and across the lower classes. Mutual perceptions and both positive and negative discourse arose out of these complex relationships in a sort of game of mirrors that revealed both different and shared mental attitudes. Even hostile representations, accusations, and strife were part of this exchange system. In this context, proximity and difference created a lived situation that we might define as "familiar otherness".

The history of Jews and Christians is a history in which minorities were not disconnected islands isolated from the majority mainland. This history is instead characterized by exchanges and intertwined institutions, societies, and cultures that are impossible to separate. From this point of view, new studies that focused on the active period of the ghettos (the 16th–19th centuries) reflect this important shift in historiographical perspective, bringing out new and unexpected results based on very detailed documentary research in previously overlooked sources and archives. The study of Jewish history and that of Italian history have long been carried out separately, in almost complete isolation. Consequently, although the Jews lived embedded within Christian societies, they are almost invisible in the general historical narrative. This has meant that we missed the valuable insights that analysis of Jewish institutions, norms, and practices could yield for the comprehensive reconstruction of European and world history.

The new method of "entangled" history makes use of data preserved in administrative, notarial, criminal, and inquisitorial sources along with legal sources and treatises. This approach allows historians to fully integrate Jewish history into the overall history of early modern Europe and its great processes of transformation. Jewish history is revealed as an integral part and a fundamental aspect of broader phenomena. For example, Jews were caught up in the definition of heresy, the censorship and prohibition of dangerous books, the understanding of witchcraft, the history of emotion and affectionate or sexual contacts, and the construction of a "lexicon of prejudice" and discrimination. Politically and economically, the Jews were involved in the discourse over rights and citizenship, the development of trade and of international financial networks, the birth and roles of mercantilism and of capitalism, and so on.

Ultimately, bonds of friendship, forms of collaboration, imitation, exchanges, and alliances were all part of an intense interaction between Jewish and Christian society, well before the emancipation of the late 17th and 18th centuries and the end of the ghetto system. Some historians have gone so far as to identify this interaction between majority and minority as the source and origin of the capitalist system's role as a primary factor in changing religious and cultural barriers. Of course, the cosmopolitan rhetoric of international trade should not be confused with harmonious intercultural tolerance or with assimilation – at the time these were still nonexistent. However, it is worth reiterating that the image of insular minority communities, ruled only by their own sealed, static moral and economic norms and opposed to or unable to adapt to the march of the modern economy, is neither accurate nor useful.[3]

There is, then, no "history of the Jews" that stands separate from Italian and European history – a self-referential history for the Jews that is irrelevant for non-Jews, with the exception of the *Shoah* – not during the centuries of the modern era, nor later in the 20th and 21st centuries. There is only a single history, no longer divided, and above all interconnected and global.[4] The history of the Jews and their centuries-long relations with Christians thus represents an essential part of the broader history of the difficult coexistence among different religions and cultures, and problems that are linked to relations between majorities and minority cultures.

A history of the Jews in early modern Italy must take into account the modalities of interaction within defined geographic and spatial contexts while also providing a comparative framework for the different situations and conditions particular to Jews. One of the main threads in this work will not be separation, but rather the exchanges, reciprocity, and transformations of identity that sprang from such exchanges. A second element will focus on the intrinsic trait of mobility. Beyond the emigration imposed by the diaspora, a high degree of mobility characterized a wide range of activities – more than just economic – that were based on close-knit relationships of kinship, solidarity, and trust, as well as shared culture, religion, and "nation", no matter how scattered across the world they might be. The choices and decisions made by these groups will be presented in the context of relational mechanics and dynamics and of individual and familial as well as collective and group networks. In short, connection and mobility – not isolation – are the essence of this Jewish history.

Notes

1 Della Pergola, "La popolazione ebraica in Italia," 898.
2 Caffiero, *Legami pericolosi*, 10ff.
3 Trivellato, *The Familiarity of Strangers*.
4 Caffiero, *Legami pericolosi*, 12–14. On "connected history" see Subrahmanyam, *From Tagus to the Ganges*; *Three Ways to be Alien*.

Part One

The Geopolitics of Italian Jewry between the 15th and 16th Centuries. The Structures

1 Demography and Geographic Distribution

How Many Jews Were There in Italy?

Jews have lived continuously in Italy, and in particular in Rome, for more than twenty-two centuries. This is unique in the European context. At the start of the early modern period, the Jewish population in Italy fluctuated, numbering 35,000 in the 15th century and 50,000 in the 16th century, out of a total population estimated, respectively, at 8 and 9 million inhabitants. In other words, Jews formed between 4.4 per thousand of the population for the 15th century and 5.6 per thousand for the 16th century.[1] What is worth noting is that these tallies represent the high point of Jewish population numbers compared to both the Middle Ages and the modern and contemporary periods.[2] Only between 1900 and 1938 did the number of Jews in Italy once again exceed 40,000. Italy's Jewish population had declined sharply in the 17th century, partially rebounding in the 18th and 19th centuries.

The causes of the rapid growth of the Jewish population between the 15th and 16th century can be found in the waves of immigration which started in the 14th century, bringing Jews to Italy from France, Provence, and Germany. Of course, the great expulsions from the Iberian Peninsula and from the Spanish dominions in Italy after 1492 (about which we shall have more to say below) played a very important role, triggering very significant immediate and long-term consequences. Approximately 25,000 Jews arrived in Italy from Spain, more or less permanently. So, at least for a short period, the total number of Jews on the peninsula would reach 75,000. The sharp decline in the 17th century can be attributed to the general decline in the European population, and to the institution of the ghettos and enforced segregation and everything they brought with them: more or less forced baptisms, local expulsions, and the imposition of rigid inquisitorial controls over the Jews. Thus, Italian Jewry was reduced to about 21,000 people over the course of the 17th century, mostly living in the large- or medium-sized cities with ghettos.

In 1700, the number of Jews in Italy rose to 26,500 out of a total population of 10 million, and in 1800, the number had reached 31,400 out of

DOI: 10.4324/9781003188445-3

Figure 1.1 The principle Jewish settlements before the expulsions and the age of the ghettos (drawn by the author).

17,860,000 inhabitants. The percentage thus remained at 2 per thousand of the population.[3] Rome remained one of the most important Jewish communities, demographically and otherwise, although at a certain point it was superseded by Livorno. The Jewish population of Rome, which in the 18th century varied in number between 3,000 and 5,000, was the largest on the peninsula. Even so, Jews were only about 3% of the city's population.[4] But most importantly, Rome served as the cultural and religious reference point for all other Jewish communities, whether Italian or European, for the entire early modern period.

Where Were They? The Great Northward Migration

Immigration and emigration, the policy of expulsions and the demographic developments that depended on these two factors also had important repercussions on the geographical distribution of settlements and Jewish centers on the peninsula, as well as on the socioeconomic system and productive activities. Of the roughly 50,000 Jews who lived in Italy just before the expulsions from the Iberian Peninsula (Spain, 1492 and Portugal, 1497), half of them resided in Sicily, one third in the central and northern areas, and the rest in other southern regions.[5] So, for centuries, the Jewish population was concentrated in the south-central part of Italy. During the 16th century, however, the geography of Italian Jewry changed profoundly, in a resounding reversal that was not without major social and economic consequences.

The expulsion from Sicily decreed by the Spanish rulers in 1493, and the following expulsion from the kingdom of Naples in 1541 led to the disappearance of these southern Jewish communities, and relocated the axis of Jewish settlement to the central-northern end of the peninsula. Some abandoned Italy altogether for more welcoming lands, for example the countries of the Mediterranean Levant. In fact, Jewish settlements had already begun to proliferate in central Italy (modern day Lazio, Umbria, and the Marche) and further north (Tuscany, Emilia–Romagna, Veneto, Lombardy, and Piedmont) as early as the end of the Middle Ages, and especially from the 13th century on. Settlers included Jews from European countries like France and Germany where expulsions had been in place for a long time, as well as from Rome and the south of Italy. Merchants from Rome and the south relocated with their families to the central-northern regions at the invitation of Italian cities in order to engage in moneylending – that is, pawn broking. This sizable and widespread phenomenon also extended to small towns. It has been found that between the 14th and 15th century there were at least 600 locations in which one or more Jewish families lived[6] and, in any case, Jewish settlements in northern and central Italy were by then established. At that point, almost all Italian Jews lived in, or north of Rome.

Contrary to what was happening in these areas, the situation of the Jews in the Italian south had already begun to deteriorate by the end of the 13th century, as Angevin policies oscillated between protection and persecution. In 1442, when the Aragon dynasty gained control over the southern part of the Italian Peninsula, Jews once again enjoyed a period of tranquility. They were granted full citizenship and the right to engage in a variety of professions other than moneylending, with the possibility, for example, of practicing medicine or taking up the new craft of printing. Ferrante I of Naples, though a cousin to Ferdinand the Catholic, who expelled the Jews from Spain, acted quite differently than his famous relative; he welcomed Spanish, and then Sicilian Jewish exiles into his kingdom, even over the growing hostility of his subjects. With Ferrante's death in 1494, however, the status of the Jews was affected by general historical developments.

Charles VIII of France, Angevin pretender to the throne of Naples, arrived in Italy. His taking of the city, apart from unleashing Christian violence, with sacking and massacres, meant the end of the policy of tolerance. Once Spain assumed direct rule over the southern peninsular kingdom in 1503, waves of expulsions – and conversions – followed, until Jews were definitively banished in 1541.

On the other hand, in Sicily, which like Sardinia had been a direct subject of the Spanish Aragonese crown for some time, and where the Jewish presence was economically and numerically significant, expulsion took place as early as January 1493. As a result, the once flourishing and numerically dominant Jewish communities of the South vanished.[7] Thus, it was political and military events and rulers' decisions that would seal the fate of the Jews in the kingdom of Naples and the South. There are other factors that also played a role such as anti-Jewish preaching by Franciscan and Dominican mendicants, the condemnation of usury, conversion policy, and popular hostility not only to moneylending but also to all Jewish business activities, and to the privileges Jews often obtained from the authorities.

The Jews of southern Italy who did not convert ended up choosing the road, either heading to Rome or to the north, or they left the peninsula in the direction of the cities of the Ottoman Empire.

Legal Status and Relations with the Christian Authorities: the Issue of Moneylending

The immigration of bankers, who with the support of the papal Curia itself, moved northward from Rome to set up lending banks, resulted in a large number of settlements within the Papal States, in particular in what are now called The Marches and Umbria. It should be recalled that Rome's urban statutes had prohibited Jews from pawn lending in the city since 1363, protecting Roman merchant families from competition. This policy, which would remain in effect until 1521, contributed to a massive emigration of Jewish merchant bankers out of Rome and towards locations in north-central Italy where their capital was in demand. Families of merchant bankers from the center of the peninsula expanded into Tuscany, Urbino, and the duchies of Mantua, Ferrara, and Milan. However, alongside and parallel to the migratory current from the south, which was composed of *Italiani* Jews, of Italian origin, there was another current from the north, consisting of Jews from France and especially Germany ("Ashkenazi" from *Ashkenaz*, the Hebrew name for Germany). This second group, also responding to the rising demand for credit, settled in Veneto and Friuli, and subsequently in Piedmont. The current Emilia-Romagna represented the dividing line between emigration from the south and from the north: members coming from both directions could be found in Modena, Ferrara, Reggio, and the small adjacent towns.[8]

First of all, however, there are two questions of a more general nature that must be addressed: the first is that of why Jews were admitted to Christian states, and in particular to the papal territories; the second concerns the Jewish specialization in the field of moneylending.

Regarding the first question, it should be noted that the presence of Jews in Christian society was tolerated by the Church based on the doctrine elaborated by St. Augustine. This doctrine had always remained the basis for the attitudes of the popes and the ecclesiastical authorities and was accepted by jurists, both canonical and secular, as well as by Christian secular rulers. This doctrine says that the Jews, because they had rejected Christ and were responsible for His death (deicides), were no longer the chosen people of God. God punished them with the destruction of their Temple in Jerusalem and the diaspora (70 CE), replacing them with the Christians who became, through Jesus, the *verus Israel* – the true Israel. Nevertheless, the Jews should neither be exterminated nor expelled, since their degraded and unhappy condition of exile and discrimination constituted living proof of Christian truth. The Jews were necessary as witnesses of that truth. In addition to this concept, based on the theology of replacement which taught that Christians had replaced the Jews as the Chosen people, and had become the true Israel,[9] there was the added duty – almost an obsession – to convert the Jews. This idea was also central to the very identity of the Catholic faith as well as to its claims to truth. Conversion was also inscribed within a precise theological framework, related to the eschatological-millenarian belief that the second coming of Christ on earth to inaugurate the 1,000 year Kingdom would be announced by the religious unification of the world, and in particular by the conversion of the Jews.[10] As a result of this theological construct, which also dictated the conditions for their presence, the particular legal status of the Jews in society involved provisions and regulations that swung between privilege and discrimination.

As for the second question, regarding the Jewish specialization in banking, it should be emphasized that the origins of Jewish settlements in the cities north of Rome were rooted in the practice of lending money at interest. However, the dynamics and causes that led to this phenomenon require explanation.

Throughout Christian Europe in the Middle Ages, the use of the small consumer loan was quite widespread; they were generally based on pledged collateral, with a corresponding collection of interest (termed *foenus* or usury). This sector – the only one out of the various commercial and financial sectors to explicitly allow the charging of interest for the simple repayment of loaned money – was condemned by the Church and disparaged by all of society. Usury was widely believed to be a morally illicit pursuit, and usurers were considered public sinners by the Church and were excluded from the sacraments. The Church was thus hostile to lending banks and fought all moneylenders, whether Christian or Jewish, even though between the 12th and 13th century, a period of strong demographic growth, it was forced to grapple with the futility of its prohibitions. However, contrary to common belief, there were no religious or ethno-national distinctions in the field of moneylending, nor were the Jews the ones who promoted the moneylending business. Jews were following the model of a very active Christian market.[11] Then, during the two centuries between 1300 and 1500, we see what has been called a "changing of the guard", as Christians were replaced by Jews,[12] and Jews achieved a near-monopoly on this kind of banking activity. Jews gradually displaced gentiles who abandoned the field for a variety of reasons, not the least of which was the infamy and social disrepute it entailed.

From the Church's point of view, allowing moneylending as an open, and predominantly Jewish, practice offered clear advantages. On the spiritual level, Christians would not be damning themselves. Even more important, from an economic point of view, the Jews could be blackmailed, and were possible targets for various taxes and liens. The situation also changed relative to the exigencies of the myriad of small feudal holdings, especially in northern Italy, which required access to credit in order to support themselves and strengthen their economic lives. In the end, papal opposition faded, and instead the papacy encouraged the settlement of Roman Jewish bankers in Lazio, in Umbria, in the Marches, and in other areas directly or indirectly subject to the temporal power of the Church. From the end of the 13th century, we see the public practice of Jewish moneylending expanding in towns both large and small across central-northern Italy.

Local authorities regulated Jewish settlement through a bilateral agreement or contract between the established powers and the bankers. The contract, called a *condotta*, was approved by both parties and subdivided into precise paragraphs (*capitoli* or chapters) dictating the terms of residency and the practice of moneylending. This gave the bankers a dominant role within Jewish society, even when banking was not their only profession, which many still believe was the case. In fact, in many instances, these men were primarily merchants and only later became bankers, using moneylending in order to support their wider ranging commercial and professional initiatives. The preponderant image/stereotype of Jews as strictly moneylenders and usurers is a true cliché that was widespread at the time, but which is also shared by many historians to this day. Contrary to that image, it was trade that was really essential to the Jewish economy, even as the credit sector became the focus of rapidly rising interest among the Jews. Credit and commerce were almost always complementary occupations, especially for the most affluent, and were not mutually exclusive.[13] Moreover, archival findings confirm that Jews violated the prohibition on engaging in the agriculture business, which involved using Christian manual labor. In those same sources, we can easily find Jewish bankers who rented and directly managed agricultural land and pastures, even in regions subject to Church rule.[14]

The *condotta* contracts, besides specifying the procedures for credit – rates of interest, requirements for care of the pledges, bookkeeping procedures, etc. – guaranteed the right of residency for the merchant bankers, their families, and other associates for a certain number of years, along with the right to practice their religion. Often these privileges and specific rules for Jews were also included in late medieval city statutes that were still valid years later, sometimes including exemptions from canon law. The city of Rome's statutes of 1363, for example, included specific provisions concerning the Jews which, despite the fact that some of the provisions were discriminatory, did protect the minority from potential abuses.[15] Other concessions followed: permission to maintain synagogues and cemeteries, for example, as well as the right to observe ritual practices, including those related to kosher food (*kashrut*). Equally important was the recognition of the community as a *Universitas*, which endowed the group of Jews with a legal status analogous to that of the artisans' guilds. This allowed the Jews a great deal of autonomy in their internal organization.

The downside, however, was that Jews' position in Christian society remained one of absolute inferiority, exposing them to discrimination and persecution. There was extraordinary taxation; restrictions on their right to testify in court against Christians; attempts at forced baptism; prohibitions on relationships of any kind with gentiles, especially marital or sexual; prohibitions on holding public office, on proselytizing, or attempting to bring converted co-religionists back to Judaism. The penalties were very harsh in these cases. Over time, special laws, both secular and ecclesiastical, were developed to regulate the Jews; legislation that was exclusionary, socially degrading, and increasingly severe. This included the obligation, for instance, to wear distinctive markings and the imposition of separate Jewish quarters, a prelude to the ghetto. During the 15th century the Jews' exclusion and separation from the body politic was exacerbated by the anti-Jewish preaching of the Observant Friars Minor – from Bernardino of Siena and John of Capistrano to Bernardino of Feltre. Furthermore, starting in 1462, this exclusion was worsened by the widespread establishment of *Monti di Pietà*, lending banks that were meant to supplant those of the Jews. The bankers themselves, however, were often granted exemptions from wearing the badge, permission to employ Christian wet nurses and servants, and recourse to specific judges and courts: for example, in the case of Rome, to the cardinal *camerlengo*.[16]

Until the 1500s, the legal condition of the Jews in north-central Italy remained favorable as a whole. Though civic law only rarely recognized Jews as citizens (*cives*), the holders of the *condottas* in Italian towns obtained a kind of "citizenship pro tempore", with the associated privileges.[17] However, the issue is not entirely clear. Some authors maintain that the Jews were considered *cives* on par with other citizens even in the Middle Ages, as exemplified by Rome.[18] For other authors, the perception of Jews as "infamous", "unfaithful to God", and by nature incapable of the true faith rendered their citizenship highly ambiguous, and at best incomplete.[19] Ultimately, the Church continued to teach the theological doctrine that Jews were condemned to perpetual servitude. This doctrine, which dated back to the apostle Paul and was reaffirmed by Thomas Aquinas and the popes, was even included in canon law. In the early modern period, Jews' status as residents did not include citizenship nor equality of civil rights. Well into the 18th century, even Benedict XIV, the jurist and canonist pope, referred directly to the theological thesis of Jewish servitude in some of his official documents regarding the forced baptisms of Jews.[20]

Jews in Court

Jews were subject to both the secular and ecclesiastical laws and courts of the jurisdictions in which they lived. However, it is not a simple task to disentangle the various judicial authorities, which were often in competition and in tension with one another. In the 1500s, in the territories of the Papal States, the Jews who remained in the outlying communities of the Papal States and who, as we will see, remained there even after the establishment of the ghettos in Rome and Ancona, saw local civil authorities gradually cede control over them to the diocesan bishop, almost always in connection with the Roman inquisitorial court. With increasing frequency, it fell to the episcopal criminal and civil courts to deal with cases involving Jews.[21] Here, we find a significant indication of the extent to which the Jewish question itself was taking on a religious connotation, particularly that of controlling Jewish differentness, and no longer just economic and social activity. It also shows the degree to which the perception of Jews, especially in Counter-Reformation Italy, was changing in the direction indicated by Rome.

The situation in Rome itself is illustrative. Here, ecclesiastical appropriation of jurisdiction over the Jews had begun already in the 16th century. From 1550 onwards, we see jurisdiction over the Jews increasingly falling to the cardinal vicar, the vice-bishop of Rome, who also had authority over converts. However, in reality Jews were subject, just like other Romans, to all of the city's existing courts. And over time, the vicar's authority was progressively eroded by competition among various ecclesiastical tribunals and the many other jurisdictions that concerned themselves with the Jews. In the reform of the courts instituted by Paul V in 1612, jurisdiction over the Jews in spiritual and disciplinary matters (conversions, compulsory attendance at sermons, relationships between Jews and neophytes) belonged to the cardinal vicar and his court, while the courts of the Governor and the Senator prosecuted civil and criminal misdemeanors, and the cardinal *camerlengo* intervened in economic matters (pledged collateral, Jewish bankers, licenses for participating in fairs). The sentences most frequently handed down by the governor's criminal court ranged from fines to the most serious penalty of exile; apparently capital punishment was avoided.[22] The vicar's court and the Senator's court had equal authority over common crimes in which both Christians and Jews were involved.

However, this legal regime was complicated by the increasingly oppressive and all-encompassing intrusion of the Roman Inquisition (founded in

1542) into the most sensitive cases involving spiritual matters: disrespect for the Catholic faith, blasphemy, magic, possession of the prohibited *Talmud*, censorship of the press, illicit relations between Jews and Christians, apostasy by the converted, and accusations of ritual murder. Such inquisitorial interference even extended into the economic sphere.[23]

As we shall see below, the reasons for the increasingly pronounced interference by the Congregation of the Holy Office are quite indicative of the hardening of anti-Jewish attitudes in the early modern era. What should be noted here is the tangle of jurisdictions and the constellation of institutions all claiming authority over the Jews. This effectively opened up spaces of opportunity for Jewish individuals and communities. Litigants would play upon the tensions among the various courts, choosing to approach the authority they thought most favorable to themselves in each particular case. A system of negotiation thus emerged, in which the Jewish communities were far from passive, immobilized, and closed off in a defensive posture; instead, they were proactive and ready to take the initiative or lodge a protest. In connection with cases of forced baptism, for example, research has shown the Jews' ability to act in the social dynamic as a recognized social body, the *Universitas Iudaeorum Urbis*, and to play upon an articulated front of different institutional representatives and authorities. They did so with great determination, both for the resolution of conflicts with the external world and to settle their frequent intra-communal quarrels.

Jews' regular appeals to Christian authorities and courts through supplications, denunciations, and Memorials reveal an ongoing pattern of communication with the external majority world, and rebut the stereotyped image of two groups, each alien, closed, and impenetrable to the other. This is a misleading picture which among other things implies both the idea of the Jewish communities' substantially victimized passivity with respect to their political and social surroundings, and the idea that Jewish identity could be defended only through the instruments of renunciation – closure, absence of communication, and self-absorption – that we discussed at the beginning. As we shall see, recourse to Christian authorities was not only extremely common for addressing specific protests and claims, but was actually essential for the sort of collaboration that had to be established between Christian and Jewish authorities to maintain equilibrium, order, and social stability in the relations between the two groups.[24]

If we look beyond Rome and the Papal States to the rest of north-central Italy, the legal condition of Jews was much the same, even though in those area sovereignty belonged not to the pope but to secular governments. Though influenced by the Church and by legislation on Jewish matters, these governments could often distance themselves from papal bulls and follow their own specific interests and political relationships. Jews could be subject to particular judges, to their deputies, or to the ordinary courts for civil and criminal cases. Here too, episcopal courts were active in questions of religion or of morals, often clashing with local representatives of the Roman

Inquisition.[25] However, for civil matters and cases involving only Jews, there were also internal State courts that resolved disputes based on Jewish law, for example in cases involving personal status such as matrimony, inheritance, dowries, and so forth. In many cases, such as in Venice, there was clear competition between the regular presiding magistracies that claimed authority over crimes committed by Jews and the ecclesiastical courts, especially the Holy Office. In Venice, though, the State jealously guarded its prerogatives against any intervention by the Church, and the particular structure of the Venetian inquisitorial court, which included a strong presence of secular representatives from the Republic, succeeded in limiting the Church's sphere of jurisdiction and therefore its ability to intervene.

Notes

1 Della Pergola, "La popolazione ebraica," 905.
2 For an overview of Jewish medieval history see Veronese, *Gli ebrei nel Medioevo*, and the many titles in the bibliography there. Cfr. now Todeschini, *Gli ebrei nell'Italia medievale*.
3 Bachi, "La demografia dell'ebraismo," 263 and 328. This figure is accepted by Milano, *Storia degli ebrei*, 335; and by Harris, "La demografia del ghetto," 9. Bachi and Della Pergola, "Gli ebrei italiani," 158 differs only a little from this.
4 For the 1700s, cf. Harris "La demografia del ghetto," 10. Quantitative data for Rome are uncertain and debatable, as demonstrated by the different figures found in various sources: Milano, *Storia degli ebrei*, 292, 336 mentions 6–7,000 as well as 5,000; Bachi, "La demografia dell'ebraismo," 290 and 295 mentions 4,000; Livi, *Gli ebrei alla luce*, 266f. and tab. 1, calculates some 3,000 for the years 1775–1800. A census of 1796 mentions a total of 3,617 individuals, among them 778 heads of family, found in Archivio di Stato di Roma, *Camerale II*, Ebrei, b.x, f. 17. A census of 1733 mentions 4,059 individuals: Groppi, *Gli abitanti del ghetto*.
5 Della Pergola, "La popolazione ebraica," 914.
6 Veronese, *Gli ebrei*, 29.
7 On the Jews in the south of Italy as well as Sicily, see Abulafia, "Le comunità di Sicilia," 45–82, as well as his many other studies.
8 Simonsohn, *The Apostolic See*, 102.
9 Stefani, *L'Antigiudaismo*.
10 On the centuries-old myth of the conversion of the Jews in eschatological terms, see Caffiero, *La nuova era*, 71–131.
11 Luzzati, "Banchi e insediamenti," 173–235.
12 Luzzati, "Banchi e insediamenti," 179.
13 Veronese, *Gli ebrei*, 65; Boesch Gajano and Luzzati, "Ebrei in Italia".
14 Simonsohn, *The Apostolic See*, s.v. Imola, Forlì, Raenna, Romagna. Agricultural loans are also to be found in Ancona, the Pontifical Marches, Ferrara, Pesaro, and the territories of modern Lazio.
15 Esposito, *Un'altra Roma*, 192–3; "Normativa statutaria," 98–101.
16 Simonshon, "La condizione giuridica," 106.
17 Veronese, *Gli ebrei*, 84.
18 Esposito, *Un' altra Roma*, 126, Chapters of the Statute of 1402.
19 Todeschini, *Visibilmente crudeli*, 178–83; Romani, *Storia economica e storia degli ebrei*.
20 Caffiero, *Forced Baptisms*, 52–3.
21 Canonici, "La presenza ebraica," 102–3.

22 Esposito and Procaccia, "Sicolorum de Urbe", 18.
23 Caffiero, *Forced Baptisms*, 14–15. On the tribunals see Di Sivo, "Giudicare gli ebrei," 81–102. On the Inquisition, economic life and the Jews, cf. Maifreda, *I denari dell'Inquisitore*, 289.
24 Cfr. Caffiero, *Il grande mediatore*.
25 See Caffiero, "Tra due fuochi".

2 Settlements and Networks. The Topography and Characteristics of Italy's Judaisms

Even a quick examination of the geography of Italian Judaism – or better said, of the different Italian Judaisms – in the early modern age must not overlook an important consideration, which, along with mobility consti-tutes one of the specific and particular traits of the history of the Italian settlements. This is the vast Jewish network of familial, economic, cultural, and even political relations which extended to include communities that were located in different and even distant state and economic contexts. The regional network of Jewish bankers – for example from the Marches and Tuscany – was connected by family relationships, kinships, and endoga-mous marriages and shared channels of communication and information between the various nuclei, responding to a precise strategy of territorial rootedness. Local roots were necessary for conducting various economic activities, and contributed as well to growth in the number of settlements and economic ventures, and not only for strictly material reasons.

In fact, the fabric of relationships represented an important network of protection built through matrimonial unions, which allowed bankers and merchants to rely on greater opportunities for refuge, support, and reloca-tion should local conditions worsen because of expulsions, political change, or revocation of a *condotta*. The network, the family agreements, and the proliferation of connections and support became part of a comprehensive, all-encompassing socio-economic strategy. Accordingly, the history of each individual Jewish settlement can only be written in the context of this broader system, and on the other hand, this is the only way to explain how Jewish lenders succeeded at operating even in very small locations. From the per-spective of analyzing Jewish choices, the increase in the number of *condottas* and banks from the 1300s to the 1500s is not only a reaction to the economic and financial needs of the city governments, from the smallest up to the States. It also reflected the Jews' active, not passive, and effective strategic plan.

In the Papal States: The Marches

It is possible to draw a reasonably precise "atlas of Jewish presences"[1] in northern-central Italy between the end of the Middle Ages and the start of

DOI: 10.4324/9781003188445-4

the modern era based on the great deal of research into local realities that has been done in recent decades. Thus, it is worth making a quick survey of these settlements, starting with the current regions and focusing especially on the territories that formed the Papal States in the early modern period. Paradoxically, in fact, until the mid-15th century, the papacy was rather generous with concessions to Jews, who lived in great numbers in its territories, and generally opposed the extremist approaches of the Spanish and Portuguese national Inquisitions. The papacy never subscribed to a policy of total expulsion from the territories of the State, instead choosing the completely different strategy of segregating and separating the Jews from Christian society.

One particularly important area for Jewish settlement in these years was the region known today as The Marches, where Jews lived in at least sixty towns. These settlements were of great significance both for their number and wide diffusion in the region,[2] and especially for the particular importance of the economic functions they performed. Far from being limited to moneylending at interest, which was of course very widespread, Jews also operated in other commercial sectors and were entrepreneurs in a broad range of activities.[3] This was particularly the case in Urbino where, before the duchy came under the direct rule of the Papal States in 1631, Jewish finance had become a key pillar of the Della Rovere dukes' administration, which had granted Jews especially favorable conditions.[4] The same was true in Pesaro[5] and Senigallia, again under Della Rovere rule, and above all in Ancona.

In Ancona, the presence of the port and the associated international commercial activity, which extended to the Levant, along with the presence of ethnically and religiously diverse communities of merchants made the city very prosperous until the 16th century.[6] In the course of the 1500s, the arrival of Iberian Jews, recent converts (*conversos*), and marranos swelled the Jewish settlements of The Marches, especially at Ancona. In 1532, however, the city lost its status as an independent city and came under direct papal rule, although it obtained a special autonomous status and provisions for exceptions linked to commercial traffic at the port. The Jews also enjoyed favorable conditions because of their primary role in local and international trade. In 1547, Pope Paul III invited both Spanish-speaking Jews of the Levant (*Levantine*) and Portuguese New Christians (*Ponentine*) to settle in the port by issuing a very liberal brief soliciting the merchants of any nation who might wish to settle in Ancona or in other cities of the Marche. This even included Portuguese *conversos* suspected of being marranos, that is, false Christians.[7] At mid-century, however, papal policy would be totally reversed with the launch of a strict anti-Jewish policy that was a fundamental aspect of the new ideological line of the Counter-Reformation; the great reorganization of the Church begun in the mid-16th century in response to the Protestant challenge.

What followed was an escalation of anti-Jewish regulation with very serious consequences. In 1543, a Casa dei Catecumeni (House of Catechumens) was established at Rome for the confinement of potential Jewish converts. In 1553, the *Talmud* was condemned and banned, then publicly burned in Rome's Piazza Campo de' Fiori. On July 14, 1555, Paul IV instituted the ghetto with the bull *Cum nimis absurdum*, which imposed a set of severe, detailed rules to control the lives and livelihoods of the Jews in the Papal States, and forced them to concentrate in certain areas of just a few cities, including Rome and Ancona. In 1569, the bull *Hebreorum gens sola*, promulgated by Pius V, expelled the Jews from all localities within the Papal States except for the two "cloisters" in Rome and Ancona. Finally, in 1593, Clement VIII issued the bull *Caeca et obdurata*, which definitively reduced the number of ghettos where Jews could reside in the Papal States to three: Rome, Ancona, and Avignon. These provisions triggered conversions and above all generalized expulsions and Jewish flight from all over the State, including from the Marche. Dozens of Jewish communities, some of which had been settled for generations, were abruptly dissolved in this way.

The climate of hostility led to the dramatic episode in Ancona of twenty-four (and according to some twenty-five or even twenty-six) Portuguese marranos, including a woman, being burned at the stake in 1556. The subsequent expulsion of the Jews resulted in a much reduced area – but not the disappearance – of Jewish settlement in the Marches. Many Jews fled, for example, to Ferrara. Still others remained in the duchy ruled by Della Rovere – in Urbino, in Pesaro, and Senigallia – though these communities would also be ghettoized when the area became part of the Papal State in 1631. But in reality, settlements of Jews outside of the ghettos, especially involving bankers, never completely disappeared.

Regarding the burning of the marranos in Ancona, one contemporary chronicler reported: "The pope had 26 of the said prisoners burnt and most of them, who never wished to convert nor recant in any way, declared themselves among those who had earned merit in the next life through their constancy and by dying as Jews for their faith".[8]

The Case of Ancona: A "Trading Nation", or the Privileges of the Levantines

The case of Ancona is quite unique, and as such merits special attention. This port city, like the better-known Livorno (Leghorn), offers a prime example of intercultural commerce and the "trading diaspora". This phenomenon, which has recently come to the attention of historians, refers to mercantile communities, not only Jewish, that were part of distinct ethnic-religious groups, characterized by high mobility, and lived in "other" societies. These merchants survived there by maintaining close ties within their own circles as well as through external trade and business partnerships with other groups, partnerships that were capable of crossing and overcoming cultural barriers.[9] However, the coexistence and cultural exchanges between the majority society and these minority groups did not necessarily entail harmonious integration, nor assimilation or tolerance, and certainly not the overcoming of prejudices, as was also true with the Jews.

Definitively coming under the sovereignty of the Papal States in 1532, Ancona had long had relations with the Ottoman Empire and maintained its own consul in Constantinople. Now, the pontifical authorities sought to attract ethno-religious groups who could mobilize long-distance connections in order to expand the city's trade. As a result, thanks to the preferential agreements negotiated with the principal mercantile "nations" that had settled in Ancona, and in particular thanks to the concessions granted to the Levantine and Portuguese Jews in 1534, and renewed in subsequent years, a regime of great economic freedom prevailed in the city during the 1540s. Venice's Adriatic hegemony and fierce competition notwithstanding, by mid-century the very much smaller "Doric City" – 18,000 inhabitants as compared to Venice's 160,000 – saw extraordinary economic growth. Ancona served as a trade bridge between West and East, with the Balkans and with the Levant: the route from Ancona to Ragusa (modern Dubrovnik) vied with the analogous Venice-Split route for control of the land and sea routes in the Balkans.

Another element contributing to this growth was Ancona's favorable geography, since the city was located at the intersection of two great land trade routes: the first linked with the north through Ferrara, Milan, and Basel all the way to Antwerp and London, while the second ran northwest to southeast – that is, from Lyon, Marseilles, Genoa, and Florence towards the Balkans and the Ottoman Empire.[10] In short, Ancona found itself at the center of a well-developed Adriatic trade system that collected and distributed both goods and capital. During the 16th century, with the active contribution of their various composite Jewish communities, Venice and Ancona served as the two points of convergence in Italy for international trade between West and East. They would later be joined by Ferrara, whose river port operated as a hub for the passage of merchandise traveling from London, Antwerp, and Lyon towards Ancona, to be exchanged there with goods coming from the Balkans.[11] The connections between Ferrara's Portuguese "nation" and the one at Ancona were well developed, as demonstrated by the presence of the same families of merchants and bankers in both cities: the Pires, the Pintos, the Rubios, and the Mendes.[12] But complementary and trusted economic relationships were also forged among Sephardic, Italian, and Ashkenazi Jews.[13] The Sephardim, hailing from the Iberian Peninsula, took their name from *Sefarad*, the medieval Hebrew term for Spain, while the Ashkenazim, as has been mentioned previously, took theirs from *Ashkenaz*, the Hebrew word for Germany.

Towards the end of the 16th century, this period of expansion ended, and Ancona entered a period of economic stagnation that lasted until the early 18th century, when the proclamation of Ancona as a free port in 1732 once again brightened the city's prospects. Stagnation had somewhat obscured Ancona's multiethnic identity and lively cosmopolitanism which, for example, was also partly due to a substantial presence of Greeks and Armenians. Still, the economic decline translated into an advantage for consolidating the Jewish presence.[14] The Jews of Ancona in particular, divided among Italians, Levantines, and Portuguese, and confined to a ghetto as of 1555, enjoyed special privileges compared to those of other Jews in the pontifical Marche, privileges that would endure well into the 18th century. And although many Portuguese Jews had left after the burning of the marranos in 1556, the Levantine Jews remained, becoming the linchpin for exchanges with the Levant. Their prerogatives were renewed even by the popes who were the harshest towards the Jews, like Pius V and Clement VIII. As noted already, Clement VIII's severe bull *Caeca et obdurata* (1593) had required Jews to leave all localities in the Papal States within three months, excepting only Rome, Ancona, and Avignon. And yet only one year later, the Levantine Jews' special privileges were not only confirmed by the pope, but a new permission was added, and extended to all the Jews of other nations living in Ancona, to "freely go to any place of the State to collect their credits for the aforementioned merchandise, and so they may not be molested by anyone".[15] Thus, all the Jews of Ancona had the opportunity to move freely within the entire territory of the Papal States, and were even allowed to stop in towns without ghettos, though naturally only with permission from the local authorities. Jews were also granted the option to wear the "black cap, or hat" in public places while traveling in the ecclesiastic State, as Christians did, thus forsaking the obligatory yellow badge on their headgear.

There is a rough analogy between these special measures, confirmed by Paul V in 1606 and maintained for two centuries, and the even more radically favorable measures enacted in the same years in Livorno – provisions that also included Ancona in the system of exceptions.[16] What is certain is that both show that the ecclesiastical authorities were fully aware that mobility was indispensable to the Jews' economic activities, along with the accompanying need to make exceptions to the rules dictated by religious motives and minority control. Economic needs were given *de facto* priority over religious considerations. Jews were able to take advantage of these permissions, remaining in towns where they had come to trade, setting up small shops and dwellings, and disobeying the requirement to live in a ghetto. This was what actually happened, especially in periods of greater freedom for Jews: for example, at the end of the 18th century, at the time of the founding of the Republics, when the free settlement of Jews in various places that did not have ghettos gave rise to numerous Catholic protests.

Ancona's liberal policy towards Jews was no trivial matter, considering that it was, after all, the second city of the Papal State. Historians have only recently recognized how this changes our overall perception of the Jews' concrete situation in Italy. Ancona's distinct profile should now be considered alongside the exceptional situation of Livorno and the more "liberal" context of Venice. Ancona's laws favoring the Levantine Jews and the legal framework accorded to them would remain unchanged for the following two centuries. Of course, this regime of exceptions did not rule out a continuing role for purely religious considerations. In fact, the privileges granted and the possibility of interacting with Christians while carrying on daily commerce, setting aside different religious memberships, were also meant to push the Jews to convert.

Immigration and the concentration of Jews living in the Marche into the ghetto combined to make Ancona the region's most sizeable Jewish center. According to some historians the Jewish population reached 3,000 by the mid-16th century. This number was destined to fall sharply – by more than half – in the following century. Thus, in 1618, there were 1,443 Jews, 13.9% of a total population of 10,375. By the end of the 1600s, their numbers were further reduced to 1,061, equal to 11.4% of the population, but rose again in the mid-18th century to approximately 1,400 after the establishment of the free port in the city.[17] Though they were a minority of the population, the Jews played a decisive economic role and were the most active element in the city's economic fabric. They were organized into various "nations", each with its own specializations and networks of contacts: the Italian Jews engaged in local moneylending; the Levantines and the Portuguese – each with their privileges – were instead active in long-distance trade. But the boundaries between the respective activities and between the groups were not clear-cut.

Representative of this milieu is the example of one of the most important merchant-bankers of Ancona, the Portuguese marrano doctor Francisco Barboso (Chaim Rubio or Ruvio), who arrived in the city in approximately 1544, after 18 years spent in Portuguese India.[18] Involved in multiple enterprises and at the center of a dense web of relationships – at Ferrara, Antwerp, and Salonika – Barboso was a moneylender, working with small private credit and through the lending banks, as well as a financier and merchant active both in the surrounding area and in long-distance trade. He thus combined the specializations of both the Italian and the Portuguese Jews. The conclusion of his story is also significant. He escaped the condemnation that weighed down on the city's marranos after the events of 1555–56 thanks to the support of his professional connections, and especially due to his decision to reconcile with the Church. He managed to avoid imprisonment and flee Ancona in the direction of the more welcoming Salonika. There, in the largest Sephardic center in Greek lands under Ottoman rule, he could avoid wearing the humiliating robe (*abitello*) imposed on penitents by the Holy Office.[19]

Further demonstrating how the history of the Jews in Italy was characterized by great mobility, and how cosmopolitanism was the chief characteristic of Ancona's Jews, it should be noted that "German" or Ashkenazic Jews like the Tedesco and Morpurgo families also migrated to Ancona, particularly in the 17th and 18th centuries, establishing a deeply rooted presence that would last until the 19th century. On the other hand, after the persecutions unleashed in Ancona, many Portuguese marranos settled in friendlier Ferrara, which also welcomed the exiles from Pesaro, who themselves had been expelled by the duke of Urbino in 1558. In retaliation for the burning of the marranos, Jews in the Ottoman Empire launched a boycott of the Ancona port, and the sultan, at their request, seized the goods of Ancona citizens who traded with the Levant. But the blockade of Ancona, which should have revitalized Pesaro, where many of the Ancona marranos had taken refuge, ended up primarily benefiting Venice.

Multiple Identities. The Marranos

Who were the marranos? Why did they create so many problems, and why were they referred to as marranos? Who, exactly, did the word refer to? The term "marrano" was coined in Castile in the 1400s as a pejorative – the word was synonymous with "pig" – for *conversos*, or New Christians, that is, Jews who had more or less willingly converted to Catholicism. The term then spread throughout Europe. The word implies the juxtaposition with "Old Christians", that is, original Christians, and has a strong subjective component: it is in fact a way of negatively branding individuals because of their Jewish descent, either direct or from their ancestors, which was believed to be masked by an insincere conversion to Christianity. This classification was therefore imposed by the majority society, and does not reflect the self-image of the group so defined. This categorization had legal implications related to the suspicion that marranos engaged in the crime of judaizing. But it also had a biological aspect, since according to the underlying theory, Jews and their descendants inescapably remained Jews, even if they converted to Christianity; the "stain" was transmitted by blood. This early racist theory, which brands the New Christian as biologically and ethnically tainted, found its full practical application in Spain with the so-called Statutes of *limpieza de sangre* (purity of blood) that prevented *conversos* from holding offices and from employment in religious and civil institutions.[20] However, the term "marranos" was often ambiguously used as a pejorative for actual practicing Jews, as happened in Rome, for example, with the arrival of the Iberian exiles.[21]

With the passage of time, and with the expulsion of the Jews from the Spanish dominions in 1492, the word "marrano" acquired a specific connotation, understood by Christians as synonymous with crypto-Jew and judaizer, and thus a two-faced person, deceptive, treacherous, and untrustworthy, who pretended to be Christian in contexts where Jews were not tolerated. These are the origins of the term's negative significance, which endures to this day. Just as in Spain, after the forced mass conversion of Jews in Portugal in 1497, the New Christians, or *cristãos novos*, were suspected of judaizing. The wave of fierce repression unleashed against marranos and judaizers by the Portuguese inquisitorial court after its establishment in 1536 triggered a massive exodus and continuous flow of New Christians towards more hospitable lands, particularly in the Levant, but also to the West. In the end, these refugees would travel to any destination where commercial and financial interests, familial ties, and ethnic-cultural solidarity guaranteed the possibility of settlement. The term "marrano" spread along with the Sephardic diaspora throughout the West, both of which reached Italy with the migrations of Jews, converts, and, of course, marranos.

Marranos came to be almost exclusively identified with the descendants of Portuguese converts and as members of the Lusitanian *Nação* (Nation). They were in constant flight from the Iberian Peninsula, continually wandering from place to place, and yet they often tried to return, never abandoning their interests in or ties to Portugal. Their reintegration into Judaism, when it happened, was never easy, and could not erase the mixture of their ancient religious heritage and their lived experiences as Christians.[22] Outwardly Christian – down to the new names they assumed, abandoning their Hebrew names – yet secretly faithful to the religion of their ancestors, these marranos lived on the border between two realities, bearers of a composite and ambivalent religiosity and culture. Scholars spoke of a "marrano religion" with its own unique characteristics. Women were its primary protagonists through their role in perpetuating and transmitting *converso* identity within the family. The marranos are therefore a very interesting and important example of religious and cultural syncretism and hybridism, as well as of "disguised identity".[23] They have been fittingly defined as "souls in conflict".[24] The frequent adoption of a type of religious *latitudinarian*ism by these figures has led historians to make them spokespersons for already modern identities. For the Church, of course, they had received baptism and so remained Christians, and if they were found secretly practicing Judaism, they became apostates. This exposed them to persecution and prosecution for serious crimes, as the martyrdom of the marranos in Ancona confirmed. Nonetheless, this "marrano identity" resisted and persisted.

Despite the anti-Jewish climate of Counter-Reformation in Italy many rulers, including the pope, saw the marranos, and in particular their network of international contacts, which extended from the Levant and the Far East to the Americas, as a very important resource for expanding commerce and industry. It was also important to prevent them from going to enrich the hospitable Ottoman territories. Thus, they were welcomed in Ferrara, where Ercole I had first invited them to settle as early as 1492, and where Portuguese New Christians from Antwerp chose to migrate in the early 1500s.[25] Ancona, the papal port city, hosted Levantine Jews from the Ottoman Empire as well as Portuguese New Christians, at least until the burning of the marranos in 1556, which led to their exodus from the city.[26] We also find them in Pisa and Livorno, as will be spelled out in greater detail below. In Savoy, the duke offered them privileges similar to those of Tuscany in 1572, though he had to swiftly revoke them under pressure from papal and Spanish authorities, who forced the duke to expel a "race so abominable".[27] Finally, in Venice, the *condotta* of 1589 recognized the settlement of Ponentine Jews – that is, apostate Sephardic Jews who had returned to Judaism – shielding them from the Inquisition and granting them commercial privileges. Among these Ponentine Jews, there were also Portuguese marranos, in other words secret Jews. Regardless of the distinction that must be made between these various social groups – New Christians who remained Christian, converts who had returned to Judaism, and marranos who were secretly judaizing – the institutional documentation classifies them all as marranos. The term is used to indicate the New Christian, who was by default assumed to be a judaizer, as well as the openly apostate Sephardic Jew and the secretly practicing Jew. Indeed, in a further broadening of the term's semantic value, the term "marrano" was often used to refer more generally to Jews of Iberian origin occupied with trade, while also identifying them for the most part as "Portuguese".

Much more than simply a synonym for crypto-Judaism, marranism should be understood as a mental attitude, springing from the interaction of the various experiences typical of the New Christians. Origins and language along with social and economic practices built a shared sphere of relationships whose common link was *"portoghesità"*: "Portugueseness".[28]

Bologna under the Popes and Ferrara under the House of Este

Continuing our survey of the territory of the pontifical State, we now turn our attention to the area referred to today as Emilia-Romagna. Jewish moneylenders arrived here in the middle of the 14th century from Rome, Umbria, the Marches, and Tuscany, and later also from the North, through Lombardy and the Veneto. The earliest Jewish settlements were established along the Adriatic coast, for example in Forlì and Rimini. Among these was Bologna, which soon became the largest settlement in the region. The capillary expansion of Jewish banks throughout the region suggests that between 1350 and 1550, the number of settlements reached nearly one hundred. Here again, economic activity was not limited to extending credit, but expanded to include land management, farming, animal husbandry, and the processing of agricultural products, for example hemp. In Bologna, where a dozen banks were active, the favor of the Bentivoglio family, lords of the city, though within the framework of papal sovereignty, enabled the Jews to strengthen their position throughout the 15th century. But the transition to direct papal rule in the early 16th century overturned that situation, culminating in the expulsion that followed the general decree that expelled the Jews from the dominions of the Holy See in 1569. The Jews, starting with the proprietors of the most important banks – the da Pisa, the Norsa, and the Sforno – fled with their families, taking refuge in the territories of the Este dukes (Ferrara) and the Gonzagas (Mantua), in Pesaro, and in Urbino. The pope, in a highly symbolic act, authorized the Dominican sisters of *San Pietro Martire di Bologna* to take possession of the Jewish cemetery and utilize its tombstones.[29]

The Estense States played a central role in the history of Italian Jews of the early modern period. It is particularly worth focusing on the unique, and at the same time exemplary, story of Ferrara. Until it came under direct papal rule in 1598, the city offered a safe haven for Italian and European Jews, as we will see. From the mid-12th century, Ferrara hosted families of Jewish bankers under renewable moneylending licenses (*condotte*). These were Italiani Jews originating from central Italy and Ashkenazim from north-central Europe. They enjoyed freedom of worship, while only the bankers were granted citizenship and exemption from the wearing a distinguishing mark – the *rotella* (wheel-shaped badge) or a yellow or orange cap – and they practiced the "craft of *strazzeria*", that is, small-scale trading in used garments and goods.

The arrival and settlement of one of the largest Sephardic communities in Italy made up of large groups of Spanish and Portuguese refugees marked a turning point in the story of the Estense Jews. The dukes made Ferrara a main Jewish center, a place of guaranteed acceptance long defended against Roman and inquisitorial intolerance. In fact, since the fateful year of 1492, the date of the general expulsion of the Jews from Spain, Ercole I d'Este had invited the Spanish exiles who were just arriving in Genoa to settle in Ferrara, offering them excellent conditions, including permission to practice medicine as well as any other craft or profession, with the exception of moneylending, which remained reserved for local Jews. Wrote the duke: "We are very well content that they come to live here, with their families, and that they bring their goods here".[30] The Sephardic Jews – frequently referred to as marranos – constituted a separate "nation" with their own synagogues, distinct from the Italian and German Jews.

The Case of Ferrara, a Tolerant City and Its Marrano Community

Ferrara was home to a sophisticated court, and the capital of a small state that was strategically situated, bordering the Papal States (whose vassal it was), the Venetian territories and the Imperial lands. At the Ferrarese court, the duchess Renata or Renée, daughter of Louis XII of France, openly sympathized with the ideas and men of the Reformation, thereby attracting the watchful gaze of Rome.[31] In the context of this tug of war with the pope, Duke Ercole II d'Este conceived his plan to transform Ferrara into a mercantile and entrepreneurial city that would attract investment from wealthy Sephardic *conversos*, and in particular Portuguese New Christians, including marranos suspected of crypto-Judaism. The idea was to position Ferrara as a stopover on the Antwerp-Ancona-Ragusa (Dubrovnik) trade route. Thus, in 1538, Ercole II sent an ambassador to Antwerp and London, bases for the most important New Christian businessmen, with the task of inviting the Portuguese merchants in those cities to relocate to Ferrara, offering them the prospect of living as they pleased, whether as Christians or as Jews. They would thus be able to practice Judaism openly and free of harassment even if they had been baptized and were therefore apostates. Some high-profile merchants, already engaged in trade with the Levant through the port of Ancona and throughout the Portuguese empire, took up the invitation. The main source of immigration was Antwerp, but others came from Naples, from Venice (which had expelled the marranos in 1550), and from Portugal itself. Others arrived later from Ancona after the destruction of its marrano community.

Antwerp, a major port city in the orbit of the Habsburg Crown, was an important haven for Portuguese New Christians. They had been authorized to settle in the city by an imperial order in the 1520s, though they had to continue to declare themselves Christians, even if they were inclined to returning to Judaism, since the city did not officially admit Jews. However, this haven was soon abandoned for other destinations after 1540, given the pressure on New Christians, who here too were suspected of crypto-Judaism and marranism. They were wealthy merchants, active in the trade of fine fabrics, gold, precious stones, sugar, and spices, in contact with the nearest markets, like Ancona and Venice, Ragusa (Dubrovnik) and the Levant, and connected to networks that spanned West and East.[32] Diogo Mendes, a very wealthy monopolist in the spice market nicknamed "the pepper king of Europe", was an especially prominent figure. Also referred to as *Homens de Negocios* (businessmen) or *Homens da Nação* (men of the Lusitanian Jewish nation), these Portuguese Jews, even after the general forced conversion and the suppression of their communities in Portugal, were able to maintain a strong national identity, great cohesion, and an efficient organizational structure in the States where they sought refuge from the Inquisition. Naturally, as soon as it was possible, most of these New Christians took back their original names and returned to Judaism.

However, getting to Ferrara from Antwerp was not at all simple unless passing through relatively friendly France, and could turn into a harrowing experience. The cause of the trouble lay in the obstacles placed by the Habsburg emperor, Charles V, who was hostile towards the Antwerp Portuguese, whom he suspected of marranism, though he simultaneously sought to keep them from leaving for fear that they would take all of their capital to the Levant, the lands of his enemy the Ottoman Empire. Thus, in 1530, Charles created what amounted to a special police force, empowered to halt any "false Christians" traveling to Ottoman lands via imperial territory and seize their goods and property. This circumstance set in motion adventurous escapes led by a genuine underground organization called *Sedaqa* (Hebrew for "charity") that provided relief and assistance for refugees.[33] The organization, in which the wealthiest merchants were active, financed the travels of the Portuguese from Lisbon to Antwerp, paying the ship captains for the trip, and then sending them over land from Antwerp to other destinations such as Ferrara. The clandestine travelers followed the Rhine by carriage and boat, crossing Germany and then the Alps, and continued along the roads and the rivers of today's Lombardy, which was then still under Spanish dominion, until finally reaching Estense city. But the mountains, roads, and rivers were monitored by imperial agents, who arrested the fugitives and tortured them, forcing them to reveal the names of their protectors.[34] Between 1539 and 1540, dozens of Lusitanian New Christians were arrested in Milanese territory, most of them artisans of modest means. They were stripped of all their possessions, and forced to denounce the most prominent Portuguese merchants of Antwerp as judaizers and as financial backers of this Jewish rescue organization.[35]

In the same way, officials also tracked down goods sent by Portuguese merchants in Antwerp to Italy, in particular to Ferrara, and to the Levant: the goods were seized, creating serious economic repercussions. Here again, the clandestine protection organization intervened, arranging for merchandise to be shipped under the names of friendly Christian merchants. Only a decisive diplomatic and political intervention resolved the situation, when Ercole II d'Este protested to the governor of Milan and requested safe-conducts and travel permits for representatives of the big merchant houses and their large retinues. Thus, in 1548, free passage through Lombardy was granted to Portuguese New Christians and their merchandise, at the price of one *scudo* a head.

Despite the troubles and travails, many New Christians did manage to reach Ferrara, and the city became an important and cosmopolitan center of commerce. Starting in the 1540s, one of the largest Sephardic communities in Italy took shape in Ferrara, with a notable Portuguese contingent. The duke's favorable attitude was also motivated by political as well as economic considerations. Ferrara and its territory were a typical *example of an aristocratic court*, and the duke was well aware of the urgent need to introduce manufacturing as well as commercial and entrepreneurial activities.

After a brief expulsion in 1549, following an outbreak of plague for which they were blamed, the Portuguese who had returned to Judaism formed a stable community in Ferrara, and enjoyed particularly favorable economic privileges guaranteed to them by a general safe-conduct in 1550. They would not be harassed for returning to the faith of their fathers, even though they had certainly been baptized in their homeland (something to which the authorities turned a blind eye). They could engage in textile manufacturing and related commerce, and they even obtained from the duke a number of contracts for tariffs and duties – that is to say, they worked in the delicate area of state tax collection. The lending banks, however, remained reserved for local Jews – Italians and Germans.[36] So, we see a sort of division of activities and economic specializations. The duke himself set up commercial companies with rich Portuguese Jews, such as the Pinto, the Nunes, the Pires, and the Mendes families, seeking to exploit their international networks, especially in the spice trade.

During the 1550s, Jews and New Christians were frequently granted safe-conducts which protected them from any denunciation. Paradoxically, these concessions were modeled on those issued in 1547 by Pope Paul III, when he invited and welcomed merchants of any nation who wished to settle in Ancona or in other cities of the Marches, including Portuguese New Christians, that is, the hated marranos. The pope had decided, as would Duke Ercole II in turn, to consider all potential arrivals as Jews, not Christians, thus permitting them to live according to their law, in effect ignoring the fact that they were actually baptized and therefore apostates.[37] Although the papacy under Paul IV revisited these decisions, radically overturning this policy towards the marranos, Ercole II openly reaffirmed his position. In December of 1555, a mere two years after the public burning of the *Talmud* in Rome, and in defiance of the pope who had instituted the ghetto only a few months earlier (July 14), the duke reaffirmed the privileges of the Portuguese "nation" to live as Jews even if "in other times they had lived as Christians", and even if they had not been truthful regarding their faith.[38] This effectively shielded them from any accusations or prosecution for apostasy.

This policy decision, which reaffirmed the duke's controversial policy differences with the pope, is all the more astonishing if we recall that the burning of the marranos at Ancona would occur just one year later. Indeed, in a further challenge, in the document, he openly refers to the privileges granted by Paul III to the Portuguese of Ancona – privileges which had just been revoked by the new pontiff – claiming that he wanted to imitate those papal concessions.[39] This decree, named the *Privilegio della Nation Portughesa* (Privilege of the Portuguese Nation), served as the model that would later inspire Ferdinando de' Medici (1593), Charles Emmanuel of Savoy (1648), Francesco I of Modena (1652), and also to a certain extent Venice (1573). Many "marranos" who fled from Ancona found refuge in Ferrara, and Ercole's son and successor, Alfonso II, refused the pope's call for their extradition for crimes of judaizing heresy.

The Portuguese newcomers included many intellectuals – doctors, jurists, and writers. Besides business connections and capital, they brought a broad heritage of knowledge, skills, and erudition with them to Ferrara. In this climate of cultural fervor and faithfulness to their ancestral religion, we soon find booksellers and printers obtaining licenses to publish Spanish books in Ferrarese editions. In 1553, the year in which the *Talmud* was publicly burned at Rome and in other Italian cities, the celebrated Spanish translation of the Bible, the *Biblia en lengua española*, later known as the "Ferrara Bible", was published under the auspices of the converted Portuguese printer Abraham Usque, *alias* Duarte Pinel. This allowed Sephardic exiles who were former *conversos* to read the sacred text though they no longer knew Hebrew. Therefore, texts were openly being printed for a marrano clientele who had resumed reading their own sacred books. Several prelates at the Council of Trent had even opposed Usque's venture and asked the duke to suspend the publication, but Ercole II refused.[40] Significantly, the book was published in two editions, one for Christians, dedicated to the duke, and one aimed at Jews, and dedicated to the woman who had underwritten the costs of publication, a marrano who had returned to Judaism, Gracia Nasi, or Beatriz Mendes de Luna, the name she took as a New Christian. We will tell the story of this exceptional woman below.

Thanks to Ercole II, who also consented to the establishment of a center for Jewish studies, the first Portuguese nation of Western Europe to be officially recognized was formed, a true model for successive Sephardic communities in Italy and Europe, especially in Ancona, Pesaro, and Venice. A center and a crossroads for the Sephardic diaspora, Ferrara maintained close relations with the other Italian centers, but was integrated into a still wider network of contacts and interests that reached beyond Europe to Portuguese India, the Dutch Indies, and Brazil.

However, things changed at the end of the 1500s, even in Ferrara. Yielding to the pressures of the Roman Inquisition, Alfonso II had many Portuguese arrested on the charge that they had been circumcised in Ferrara. He allowed five of them to be extradited to Rome, where they were tried by the Congregation of the Holy Office and sentenced to death. Once a large part of the Este duchy devolved to the Papal State in 1598, it was governed by cardinal legates, and the golden age that had linked the Jewish minority to Este policies came to an end. A ghetto was established at Ferrara in 1624. At that time, Ferrara's Jews numbered little more than 2,000. The dukes retained control only in the two provinces of Modena and Reggio, both imperial rather than papal fiefs, with Modena as the capital. The new duke Cesare d'Este, of illegitimate birth, preferred Modena over Reggio, and was followed by many Jews, especially the Portuguese. Significantly, the Spanish and Portuguese nation of Ferrara changed its title and dropped the appellation "Portuguese", which was synonymous with "marrano" to the Church, instead calling themselves the Spanish and Levantine nation.

The Umbria Region of the Papal States

Roman Jews who migrated northwards headed mainly for present-day Umbria, where prominent communities had settled and flourished since the end of the 13th century. The most important center was Perugia, a town which, despite several expulsions and readmissions, depended heavily on Jewish moneylending, a service vital to both the city's development and its internal political struggles.[41] It was not without disadvantages: over the years, Franciscan friars like Bernardino da Siena, Jacopo della Marca, Michele Carcano, and Bernardino da Feltre preached against the Jews and usury, and it was in Perugia that Italy's first *Monte di Pietà* was established (1462), an institutional moneylender meant to replace Jewish banks. Nevertheless, the Jewish presence in Perugia held on through the 15th century, albeit reduced to about one hundred individuals. The crisis would come in the 16th century, when the Jewish population was demographically and economically depleted, in part because many relocated to Città di Castello, closer to Tuscany. The final blow was delivered by Paul IV's bull *Cum nimis absurdum*, with the oppressive limitations it imposed on the Jews, causing many to flee and abandon their property. In 1569, Pius V decreed the expulsion of Jews from all of the ecclesiastical state except for Rome and Ancona, and when the community was reduced to just seven families, the Jews had to leave Perugia after three centuries of residence. As in other localities in the Papal States, the void left by their departure and the economic crises that ensued also induced the Umbria authorities to grant temporary dispensations and commercial licenses. Thus, Jewish settlements did not completely disappear from the area.

The Other Italian States. The Grand Duchy of Tuscany

Within the extensive confines of the ecclesiastical State, temporal and spiritual power combined in the person of the pontiff; beyond its borders, Jews had to contend with regional State governments, small principalities or city governments. These places, governed with secular jurisdiction and legislation, took the Holy See's mandates into consideration, but they operated autonomously and with their own logic, making strictly political decisions. Jews often constituted an economic resource that was difficult to give up, as well as a card to play in relations with Rome, for example, when negotiating terms for the local presence of Jews and the conditions they would be subject to. Life in the Jewish settlements in the various regions always and continuously intersected with the vicissitudes of the succession of dynasties and sovereigns that came to power, and was even more entwined with the ups and downs of local powers.

On the other hand, the widespread distribution of these Jewish centers cannot only be attributed to the economic and financial needs of those who accepted them, or to the need for greater financial liquidity, the desire to stimulate mercantile trading, nor the lure of greater tax collections. We must also take into consideration the Jews' own decisions and strategies, and therefore reverse the perspective of the traditional historical interpretation of the phenomenon, which must be read based on the Jews' specific options. Michele Luzzati has identified the active strategizing of the Jews, who sought to assure themselves of firmer footing on the peninsula and formal license to carry out their various economic pursuits, as the fundamental reason for the proliferation of *condottas* and consequently of settlements. In addition, Jews were looking for opportunities to create and widen networks of protection and alliances (by marriage and other means) among the different settlements. These represented a further guarantee of the possibility of relocating to other territories after the frequent cases of expulsions by, or deteriorating relations with the local authorities of one place or another.[42] Grids of relationships, familial understandings, and the multiplication of sources of support made up the fundamental components of a comprehensive strategy that went well beyond economic concerns, and which was certainly not the work – it bears repeating – of a passive, submissive population lacking in initiative, as they have often been described.

Leaving the confines of the Papal States, we find a variety of other situations. Small Jewish settlements, originating mostly from Rome, had taken root early – as far back as the late 13th century – around Tuscany: initially at Pisa, Siena, and San Gimignano, and later more widely throughout the entire region. Jewish banks in particular multiplied around Siena, competing with those of the neighboring Papal State. Their moneylending monopoly would last until the 16th century and the establishment of the ghetto in Siena in 1572.[43] Settlements of Jewish bankers were also widespread in Florence and its territory. As early as 1437, Cosimo de' Medici had authorized the opening of four banks in the city, and the convergence of Italy's wealthiest Jews made Florence into the true Jewish financial center of the peninsula, especially in the days of Lorenzo de' Medici.

The fortunes of the Florentine Jews, who gained unusual social respect and enjoyed broad freedoms and privileges,[44] seem linked to the political fortunes of the Medici, whose fluctuating fortunes (expulsions and returns) they followed closely. After ups and downs, starting in 1547 under the new Medici Duchy of Cosimo I, and therefore a benevolent state power, the Jewish bankers regained their positions and were permitted to open additional banks throughout the duchy, at least until the institution of the ghetto in Florence in 1571.[45] But even following the establishment of the two ghettos of Siena and Florence, and the related prohibition on residence in other parts of the duchy, Jews did not disappear from the rest of the region. A few Jewish settlements linked to banks remained in some of the localities bordering the Papal States which exercised jurisdiction as feudal lords to whom the Medici had granted wide margins of autonomy: for instance, in the marquisate of Monte San Savino, in the county of Pitigliano and in the principality of Piombino.

Tuscany became one of the most hospitable Italian areas for Jews in the early modern period, especially for Sephardic immigrants, chiefly due to the establishment of two large, free mercantile settlements *without* ghettoes, in Pisa and especially in Livorno.[46] The act which inaugurated a secular policy of openness and concessions was the so-called Privilege of 1549, with which Cosimo I encouraged the immigration of Portuguese New Christian merchants, mostly crypto-Jews or marranos, to Pisa. He promised that if they openly returned to their ancient faith or there were other crimes of a religious nature, they would be judged by state courts rather than by the Inquisition, and given broad legal guarantees. The Portuguese New Christians were treated as subjects on a par with native Tuscans, and they enjoyed exemptions from duties and other broad economic concessions.[47] Moreover, in this same period, as we have noted already, the papacy also tolerated the settlement of the Portuguese in its realms – even in Rome – because of their economic usefulness, as demonstrated by the aforementioned brief by Paul III from 1547, which invited the New Christian merchants while assuring them that they would not be harassed for religious reasons. This is why Cosimo I's Privilege did not elicit excessively negative reactions when it was presented to the pope. But as we know, in the span of only ten years, papal attitudes would profoundly change, and policy towards the marranos would be completely overturned.

Tuscany, however, was a different story. In 1556, a year after the papal regulation establishing the ghettos in the Papal States was issued, and while Paul IV's hardline policy broke faith with the Jewish refugees from Iberia, beginning the persecution of marranos which would culminate in the *autos-da-fé* at Ancona, the grand duke, ignoring the protests of Portugal and Rome, went so far as to grant a secret safe-conduct to Portuguese New Christians, including the fugitives from Ancona, who wanted to live as Jews in Tuscany. He thus permitted their open return to the ancient faith without any danger of prosecution.[48] Finally, the famous "Livornina Constitution" would be issued in 1591.

The Exceptional Case of Livorno, the City without a Ghetto

In Italy, the position enjoyed by the Jews of Livorno was absolutely exceptional. Originally a small village, with the Medici's support Livorno became one of the Mediterranean's principal commercial ports, trading with both the Levant and northern Europe. It also gained the reputation of being a tolerant and open city. In launching the port, the Medici were seeking to actively insert themselves into the great international trade routes, hence their interest in attracting Iberian Jews, and in particular the Portuguese *conversos* with their extended family and commercial networks. In 1591 Ferdinando I issued the "Livornina", a charter which established the free port and granted special immunity and exemptions to merchants of every nation and faith, guaranteeing them freedom of religion and worship. Numerous foreign communities thus took root in the city – Armenian, Greek, English, and French – where for administrative purposes they would be organized into "nations". The new legislation included considerable advantages for Spanish-Portuguese Jews, the so-called Ponentines, who had been expelled from the Iberian Peninsula at the end of the 15th century, as well as the Levantines, who came from Muslim lands. Their commercial experience and abilities were considered useful to the development of the city and the State, and the primary goal of these concessions was to use them to gain access to trade with the Levant and the Iberian empires. Jews were allowed to reside in Pisa and Livorno and to buy real estate there, and marranos were assured protection in their dealings with the Inquisition. A second edict, the Livornina of 1593, broadened these concessions.

To understand the significance of these decrees, they must be placed in the context of the growing anti-Jewish climate of those decades, mainly instigated by Rome. So, it is worth noting that in the same year, 1593, the powerful religious Order, the Society of Jesus decided to exclude New Christians and their descendants from its ranks, conforming to the Spanish decrees of *limpieza de sangre* (purity of blood), racist before their time, which excluded the descendants of converted Jews from offices and appointments. Again in that same year of 1593, Pope Gregory XIII issued the bull *Antiqua Judaeorum improbitas*, definitively confirming the Inquisition's jurisdiction over Jews, especially in cases of apostasy and judaizing.[49]

Thus, it is highly significant that the most important privilege granted by the "Livornina", truly exceptional for the era in fact, was that it allowed converted Jews to return to their ancestral faith without facing the crippling accusations of judaizing and apostasy in inquisitorial courts. Other prerogatives granted were recognition of Jews' full ownership of real property, a special judge for disputes between Jews and Christians (the community lay leaders, the *massari*, would have jurisdiction in cases between Jews), the right to earn a degree from the University of Pisa, permission for Jewish physicians to treat gentiles as well as their fellow Jews, permission to employ Christian domestic servants and nursemaids; religious concessions included the right to have a synagogue and the recognition of religious holidays. Above all – and this was of primary importance in a Catholic culture obsessed with conversion – the decree assured that no Jewish child under the age of thirteen could be taken from its parents to be baptized.[50] In short, the bull *Cum nimis absurdum* of 1555, which established the ghettos, and was brimming with restrictions and sanctions for the Jews, never really arrived in Livorno, and almost none of its prescriptions were applied there. Even the Roman Inquisition found it was severely limited in its ability to operate there.

However, it would anachronistic and misleading to speak of "tolerance" and "modernity". The privileges granted to the Jews and marranos harken back to the long-standing tradition of the *condotta* and originated both from the specific material and geographic condition of Livorno (a "new city"), as well as from the strategic and self-interested decision to disregard the religious membership of the Portuguese and Spanish exiles that were pouring into the city. This was not at all a case of the Tuscan authorities abandoning the Catholic values of the Counter-Reformation. Rather, they were adopting a pragmatic and effective strategy; all of the concessions were aimed at commercial and financial goals, and responded to very substantial interests. As we have seen, similar privileges and licenses were even issued on papal soil for the Jews of Ancona, notwithstanding the otherwise rigidly anti-Jewish decrees.

Large numbers of Iberian Jews made their way to the port of Livorno, attracted by the guarantees offered by a situation wholly unique in Italy. Naturally, the Roman authorities objected, and tried to use the Inquisition to control the main centers of Sephardic Jewry in Italy (Ferrara, Venice, Livorno, Ancona), and especially the phenomenon of marranism, which was viewed with strong suspicion. Livorno became one of the capitals of the western Sephardic diaspora, especially for the Portuguese, and an essential hub in the business networks of Sephardic merchants and their families who established themselves in the city starting at the end of the 16th century, and through the following centuries up to the 1800s.

Livorno was granted the status of a city in 1606, freeing itself from Pisa. Its Jewish community surpassed that of Pisa in size, constituting a broad part of the economic and international fortunes of the city. The community in Livorno numbered over a 1,000 members in the first half of the 1600s. For the rest of the century, it would continue to attract Portuguese marranos fleeing from their homeland, who could now choose their religious identity and return, if they wished, to Judaism. This worried the inquisitors, who lamented the large number of Iberian New Christians "who come to Italy to live as Jews and judaize".[51] A long decline began around 1715 due to competition from the port of Marseilles, but Livorno would continue to enjoy considerable prestige for another two centuries. Its synagogue, damaged during World War II and later demolished, was one of the largest and most beautiful in Europe.

For a long time, the history of the Jewish presence in Livorno and the history of the Portuguese coincided. The liveliness of Jewish Livorno also translated into a mental willingness able to surmount the rigid borders between the Christian and Jewish worlds, and openness to experiences that allowed for blending and often hybridization of the two cultures and religions or, at least to a universalistic acceptance of the redemptive value of both.[52] In this sense the career of Jacob Rosales is exemplary; he was a key figure in the Sephardic diaspora, a Portuguese New Christian who was a scientist, diplomat, and physician, and in contact with Galileo Galilei. In the mid-1600s, already an old man, he chose to relocate from northern Europe to Livorno and, possibly influenced by the ideas of Jewish messianism (Sabbatianism), declared "that he was a Jew and professed the law of Moses" but "that in his heart he was convinced that followers of the law of Christ would also be saved".[53] The religious *latitudinarian*ism typically adopted by such figures has led historians to draw connections between the marrano experience and aspects of modernity.[54]

Sephardic commercial, financial, and entrepreneurial experience was equally significant and important on the economic level, strengthened by the dense networks of relations that linked the principal Sephardic families of the city through matrimony, and especially by the mercantile alliances stretching into the Levant, northern Europe, across the Atlantic, and even to Asia. These leading families maintained firm control over communal offices (those called *massari* or seats on the councils). They created an economic group that arose from the ties they maintained with markets in their countries of origin, especially Portugal and its colonial empire. The processing of Mediterranean corals was completely in Jewish hands, and the finished product was shipped to India, Russia, and China in exchange for diamonds. Such was the case with the recently studied Ergas and Silvera families.[55] The connections established by these Sephardic merchants were the basis for a transcultural network with Catholics in Portugal and Hindus in India. Theirs is a "global history", in which commercial diasporas appear woven into networks that include unusual and diverse partners and business associates. The two families mentioned above, bound by marriages as well as by business ventures, enjoyed the highest social prestige, imitating the habits and customs of Christians; they had coats of arms, drove in carriages, and kept private boxes at the theater.

The wills of these merchants also reveal far-reaching business affairs. Often a member of the family or an associate would settle at one of the various centers of business in order to monitor trade: in Genoa, Venice, Florence, Amsterdam, Smyrna, Constantinople, Tunisia, Marseilles, Goa, New Spain, in the Americas, and in Mexico.[56] But the Livornese were not only merchants. Through the appropriation of the lucrative tobacco concession, a luxury good in growing demand, and real estate investments in homes and land, groups of entrepreneurs developed. For these Jewish families land ownership functioned as a means of ever greater integration into the majority society. This process would be confirmed in 1780 following the grand duke's reform of the municipal government, when the Jewish nation was granted a representative in Livorno's town council with the right to vote, an honorarium, and a seat equal to the Christian representatives. Landowning Jews thus began to get involved with the link between property ownership and citizenship that was typical of the bourgeois societies of the 19th century, and which was eventually confirmed for Jews by the processes and laws of emancipation. Participation in the economic sphere and the assimilationist role of money enabled integration with local elites, as well as extra-economic forms of recognition and relationships with the majority society. In Livorno, for example, Jews were able to join various associations, one of which was the Masons. We can also see the role of money in fostering social and economic integration and cultural assimilation in the Jews' adoption of typical Christian mechanisms for preserving status, for example, the *fideicommissum* established for real estate assets. We find numerous acts of that sort drawn up in Livorno as early as the end of the 17th century and through the following century.

The Livornese community was dominated and administered by a restricted Spanish and especially Portuguese Sephardic oligarchy that excluded Italian Jews. This situation remained substantially unchanged until the early decades of the 18th century when, in 1715, the grand-ducal authorities extended participation in the offices of community government to Italiani Jews. Nonetheless the political, economic, and cultural dominance of the Sephardim continued for a long time. The families of the "Sephardic nobility", leaders of the community, withdrew from large international trading over time, leaving this to newcomers and living on the income they derived from the large real estate holdings they had accumulated. The "Jewish nation" soon became the most numerous and most economically important of the various foreign "nations" established at Livorno.

Uniquely for Italy, Livorno never had a closed ghetto; rather it had a Jewish neighborhood gathered around the synagogue, where the wealthiest Jews did not actually reside. Demographic growth was rapid. The 134 Jews of 1601 had become 1,250 by 1645 and more than 2,000 in the mid-17th century, when Livorno constituted the largest European Jewish community of the Western Sephardic diaspora after Amsterdam. They made up between 7% and 13.5% of the city's population between the start of the 17th and the end of the 18th centuries. Over the course of the 18th century and into the first years of the next, this Jewish community became the most populous in Italy – perhaps even larger than Rome's – and one of the largest in Europe, rising from 3,476 total in 1738 to almost 5,000 in 1809, equivalent to 10% of the city population.[57] The demographic growth was naturally due to the continued influx of immigrants. In the same period, Rome had about the same number of individuals (from 3,000–3,500 to 5,000), which was equivalent, however, to just a little more than 3% of its population.

Northern Italy. Lombardy, Piedmont, Liguria

In Northern Italy, the geographic reach of Italian Judaism extended to Lombardy, Piedmont, Genoa, and to the eastern territories of Veneto and Friuli. Jewish moneylenders, for the most part of German origins and hailing from beyond the Alps, settled in Lombardy towards the end of the 14th century.[58] The rather significant number of towns – more than one hundred – in which they settled and where they pursued trade, manufacturing, and agriculture, in addition to banking suggests that their presence made an important contribution to the region's economic development. The first authorization for a bank was issued in 1386, by the Gonzaga *signoria* at Mantua. Almost simultaneously, the duke of Milan, Gian Galeazzo Visconti, allowed a group of German Jews to settle in his State. Between 1450 and 1500, the number of Jewish settlements multiplied, expanding to the major cities and the minor towns, where they engaged in a wide variety of enterprises. Nevertheless, life in the region was not peaceful for Jews, due to violent attacks by the Friars Minor of the Observance and the ruling classes that were opposed to Jewish moneylending. An acute crisis arose in 1488, during the Sforza dynasty under Ludovico the Moor, when 40 Jewish residents were tried for possession of books considered offensive to the Christian religion. Nine were condemned to death and the others were sentenced to seizure of their assets and expulsion. These severe measures were only averted with the payment of an enormous sum of money from the Jews. The Jews of the Duchy of Milan, which in 1535 had passed under direct Spanish rule, suffered the consequences of decades characterized by great political and military upheavals, which led to a reduction in their activities.

Here too, the turning point was a consequence of the expulsion of the Jews from all Spanish controlled lands, which included the definitive expulsion from Milanese territory declared in 1590 and concluded seven years later in 1597. The wave of migration flowed mainly towards the Gonzaga Duchy, but also towards the Savoyard State and Tuscany. In the Lombard region, the real exception was the Duchy of Mantua, where Jews enjoyed a degree of tranquility under the Gonzagas throughout the 1600s, along with the opportunity to engage in all sorts of businesses and even entrepreneurship. Until the establishment of the ghetto in 1610, the Duchy proved to be the safest, most welcoming place for Jews in Lombardy, as attested to by its extraordinary demographic growth: at the start of the 1500s, the Jewish nucleus numbered around 200 persons, but had increased to 2,325 by 1610.[59]

Jewish moneylenders from France and Germany began to settle in what is today the Piedmont region towards the end of the 14th century. Jews originating from Rome or central Italy were a minority. Between 1450 and 1550, the settlements multiplied even in small towns: the majority of the members of these communities were engaged in moneylending activities. In 1565, the new duke Emanuele Filiberto granted a *condotta* to the Jews that authorized them to reside anywhere in his State, and to carry out their business under the ruler's protection: this inaugurated a line of Jewish policy to which the House of Savoy would remain substantially faithful. A destination for migrants leaving the Papal States after the expulsions of 1569, Piedmont offered hospitality to the "Jewish nation" in all of its ethnic-geographic expressions. With a letter published in 1572 that offered privileges, the duke invited Italian, German, Spanish, Portuguese, and Levantine Jews to introduce "every type of art and trade" and business relationships "with Turks, Moors, Persians, Armenians", guaranteeing them an unusually long *condotta* for twenty-five years, and an exemption from taxes for bank owners.[60] But in 1679, although somewhat late with respect to the institution of other ghettos, a *claustro degli ebrei*, "cloister of the Jews", was also set up in Turin.

The Republic of Genoa's situation was unique. Jews arriving from Northern Italy and Central Europe had been present in the capital since the Middle Ages. Already numerous in the 12th century, they played an important part in constructing a central role for the city in international trade in the Mediterranean, and remained an active factor in economic and commercial life. It's also worth noting the Jews' peculiar relationship with Genoa. In fact, the Republic's policy oscillated between concessions and rejections of the Jewish presence, consistent with an essentially pragmatic attitude; on the other hand, the Jews themselves succeeded in staying, through licenses and individual permits, especially those able to weave themselves into the socio-economic fabric of the city. Not even the arrival *en masse* of the Spanish Sephardim in 1492, which occurred, moreover, during a period of acute political crisis and economic decline for the Ligurian city, changed the situation much. There were various decrees of expulsion, which were repeated but nevertheless remained a dead letter until the mid-1500s. For example, as early as the winter of 1493 the Genovese authorities, worried by the continuing influx of migrants, issued a first edict of expulsion; however, it had little effect, as did those which followed it, repeated with the same outcome.[61]

During the 17th century, economic crisis and competition from Livorno induced Genoa to establish its free port, also open to Jews, as the government hoped to attract capital and economic benefits. It was Jews from Livorno who asked to be allowed to settle in the city, with the aim of assuring their access to this market as well. In 1658, they were granted the right to reside in Genoa and to trade freely there. Thus, a stable community arose, internally organized, with a synagogue and with its homes set inside a ghetto.[62]

Venice, the Cosmopolitan City

The history of Jewish settlement in Venice, which was late in welcoming Jews permanently, is very particular. The presence of Jewish moneylenders in the city dates back to the 10th century. In 1385, the first *condotta* related to moneylending was granted, for a ten-year period. However, an expulsion was decreed in 1394, effective upon the *condotta*'s expiration. Highs and lows in the policy towards the Jews followed; prohibited from settling in the capital, Jews started to settle in the towns of the mainland. However, the anti-usury preaching of the Friars Minor in these places spread intolerance and prejudice. Most of all, in various towns – excepting Venice and Mestre – this preaching led to the introduction of competition from the *Monte di Pietà*, non-profit credit institutions making short-term loans for small sums. In the second half of the 15th century, events related to the accusations of ritual murder at Trent (1475) and Portobuffolè (1490) triggered expulsions from Treviso, Vicenza, Udine, and other minor towns, which resulted in the concentration of refugees in Verona, Padua, and Rovigo.

The Jews who had been cast out of Venice at the end of the 1300s had instead gathered at Mestre, where they quietly went about their business, even in Venice, though without stable settlements in the lagoon city. During the War of the League of Cambrai (1508), however, they took refuge in Venice along with many others from the mainland cities that had been conquered by the empire. The turning point arrived with the defeat of the Venetians at Agnadello, in Lombardy (May 14, 1509), when the Most Serene Republic risked being wiped off the map by a coalition of all the major European powers, united against Venice to prevent *La Serenissima* from conquering Milan. The Jews then fled from the mainland, now occupied by the French and imperial forces, and sought refuge in great numbers in Venice, protected by the safe waters of its lagoon.

This time they managed to stay, thanks to the funds they showered on the Republic under the guise of loans or contributions for its political and military predicaments, and to the fact that the Venetian ruling class was aware that a new expulsion would have dealt a serious blow to the Venetian economy, especially in the area of foreign trade. It was at this juncture that history's first ghetto was born. Venice, in fact, granted Jews permanent and definitive residence in the city in 1516, establishing the quarter named Ghetto Nuovo in Cannaregio. The process unfolded gradually. In 1541 the Levantines, Jews from the Ottoman Empire, were permitted to settle in the city as foreign subjects for a limited time for trade. Ponentines from the Iberian Peninsula were not included in this concession, nor were New Christians, who were considered apostates and marranos. In fact, after pressure from the pope and Spain, the marranos were expelled from the city in 1550. But after the Christian victory at Lepanto in 1571, and with the dominance of the anti-papal and anti-Spanish party in the Venetian government, in 1573 the Council of the Ten invited the Spanish and Portuguese Jews who lived in the West to settle in Venice, offering them a safe-conduct for two years and immunity from accusations of apostasy. Thus began the construction of the Venice-Split commercial trade axis, which competed with the rival Ancona-Ragusa axis for control of the land and sea routes through the Balkans. In the following decade, a *condotta* was granted to the Ponentine nation in 1589 which assured the Sephardim who wished to settle in the city freedom of movement, guarantees for the security of their property and businesses, and autonomy in matters of tax collection. They were granted privileges enjoyed by Venetian merchants and their immunity from religious persecution was reaffirmed.[63] Venice's decision to also consent to the permanent residency of these Jews was dictated by the need to not be left out of the trade connected to the Sephardic network – trade that the Italian States, even the Papal States, were all competing for after the Iberian expulsions. The Ghetto Nuovo was expanded, and in 1541 the Ghetto Vecchio was added.

The community saw continued demographic growth, due also to new immigration, rising from around 700 individuals in the early 16th century to 1,694 in 1589, up to 2,378 at the start of the following century and about 2,600–2,650 in 1649.[64] In the second half of the 17th century, the population instead began to decline. The fundamental contribution to the demographic growth of the Venetian Jews came from the immigration of the Ponentine Jews, especially the Portuguese. The distinctively cosmopolitan character of the city would become ever more pronounced with time, giving the ghetto a liveliness that came from the close coexistence of diverse synagogues and rites (Italian, German, Levantine, Spanish, and Portuguese). Nor should we forget, in framing the cosmopolitanism which extended across the whole city, the presence of Armenians, Orthodox Greeks, and Muslims in Venice, the latter residing in their own quarter.[65]

From the mid-16th century to the mid-17th century, thousands of Iberian Jews arrived in Venice, which in the 1600s became one of the great centers for marranos in Europe.[66] Endogamous marriages, geographical mobility, and economic specialization built a community that was active in intra-Mediterranean commerce and very well integrated into the life of the city. As we shall see better further on, the cultural contribution of Sephardic Jewry was very important to the intellectual life of Venice and of Italy.

For the Ponentine Jews of Venice, bonds with their country of origin remained very strong, in particular with Portugal, as attested to by their use of the Portuguese language in wills, and the references and bequests to relatives who were still (New) Christians residing in the Iberian territories these contained. The implicit message in such wills is that the testators were born Christians on the Iberian Peninsula and that their relations with those lands had not ceased after their departure.[67] On the other hand, their travels and high mobility are a confirmation of the family and business networks that still tied the immigrants to their native land. These were often characterized by the camouflaging and disguising of identity: New Christians would travel in Italy as Jews, and Sephardic Jews would go to Spain and Portugal under Christian identities. For this reason, mobility should not be understood only as relocation to more tolerant countries, as is generally believed in regard to the emigration of the *conversos* from Spanish dominions, but also as a continuous circulation within the network of Sephardic settlements. Thus, there were games of identity that were a specialty not only of Venetians, but also the Ponentine merchants.

Printing Jewish Books: a Competitive Christian Business

Jewish culture was very active in Venice, starting with the printing of books. Even before the official birth of the ghetto in 1516 Jewish publishing had flourished in the city; and it would go on increasing in importance until the early decades of the 17th century, when it began to decline due to local conflicts, as we will see, and because of competition from printing houses in Amsterdam and other cities. At the end of the 15th century, the Jewish printer Gershom (Girolamo) Soncino set up shop in Venice. He belonged to a family of printers from Spira that had relocated from Germany to Italy: indeed, to Soncino, a small, wealthy city in Lombardy, in what is today the province of Cremona. However, various difficulties combined to ruin Gershom's plans to settle in Venice, in particular bitter competition from Daniel Bomberg, who had invested heavily in order to publish Jewish books. Soncino then left Venice and moved to Fano, where he began a new publishing direction, no longer based strictly on publications in Hebrew, but also on texts in Latin and the vernacular, expanding his publishing activity to many Adriatic cities: Pesaro, Ortona, Rimini, Ancona, and Cesena. He was active until 1527, when the altered situation in Italy led him to depart for the Ottoman Empire, where he continued his work at Thessaloniki and Constantinople until 1534, the year of his death.[68]

  With the field left open by Soncino, the lucrative business of Venice's Jewish press remained solidly, and solely in Christian hands. The key player was Daniel Bomberg.[69] A wealthy Flemish Catholic merchant from Antwerp, where the printing press had been present since 1482, he grasped the possibilities the new industry offered. He decided to relocate to Venice, already an established capital of the printing business, which was highly developed there; but most importantly, Venice had the most favorable geography. He had been steered towards Jewish printing by a converted Jew, Felice da Prato, a person of great intellectual stature who was also his Hebrew teacher. Such an enterprise certainly presented very favorable prospects commercially, because there was an ever-increasing demand for Jewish books from wealthy communities – not only in Italy, where so many exiles from Spain and Portugal had flocked, but throughout Europe and the East. Moreover, in these same years, Pope Leo X showed a great tolerance towards the Jews – in contrast to his predecessor Julius II – so much so, that he did not object to the installation of a Jewish printing press in Rome itself. The endeavor was even sponsored by Cardinal Egidio da Viterbo. Indeed, the pope offered Bomberg the task of building this printing house, but he refused.

Bomberg equipped his printing shop well, employing four Jewish typesetters, who were exempted from the obligation to wear the yellow cap. Erudite scholars, Jewish or converted, were hired to support the venture. The last of the great text editors who worked for Bomberg was Elia Levita, a lexicographer and grammarian, and a protégé of Cardinal Egidio da Viterbo. He left Rome following the sack of the city by the imperial landsknechts in 1527, and was welcomed to Venice by Bomberg, for whom he worked until the liquidation of the company. Bomberg thus became the most famous publisher of books in the Hebrew language in Venice. His first volume, though not in Hebrew, appeared in 1515; that the same year he obtained a ten-year exclusive from the Venetian Senate on the printing, sale, and importation of books in Hebrew. The imitation of the series of precious Hebrew characters that Bomberg had crafted was also prohibited. Bomberg was not Jewish, and this worked in his favor; as Soncino's misadventures had shown, had he been Jewish he would not have been able to obtain the privilege for the press.

In December 1516, the year the ghetto of Venice was established, Bomberg released the first book printed in Hebrew in Venice, the *Pentateuch*. Besides various prayer formularies, he also published three editions of the Bible with rabbinical commentary. The *Rabbinical Bible*, from 1524 to 1525, a true *editio princeps*, remained the model for all editions that followed, even those of today. His presses produced more than 200 works in Hebrew, and his innovations in the field of Jewish typography constituted the prototype for successive printers. Bomberg was encouraged by erudite Jews – and by some humanists such as Johannes Reuchlin – to publish the *Talmud* in its entirety (the Babylonian *Talmud* and the Jerusalem *Talmud*). Publishing the foundational text of Jewish wisdom, but also a book considered heretical and prohibited since the Middle Ages, represented an immense and risky venture, since it required a truly staggering capital investment.[70] Nevertheless, the text saw the light between 1522 and 1523 with two more printings, and remained the foundation of all subsequent editions, even the most recent. With his exquisite printings, Bomberg elevated Hebrew typesetting in Venice to such a level of excellence that it was considered the best in Europe. But this attracted envy, competition, and even counterfeiting. In fact, by the 1540s, times were becoming more difficult economically for the printer and the Jewish press in general. In 1545, the Venetian aristocrat Marco Antonio Giustinian opened a rival print shop, copying Bomberg's works with impunity.

Giustinian, aware of his competitor's pre-eminence, and of the immediate need to ensure he had competent workers, secured the collaboration of some of Bomberg's expert assistants, printers, and engravers, contributing to the Flemish printer's growing troubles. Bomberg, who had returned to Antwerp in 1538, was forced to halt his printing business in Venice in 1549. Meanwhile, the cultural climate in Italy was changing in regards to the policy of tolerance that until then had prevailed in dealings with Judaism and its books. In Venice, the Senate declared the establishment of a strict censorship of the press, entrusted to the secular courts of the *Esecutori contro la bestemmia* (Executors against Blasphemy), while the task of issuing licenses was assigned to the Reformers of the University of Padua. Bomberg never returned to Venice, perhaps not wishing to witness the end of his youthful illusion of a grand commercial firm which in reality had ruined his family fortune. The typographer, who had been dubbed the "Aldo of Jewish books", in reference to the celebrated Aldo Manuzio, passed away at Antwerp in 1553. His firm was liquidated and all the books that remained in the warehouse were seized from his heirs and destroyed. Giustinian achieved the goal of his machinations, taking Bomberg's place as the sole remaining typographer in Venice who printed and trafficked in Hebrew books. Between 1546 and 1551, he too published the complete edition of the Babylonian *Talmud*.

After Bomberg's exit from the scene, Giustinian was able to hold on to his monopoly on Hebrew printing in Venice for a short time, though without ever succeeding in equaling the typographical perfection of his predecessor. But he too would encounter a fierce competitor. The commercial struggle that would arise from their rivalry had disastrous consequences for the Jewish press and Jewish culture itself in Italy, especially in Venice. In 1550, Alvise Bragadin, another Venetian aristocrat who enjoyed the favor of the Reformers of the University of Padua, wished to set up a Hebrew print shop in his native city, also launching a far-flung trade of such books, which he would export not only throughout Italy, but to the Jewish communities of Europe and the Near East as well. The firm he established was carried on by his son Giovanni, by Giovanni's children and by their descendants until the mid-18th century, under the name of *Stamperia Bragadina*.[71] The rivalry and competition that had characterized relations between Giustinian and Bomberg escalated, resulting in even worse relations between Giustinian and Bragadin, mutual complaints and lawsuits. These commercial conflicts between the two aristocrats demonstrate what was at stake economically, given the great demand for Jewish books throughout the world of the diaspora. But the hostilities and the rivalry between these two Venetian printers sparked a crisis with destructive results for Jewish culture, and more generally for Italian culture as a whole.

Bragadin took the rivalry so far as to denounce his rival to the Inquisition in Rome itself, accusing him of having published Jewish books that contained clauses which were blasphemous and contrary to Christian religion (to wit, the *Talmud*). His quarrel with Giustinian fit in with the mounting climate of anti-Jewish intolerance in Italy. The Venetian aristocracy was not immune to this climate, in spite of attempts by Venetian printers on several occasions to oppose the application of restrictive laws that would have

damaged their very profitable businesses. In Rome, the papacy was changing its stance: though Bomberg's edition of the *Talmud* had in a certain sense
been sponsored by Leo X, Julius III, who ascended to the *Throne* of St. Peter
in 1550, had radically altered the attitude of the Church regarding Jews and
the *Talmud*, and shortly thereafter Paul IV instituted the ghetto in 1555.
The culminating moment of the new policy was the Inquisition's decree of
September 12, 1553, which ordered the condemnation, confiscation, and
the public burning of all copies of the *Talmud* for containing blasphemies
against the Christian faith. Jewish books had already been fed to the flames
in Rome's Campo de' Fiori on September 9.

When the Congregation of the Holy Office decided to extend the papal
decree to all the Christian princes and rulers, Venice quickly complied. On
October 18, 1553, the Council of Ten ordered the requisition and burning
of all copies of the *Talmud*, including summaries, compendia, or excerpts.
Those who did not comply were threatened with very serious penalties. The
book burning was carried out on October 21, 1553, in Piazza San Marco
and at Rialto. Giustinian's attempts to prevent the confiscation of copies of
the two *Talmuds* that he had recently printed were in vain, as was his paradoxical appeal to the pope for reimbursement for his losses. The *Talmud*
printed by Giustinian was completely destroyed, at a truly massive financial
cost. The company ceased all activities, swept away by the unforeseen consequences of a controversy incited only out of rivalry and personal interest.
Bragadin, who had not printed the *Talmud*, suffered minor losses, but was
likewise forced to cease printing for a short time, during which no one in
Venice held the right to print Jewish books. The two men's jealous rivalry
thus caused a cultural catastrophe.

Historians have postulated that Venetian suspicions that the Jews were
possible agents of the Turks might explain why the Republic obeyed the Inquisition's decree so promptly, given Venice's legendary independence. And,
yet the first Italian edition of the Koran was produced at Venice, published
by Andrea Arrivabene in 1547: a work with clear political aims – linked to
the French negotiations for an alliance with the Muslim empire against the
Habsburgs – that enjoyed very broad success across different social strata.[72]

In 1559, the *Esecutori contro la bestemmia* authorized the printing of Jewish texts, still excluding the *Talmud*, which was inserted into the first *Index*
of Prohibited Books (*Index Librorum Prohibitorum*) published by Paul IV
for all Christians. But by 1564, the Tridentine *Index* reauthorized the printing of the *Talmud*, provided that it was expurgated and without a title on its
cover. This easing of the pressure permitted Venetian presses that printed in
Hebrew, led by Bragadin, to resume their work, though never again reaching past heights of excellence. Later on, permission to print Hebrew books
was granted again, but subject to censorship, that "license of the Superiors"
which we find in all of the books printed in Venice from the second half of
the 16th century onwards. But by now the sun had set on the golden age
of the Jewish press in Venice, and other cities, especially Amsterdam, had

taken the lead. In 1596, the new *Index* of Clement VII definitively renewed the prohibition on and total condemnation of all these books. And yet (as we will see in Part 2), notwithstanding the misfortunes of the publishing industry, the greatest and most important exponents of Jewish culture were active right there in Venice.

Notes

1 Luzzati, "Banchi e insediamenti," 187.
2 See the map of settlements in Gasperoni, "I banchieri ebrei," 150.
3 Andreoni, "Gli ebrei della Marca," 109–47.
4 Veronese, "La presenza ebraica," 251–81; Gasperoni, "I banchieri ebrei," 149–61.
5 Colletta, *La comunità tollerata.*
6 On the Jewish community of Ancona in the 16th through the 18th centuries, see Andreoni, *Una nazione in commercio*, and the large bibliography there.
7 Israel, *Gli ebrei d'Europa*, 27. Concerning the marranos, see above, 9–13.
8 Ioly Zorattini, "Ancora sui giudaizzanti," 51. The quotation is from the 15th- to 16th-century chronicler, Bartolomeo Alfei.
9 Curtin, *Cross-Cultural Trade.* For a more recent further theoretical discussion of trade diasporas see Trivellato, *The Familiarity of Strangers.*
10 Andreoni, *Una nazione in commercio*, 53–4 ss.
11 Di Leone Leoni, "Alcuni esempi di quotidiana," 57–114.
12 Di Leone Leoni, *La nazione ebraica spagnola*, 189.
13 Bonazzoli, "Ebrei italiani, portoghesi e levantini," 727–70.
14 Regarding the economic and social history of the Jews in Ancona between the 16th and 18th centuries refer to Andreoni, *Una nazione in commercio.*
15 Andreoni, *Una nazione in commercio*, 81.
16 For Livorno, see below, 49–54. See above, 26–33.
17 Andreoni, *Una nazione in commercio*, 47.
18 On Barboso, see Andreoni, "Gli ebrei della Marca," 128–42; and earlier, Di Leone Leoni, "Per una storia della Nazione Portoghese," 27–97. On the Portuguese marranos at Ancona cfr. Ravid, "A Tale of Three Cities"; Cooperman, "Portuguese Conversos in Ancona".
19 Andreoni, "Gli ebrei della Marca," 130.
20 Dedieu, "Conversos, Spagna," 406–8; regarding the historiographical debate cfr. Stuczynski, "Marranesimo," 989–97 and bibliography. On marrano identity, in addition to the classic by Roth, *Storia dei Marrani*, cfr. Révah, "Les marranes portugais," 185–232 and Yerushalmi, *Dalla corte al ghetto*, 33–71. However the bibliography is immense.
21 See Chapter 4.
22 About new Christians returning to Judaism, see Kaplan, *Les nouveaux-juifs d'Amsterdam.*
23 Ioly Zorattini, *L'identità dissimulata*; Wachtel, *La fede del ricordo.*
24 Graizbord, *Souls in Dispute.*
25 Regarding the Portuguese at Ferrara, cfr. Di Leone Leoni, *La nazione ebraica spagnola*; Segre, "La formazione di una comunità," 779–841. For a comparison between Ancona, Venice and Livorno, see Ravid, "A Tale of Three Cities," 138–62. For Venice, cfr. Ruspio, *La Nazione portoghese.*
26 Bonazzoli, "Una identità ricostruita," 9–38.
27 Frattarelli Fischer, "Gli ebrei, il principe," 226.
28 Ruspio, *La Nazione portoghese*, 21.

29 Segre, "La formazione di una comunità," 725–6.
30 Di Leone Leoni, *La nazione ebraica spagnola*, 609.
31 Belligni, *Renata di Francia*.
32 Di Leone Leoni, "Alcuni esempi di quotidiana," 72; *La nazione ebraica spagnola* I, especially 51–4, 65.
33 Di Leone Leoni, "Sedaqua," 1405.
34 Di Leone Leoni, "Alcuni esempi di quotidiana," 80.
35 Di Leone Leoni, "Alcuni esempi di quotidiana," 81.
36 For the Jews in Ferrara, cfr. Segre, "La formazione di una comunità," 779–841; and more recently Di Leone Leoni, *La nazione ebraica spagnola*.
37 Di Leone Leoni, *La nazione ebraica spagnola*, I, 186–7.
38 Di Leone Leoni, *La nazione ebraica spagnola*, I, 515–8 and doc. 1170, II, 1033–6.
39 Di Leone Leoni, *La nazione ebraica spagnola*, I, 515.
40 Segre, "La formazione di una comunità," 813–9. On Sephardic printing in Ferrara, see Di Leone Leoni, *La nazione ebraica spagnola*, 423–61.
41 Toaff, *Gli ebrei a Perugia*; *The Jews in Umbria*.
42 Luzzati, "Ruolo e funzione dei banchi ebraici," 742–4.
43 Luzzati, "Banchi e insediamenti ebraici," 195–6.
44 Luzzati, "Banchi e insediamenti ebraici," 198f.
45 Siegmund, *The Medici State*.
46 Toaff, *La Nazione ebrea a Livorno*; Luzzati, *Ebrei ed ebraismo a Pisa*.
47 Frattarelli Fischer, *Vivere fuori dal ghetto*, 15ff.
48 Marcocci, "Itinerari marrani," 405–17, esp. 407; Frattarelli Fischer, "Ebrei a Pisa e Livorno," 93–116.
49 Caffiero, *Legami pericolosi*, 12–15.
50 On Jewish Livorno, cfr. Filippini, "La nazione ebrea," 1045–66; Frattarelli Fisher, "Reti toscane," 93–116; *Vivere fuori dal ghetto*. For an analysis from the perspective of gender, cfr. Galasso, "La moglie duplicata". Regarding international economic exchanges, Jewish and otherwise, see Trivellato, *The Promise and Peril of Credit*. For a cultural analysis of the relationship between Jews and the Enlightenment in Livorno, see Bregoli, *Mediterranean Enlightenment*.
51 Marcocci, "Itinerari marrani," 412.
52 As had happened in the New World, in particular in the Brazilian colonies: cfr. Wachtel, *Entre Moïse et Jésus*.
53 Frattarelli Fischer, "Ebrei a Pisa e Livorno," 277–9.
54 Wachtel, *Entre Moïse et Jésus*.
55 Trivellato, *The Familiarity of Strangers*.
56 On the wills of Jewish merchants in Livorno, see Frattarelli Fischer, "Reti toscane," 102–4.
57 Filippini, "La nazione ebrea," 1054.
58 Simonsohn, *The Jews in the Duchy of Milan*; Luzzati, "Banchi e insediamenti ebraici," 205.
59 Segre, "La Controriforma," 745–7; Simonsohn, *The Jews in the Duchy of Mantua*.
60 On the presence in the Piedmont, cfr. Segre, *The Jews in Piedmont*.
61 Zazzu, *Sepharad addio*.
62 Urbani, "Nuovi documenti," 193–209.
63 Ravid, "The Venetian Government," 3–30; Ruspio, *La Nazione portoghese*, 64. The bibliography on the Jews of Venice is extensive: I refer to the one cited by Ruspio.
64 Favero, and Trivellato, "Gli abitanti del ghetto di Venezia," 9–50. On the ghetto, see here further on in Part II; Calabi, "Il ghetto e la città," 125–203.
65 Calabi, *La città degli ebrei*.
66 For more on these aspects, cfr. Ruspio, *La Nazione portoghese*.

67 Ruspio, *La Nazione portoghese,* 117.
68 Tamani, "Gershom Soncino," 1–7.
69 Cioni, "Bomberg, Daniel," 382–7.
70 On the question of the Talmud and its condemnation, see Part II, Chapter 6. In particular, cfr. Parente, "La Chiesa e il 'Talmud'," 580–91, especially 541; now updated in Parente, "L'Église et le Talmud," 233–394.
71 Cioni, "Bragadin, Alvise," 659–61.
72 Tommasino, *L'Alcorano di Macometto.*

3 Women in the History of Italian Jews

Marriage, Family, and the Role of Women

The history of the Italian Jews, and in particular the story of the marranos, is emblematic on many levels: the religious ambiguity, the cultural contamination, the extreme mobility, the entrepreneurial, political, and diplomatic skill, as well as a proactive posture that once again undercuts the stereotype of Jews as perpetually resigned and inert victims. But it is also emblematic from another point of view, namely the condition and role of women in Italian Judaism, as well as in marrano culture.

There were many women who were moneylenders or even owners of merchant houses; some were intellectuals and literati, such as the Venetian Sara Copio Sullam, to whom we will return further on. Jewish women generally enjoyed a more favorable situation than that of Christian women for a variety of reasons. First of all, the tradition established that Jewish identity was passed on to children through the maternal line. Furthermore, the limited marriage market and strong emphasis on endogamy, pursued to keep resources in the family, made the dowry system fundamental, and ended up making women more valuable. Finally, rabbinical rulings had recognized a relative equality of rights between a man and woman within a family, and indeed an advantage for the daughter through the dowry system. The tendency to arrange marriages that were alliances between two parties of equal status, and the nature of marriage, which among the Jews was simply a contract, opened important negotiating spaces between the genders, within which women won margins of autonomy and freedom in managing themselves and their assets.[1]

Divorce was permitted for Jewish women, and not only as recipients of the request; women also initiated and asked for divorce. They retained control of their assets and dowry after the death of a spouse or after divorce, and had the freedom to make a will, often favoring their children. Once widows, women were the official caretakers of their children as holders of the *patria potestas*, often in association with relatives from the matrilineal line, and continued to manage the deceased husband's affairs, including lending banks. The families were not only agnatic and patrilineal, as is often

DOI: 10.4324/9781003188445-5

believed, and in the absence of male heirs the lending bank was also passed down through the female line. Thus, a banker's son-in-law often inherited his father-in-law's business from his wife. As was also true for other occupations, the banking profession was not an exclusively male activity, and women too had their roles. Finally, in some cases, young women could also oppose marriages arranged by their parents, instead arranging unions of love. Marriage and family were the main setting of the lives of Jewish men and women, within a culture that was hostile to celibacy.[2]

The marriage market was also the most important opportunity for the re-distribution and circulation of family resources, and for social exchanges.[3] Women had an advantage in this process of redistribution, given that the share of assets passed on to male heirs was smaller than the considerable dowries set aside for Jewish girls. Within a group such as the Jews, who were at least in principle excluded from real estate ownership, the dowry represented security, an inviolable prerogative sanctioned almost everywhere by common law. As such, the dowry was a resource that shielded inheritances from various threats (creditors, flights, expulsions, seizures), and was used to finance the family's business ventures. Dowries also helped to discourage conversion; leaving the ghetto meant leaving the dowry behind too. The convert Giulio Morosini, formerly Samuel Nachamais (1612–87), famously lost a legal dispute with his wife, to whom he had to return a large dowry when she remained in her faith. Not by chance, therefore, familial strategies rotated around the payment or restitution of dowries, while women often held the most significant part of the family assets.[4]

This centrality of the female line in the realm of economic strategies had a positive impact on the role of women, enhancing their importance in the family, even within a predominantly patriarchal structure. Of course, there was also the important position of the mother in Jewish culture and tradition; after all, it was she who guaranteed the transmission of Jewish identity itself.[5] Thus, the existence of a mechanism for the transmission of assets to the female line, and the fact that daughters were at an advantage in the redistribution of wealth, strengthened the role of women and especially of mothers within the family.

Furthermore, marriage was strongly endogamous, that is, intra-familiar. Jewish law recognized unions between people connected by close blood relations – for example between uncle and niece, between cousins, even first cousins, or in cases of levirate marriage, between brothers in-law – broadening opportunities in the local marriage market. Of course, this custom stood in open contrast and opposition to the prohibitions on marriages between close relatives imposed by Catholic matrimonial rules. However, if necessary, there was also an exogamous openness among Jews towards other kinship groups that allowed the circulation of women outside their own community. In this way, the importance of women was also accentuated by the fact that they constituted the basis of matrimonial exchanges between Jewish families; the networks of alliances, including economic, among different communities were kept alive by female mobility, creating kinships, and relations between dynasties of equal social and economic status (this refers to "class endogamy", similar to that in Christian societies).

Women were therefore decisive for their family and the community of origin as mediators with the outside and with other communities and dynasties, contributing to building complex networks of kinship. Recent historiography has dedicated much attention to the strategic use of marriage for building alliances, along with growing capital and keeping it in the family. Marriages between blood relatives, combined with a large dowry that was sheltered from creditors in case of bankruptcy or death of the husband, contributed to the formation of business partnerships and ensured the transmission of capital from one generation to the next.[6] It is credible to suppose that the particular role of women in Jewish society also discouraged them from the temptations of conversion in comparison to men.

Of course, marriages did not only have a purely economic value. Just like in Christian society, economic interests and religious practices and rituals intertwined in matrimony. From the religious point of view, Jewish tradition attributed – and still attributes – a leading role to women in the observance of some ritual practices that are carried out in the home, such as lighting the Shabbat candles, the preparation of holiday meals, and observance of dietary laws. The role played by women in the families of new converts and marranos taking refuge in Italy was also important. As happened elsewhere, women were central to the preservation and transmission of Jewish identity and the ancestral faith from generation to generation within these groups of crypto-Jews, maintaining respect for religious rituals and practices and the memory of the land of origin.[7]

It is a little known but noteworthy fact that in the Sephardic diaspora, and therefore also in Italy, ancient practices such as levirate marriage and bigamy were still active; for example, they were observed at Livorno until the early years of the 18th century. Levirate marriage is a divine precept (*Deuteronomy*, 25, 5–10) which consisted of the obligation for a man to marry his sister-in-law if she was widowed without children. The goal was to keep the woman and her inheritance within the family group and guarantee the deceased a descendant, since the son born from the new union was treated as the son of the deceased, carried his name, and inherit his assets. According to some interpreters and rabbis with Kabbalistic leanings, levirate marriage is linked to the doctrine of the transmigration of the soul (*gilgul*), because the soul of the dead brother temporarily resides in the body of the living brother until he releases it into the body of his sister-in-law to procreate a child with her. Thus, the child would really be the son of her deceased husband, and indeed his reincarnation.[8] In the Sephardic community, these precepts and practices were linked to Kabbalistic doctrine, which also spread in Italy after the expulsion and exile of the Jews of Spain.

Regarding bigamy, in Sephardic Judaism, a man could marry a second wife if the first wife was unable to bear children for at least ten years: the ecclesiastical authorities themselves gave Jews who found themselves in this situation permission for a second marriage. This custom was instead prohibited in Ashkenazic, that is, German Jewish communities, in which both monogamy and the rejection of levirate marriage had been fully established since the 11th century. Thus, levirate marriage and bigamy mark a central difference between Sephardic and Ashkenazic Judaism. In the Sephardic communities, however, the custom of contracting bigamous or levirate marriages persisted, two practices that are closely connected to each other, given that levirate marriage could create bigamous marriages if the brother-in-law was himself already married.[9]

The survival of these practices was determined by reasons of social and economic order (access to more dowries for the husband, ensuring the patrilineal system and retaining assets within the family by preventing the widow from marrying "outside"), as well as religious reasons (taking a second wife to fulfill the biblical commandment of procreation and levirate marriage). Once again, the key problem was that of the dowry and the risk of having to return it when a husband became a widower or a widow entered a new marriage. To avoid this danger, it was necessary to control the circulation of inheritances, and of the individuals themselves in the marriage market, and above all to minimize the possibility of having to return the dowry in case of widowhood. As we have seen, dowries were the basis of the Jewish family economic system, inasmuch as for the most part they consisted of cash, which after the wedding could be invested in productive activities.

Over time, the needs of individual freedom, protecting the rights of women and their position in the marital relationship, and increasingly strong marital ties drove the Jewish authorities to accept the revision of these religious traditions. But in 1726, Rabbi Sansone Morpurgo of Ancona was again called to Livorno to give an opinion on a case concerning a Jew's second marriage, though his first wife was alive, and he ruled on it favorably.[10] Education for women was also provided, and women were active in some confraternities, such as those in Rome that provided dowries to poor girls.

The Extraordinary Story of a Marrano Woman. Beatriz Mendes de Luna/Gracia Nasi and the Other Women of Her Family

As we have seen, the role of women in marrano culture was of great importance. The life of Gracia Nasi (or Naci or Nasci or Nassi), a woman born in Lisbon, Portugal, to a family that had become new Christians following the mass forced baptisms of 1497, is exemplary of the material and spiritual story of the marranos in Italy. A leading figure in the history of the marrano diaspora, Beatriz Mendes de Luna (this was Gracia's Christian name) was born in 1510, and was therefore part of the first generation of new Christians. Like many marranos, she was secretly educated in Judaism and probably always considered herself a Jew, an assumption borne out by the choices she made throughout her life.[11] Her daring story is very significant in terms of different aspects we have analyzed so far: the important role of women in marrano society, the ability to preserve, albeit clandestinely, original Jewish identity and reclaim it at the opportune moment, her extraordinary mobility for a woman, the entrepreneurship of women in the Jewish world, the close relations with relatives, culminating in the closed matrimonial endogamy, and the support, even financial, she gave to the cultural rebirth of Sephardic Judaism. The return to using the same names within the family is also significant, for example giving nieces the same names as aunts.

At eighteen years of age, Beatriz married Francisco, heir of the very wealthy Benveniste family (new Christians now become Mendes). In Lisbon, he worked with the long distance trade of precious goods and spices, and he had another business in Flanders, at Antwerp, run by his brother Diogo. The life of new Christians in Portugal became increasingly difficult with the opening of the Inquisition's court in 1536, and the following year Beatriz, widowed at a very young age with a daughter, Ana, and now the true head of the family, decided to leave Lisbon and to move to Antwerp. She went to her brother-in-law with her sizeable entourage and her younger sister Brianda, who would marry Diogo two years later in 1539. The Benveniste/Mendes family was very large, and internal bonds were reinforced by strictly endogamic marriages. In fact, the two brothers Francisco and Diogo married the two sisters Beatriz/Gracia and Brianda/Reina, who were also their nieces, being the daughters of their sister Philippa. Diogo directed a huge enterprise at Antwerp, which, with branches in all the most important global markets of the time – in Italy, France, Germany, and England – controlled the spice trade, especially pepper, coming from the Levant and Portuguese India, according to the typical trade specialization of the Jews and Portuguese converts.

Using their networks of relations, and under the cover of commercial traffic, the Mendes, like the other members of the wealthy marrano colony of Antwerp, helped many Jews to export their capital and move to other more tolerant countries, facilitating their departures from both Portugal and Antwerp. In fact, they played a primary role in *Sedaqua*, the clandestine organization that assisted in the expatriation of judaizers. It is very probable that, given their influence even in their native country, along with their diplomatic contacts with Rome, they managed to greatly delay the introduction of the Inquisition in Portugal. Moreover, as we will see, representatives of the Portuguese new Christians, such as Pedro Furtado and Jacome de Fonseca, were actively working to this end, even in papal Rome.

The clandestine assistance of coreligionists, judaizing, and imperial hostility made even the marrano settlement at Antwerp increasingly risky. The religious ambiguity of this group is perfectly illustrated by the presence in Diogo's home in Antwerp of both a synagogue where Jewish prayers were recited in Castilian, and a portable altar given to him by Pope Paul III, where Catholic divine services were celebrated.[12] In 1532, Diogo was arrested on charges of secretly practicing Judaism and of helping judaizers to leave the country. Upon the death of her brother-in-law in 1543, Beatriz decided to leave the increasingly insecure city of Antwerp for good, along with all of her numerous family members. In his will, Diogo had named her caretaker of the daughter he had with Brianda, who bore the same name as her aunt, Beatriz. Nicknamed *Chica*, young Beatriz was the sole heir of his vast inheritance, which was therefore left to be administered by her aunt, and not by her mother Brianda.

Beatriz requested safe passage from the pope, who granted her permission to move through his territories, as well as from the Republic of Venice. She faced a long journey with a series of stops that were typical for the marrano diaspora: first Aix-la-Chapelle, then Lyon, and finally Venice, where she was granted a safe conduct that included her, her sister, their respective children and all their employees, as many as thirty people. Venetian liberality naturally depended on the importance of the person receiving it, and in this case also on the designs of the local patriciate to get its hands on the Mendes wealth, perhaps through a marriage with one of the widows or their daughters. After all, the Mendes women were baptized and Christian, even if it was a pretense, since they remained deeply Jewish. Beatriz and Brianda, always presenting themselves as Christians, settled with their retinue at palazzo Gritti on the Canal Grande, not far from the ghetto. However, their true belief and faith is demonstrated by the fact that they arranged to have the remains of their parents and of Beatriz' husband, Francisco Mendes, shipped to them from Portugal, so that they could be reinterred in a specially built chapel in Venice. From there, however, the remains were destined for the Holy Land, on the Mount of Olives in Jerusalem.

Beatriz, as executor of the will, had inherited half of the company's capital, and so became the administrator of an immense family fortune that she too continued to grow. But her predominant role exacerbated relations with Brianda, mother of the sole heir. The strife between the two sisters led to the long legal dispute that Brianda brought before the Venetian authorities against Beatriz over her daughter's inheritance. Following the ruling against her in this case in 1549, Beatriz decided to move to Ferrara, a more secure city under the protection of Duke Ercole II. Furthermore, policy towards marranos in Venice was changing; in fact, their expulsion would be ordered shortly afterwards in 1550.

Beatriz continued to manage the family's large banking and trade business from Ferrara. She was exempted from the limits on autonomy that the city statutes imposed on the women of Ferrara, which prohibited them from administering assets without the assistance of a relative, and worked completely independently. She obtained an exemption that was unique in the city, and was therefore the only woman of her century in Ferrara who enjoyed broad decision making freedom in the management of a great family banking and commercial enterprise, commanding a large group of employees and agents.[13] Brianda also moved to Ferrara to continue the dispute. They remained there for two years, even after the expulsion of marranos from Ferrara in 1550 following an epidemic of plague which was blamed on the presence of the Portuguese converts. The pair returned to Venice in 1551 and the legal fight resumed, finally arriving at a compromise approved by the Venetian Senate. At this point, the two sisters parted ways.

The dispute with Brianda now concluded, Beatriz left Venice for Turkey in 1552. As had only briefly happened earlier in Ferrara, in Constantinople, Beatriz was able to openly return to the faith of her ancestors, and return to using her Jewish name, Gracia Nasi (or Naci). Shortly afterwards, she was joined by her husband Francisco's nephew, Juan Micas (or João Miguez), who publicly converted to Judaism, had himself circumcised and took the name of Yosef Naci. He married his cousin Ana, now become the Jewish Reina, daughter of Beatriz and Francisco. Thus, the Mendes wealth stayed within the family.

In the meantime, Brianda and her daughter, who had remained in Venice, fell under suspicion and were pressured to declare their faith. Summoned by the Council of Ten, they too abandoned the fiction of their Christianity, publicly proclaiming themselves to be Jews. Brianda declared:

> Illustrious Gentlemen, I left my country in the lands of the Emperor to escape the Inquisition, because I was fine there and because of this I sought to come to this city, thinking that with the liberty of the city and with a safe conduct I could live quietly, however I will obey your lordships as if I was Saint Francis, I have many persecutors who have always tormented me.[14]

These words are highly emblematic of the hybrid and plural identities of the marranos: the clear terror of the Inquisition is combined with the ambiguous reference, for one who was declaring herself Jewish, to the example of obedience offered by Saint Francis. Immediately afterwards, she added "that she was a new Christian and had been one of those that had been baptized by force and that she had always lived as a Jew in her heart and wished to continue doing so".[15]

In the summer of 1555, Brianda and her daughter, now openly apostate, were also forced to leave Venice and go to Ferrara, where Brianda, once again become Reina Benveniste, died as a Jew in 1556. The guardian aunt set about trying to marry off her niece Beatriz, *la Chica*, now also become Gracia, and arranged a marriage with a cousin, Samuel Naci (formerly Bernardo Micas or Miguez), the brother of that Yosef Naci who had married Beatriz' daughter, Ana/Reina. In this way, the two cousins married their cousins, who were brothers, further binding intra-family relationships. The inheritance was now largely secure. The new couple reached relatives in Constantinople, in the Belvedere Palace at Pera, with a reunion seen by those in the Sephardic diaspora as a highly symbolic event for the happy outcome of the long travails of the Mendes-Naci family, and of the entire Jewish people.[16] The family fortunes did in fact multiply when Yosef was named the Duke of Naxos and the Cyclades by Sultan Selim II, and from his role as an important mediator with Christian Europe.[17]

During her brief stay in Ferrara several years earlier, Beatriz had also returned to calling herself Gracia, and had been a leader in the cultural life of the Jewish community. She was especially active in helping forced converts to rediscover the foundations of their religion and culture, and to strengthen their bonds with Judaism again. Thus, she was the driving force behind the publication of the Bible and other Hebrew liturgical works in Spanish, the language used for the project of Jewish "re-education" since it was the language spoken by the Sephardic exiles. Ferrara became the center of marrano publishing and of the publication of Jewish works translated into Spanish, the most important of which was the *Biblia en lengua española*, known as the "Ferrara Bible", which we have already mentioned. This happened thanks to the marrano printer Duarte Pinal, who was able to return to Judaism and his real name of Abraham Usque in Ferrara, as well as the support of influential personalities who had favor in court, such as Gracia herself and the learned doctor Isaac Abravanel, grandson of the illustrious biblical commentator of the same name (1437–1509).

The Bible itself was published in 1553 in two versions, which differed in their very significant dedications: the version aimed at Christians was offered to Duke Ercole II, while the one directed at the Jews was dedicated to Doña Gracia. The double dedication thus demonstrated that, in addition to the celebration of their protectors, the text composed by the Jewish intellectuals had a dual destination, directed as it was at Jews and also at Christians. Now, there was a Hebrew Bible in Spanish available to Christians at a time, when reading the Bible in any common tongue was forbidden to them. *Consolazione delle tribolazioni di Israele*, by Samuel Usque, was published at Ferrara in 1553, and is also dedicated to Gracia. The work was printed in Portuguese and is a classic of Jewish-Portuguese literature which reconstructs the millennial history of the Jewish people and their misfortunes from the fall of Jerusalem up to the end of the 15th century. In the dedication to Gracia, who is called "the heart of the Portuguese nation", she was praised for her merit in the work of rescuing and caring for many of her exiled coreligionists.

Just as in Ferrara, Gracia had a considerable impact in Constantinople. The woman who was called the *Señora*, denoting great respect, made her triumphant and noble entrance to the Turkish city in the summer of 1553 with a western and Spanish style procession made up of four carriages full of Spanish ladies and servants, accompanied by forty horsemen. A witness at the time remarked that she had brought with her a "retinue like the Duke of Spain".[18] She successfully petitioned Sultan Suleiman I the Magnificent to allow the members of her house to wear hats and dress in the Venetian style, thus avoiding the saffron turbans that Jews had to wear.[19] She founded a rabbinical institute in Istanbul and dedicated herself intensely to assisting the poor and working with charitable organizations, without ever neglecting the affairs of the family business. She was also active in politics at the time of the tragic *auto da fé* of judaizers in Ancona, who were put to death at the stake in 1556. As we have seen, this was the most serious episode of persecution of marranos to occur in Italy during the early modern age, and it represented a radical turn in papal policy towards the new converts after Paul IV's rise to the pontifical throne and the institution of the ghetto in his States.

Gracia tried to react, working with the influential marrano community of Constantinople to establish a boycott of the port of Ancona, redirecting traffic to the port of Pesaro ruled by the Della Rovere – where many fugitives from Ancona were taking refuge – and prevailing upon the Sultan to intervene with the pope to discourage his harsh sentences, which were nevertheless carried out. All the Jewish communities of the Levant participated in the boycott of the Ancona market, and the rabbis proclaimed a ban that denied Jewish merchants access to that port: but the effort was not successful.

In the end, Gracia bought the city of Tiberias, in Palestine, from the Sultan. She intended to build a Jewish colony there and make it a center within the Ottoman Empire in which Jews of any origin could settle, thus anticipating the Zionist project. It the modern city of Tiberias, there is still a street that bears her name: *Doña Señora Gracia Street*. Gracia, no longer Beartriz, died in 1569, and the news of her passing echoed widely in the world of Sephardic Judaism. The literature about her, historical and fictional, is extensive, and has contributed to building her myth. For a long time, until 1890, in Istanbul there remained a synagogue dedicated to her and called the "*Señora*".

Notes

1 Galasso, *Alle origini di una comunità*, 27; Weinstein, *Marriage Rituals Italian Style*.
2 Weinstein, *Marriage Rituals Italian Style*.
3 Regarding the role of women in the family in Italy, cfr. Allegra, "Modelli di conversion," 912; "La madre ebrea," 53–75. For a history of matrimony among Italian Jews and the role of women, see Weinstein, *Marriage Rituals Italian Style*. See also Melasecchi and Spagnoletto, *Antique Roman Ketubot*, exhibition catalog.
4 Cfr. Caffiero, "Le disgrazie della conversione".
5 Regarding the status of Jewish women as "social protagonists", cfr. Siegmund, "La vita nei ghetto," especially 882. For other situations such as Torino and Livorno, cfr. Allegra, *Identità in bilico*; Galasso, *Alle origini di una comunità*.
6 Trivellato, *The Familiarity of Strangers*; Gasperoni, "I banchieri ebrei," 149–61.
7 Wachtel, *La fede del ricordo*.
8 On the Jewish belief in transmigration of the soul, cfr. Scholem, *Le grandi correnti*; Caffiero, *Legami pericolosi*, 93–9, 185–9; and the bibliography cited here.
9 Galasso, "'La moglie duplicata'," 417–41. Examples for Rome between the 15th and 16th centuries can be found in Esposito, "Matrimonio, convivenza, divorzio," 109–24, especially 118.

10 Galasso, "'La moglie duplicata'".
11 Muzzarelli, "Beatrice de Luna," 84. But more recently see Ioly Zorattini, "Gracia Nasci," 113–34 which contains many useful clarifications.
12 Ioly Zorattini, "Gracia Nasci," 120.
13 Di Leone Leoni, *La nazione ebraica spagnola*, I, 360.
14 Muzzarelli, "Beatrice de Luna," 94.
15 Muzzarelli, "Beatrice de Luna".
16 Ioly Zorattini, "Gracia Nasci," 128–9.
17 Roth, *The House of Nasi*; Grünebaum-Ballin, *Joseph Naci*; Calimani, *Storia del ghetto di Venezia*, 103–9.
18 Laguna, *Avventure di uno schiavo,* 190. Andres Laguna was a marrano doctor and wrote a travelogue in 1557 that is attributed to him.
19 On the Jewish minority in Ottoman society, cfr. Rozen, *Jewish Community in Istanbul.*

4 The First Trauma. The New Arrivals in Italy after 1492

The Expulsion from Spain

The complex and dramatic stories of the Sephardic Jews in Italy can be better understood, and take on greater significance and relevance if they are inserted into the general context of European history. Some Catholic States treated this active and enterprising minority much more harshly than the independent States of the Italian peninsula. Therefore, to better understand the story of Italian Judaism, we must pause briefly to look at the histories of the Jews of Spain and Portugal, which in turn had serious consequences for Italy.

On March 31, 1492, the Catholic Monarchs Ferdinand of Aragon and Isabella of Castilla issued an edict in the city of Granada, the capital of the Muslim Kingdom which had been conquered only three months earlier, requiring all Jews living in the Iberian Kingdom to leave the country by the following August 2. With the Muslim power eliminated from the Kingdom, now it the Jews' turn. The edict constituted the final act in a dramatic story of persecution, slaughter, and forced conversions of Jews which had begun as early as the 14th century, leading to tragic episodes of violence such as the massacres of thousands of people at Seville and Cordova in 1391, which were followed by many conversions. Parallel to these events legislation also became stricter, primarily aimed at a clearer separation between Jews and Christians and severe control over the *conversos*, the converted Jews who were constantly accused of judaizing, and therefore of the serious crime of apostasy. This increasingly tense atmosphere also saw the return of the accusation of ritual murder – the "blood libel" – according to which the Jews killed Christian children in order to collect their blood to be used in cooking the Passover matzah.

In this climate of hostility, the expulsion edict was published by the joint action of the monarchy and the Spanish Inquisition. The underlying reasons, however, went far back in time. The mass conversions of 1391 had created a novel problem for "old" Christians in Spain, since the new converts had begun to infiltrate various sectors of economic and public life in great numbers, holding offices in the municipal administrations or even in

DOI: 10.4324/9781003188445-6

the Church itself, areas from which Jews had always been excluded. The entrance of the new Christians into society aroused resentment and envy among the old Christians, who began to accuse the whole group of *conversos* of crypto-Judaism (marranism) in order to halt their social and economic rise. So, starting as early as the middle of the 1400s, *limpieza de sangre* laws were enacted locally, and progressively became a rule everywhere in Spain. These "purity of blood" laws prevented the full integration of the new Christians, excluding them from offices and professions based on their Jewish ancestry, even if it was ancient. The original stain was therefore not truly erased with baptism, and the appeal to hereditary blood implied a threatening use of biological and natural facts.

The court of the Inquisition, a special institution established in 1478, began prosecuting the heresy of Christians suspected of practicing Judaism. Thousands of new Christians were tried, had their assets confiscated, and often went to the stake. The essential problem that led to the expulsions of the Jews was the concern for avoiding dangerous "contaminations": that is, all contacts that still linked many converts to those who had remained Jewish had to be cut. The Jews themselves were accused of trying to bring converts back to the ancient religion. This meant expelling the Jews from the new Kingdom in order to keep the converts from feeling remorse or trying to return to Judaism. Consequently, the mass conversions of 1391 are the key to interpreting the expulsion of 1492. The expulsion of unbaptized Jews was a direct consequence of the failure of the political strategy of general conversion of the Spanish Jews. According to some, around 100,000 people were baptized, just between 1391 and 1415.[1] With the Jewish threat expelled and the heresy of the new Christians eradicated, the Jewish problem would be resolved with the integration, albeit in a perilous subordinate condition, of the Christianized converts.

Historiography has thoroughly analyzed the different motivations for the edict of expulsion, first among which was the new monarchy's political need not just for national but also religious homogenization. They had already unified the territory in an increasingly centralized Kingdom through the political union of the crowns of Castile and Aragon, and with the defeat of the Kingdom of Granada (January 2, 1492), which had eliminated the Muslim enclave from the territory of the Iberian Peninsula. But what is of interest here are the consequences of this expulsion, which ended fifteen centuries of Jewish presence in Spain, and forced the emigration of about 150,000 individuals (this number, however, is still subject to differing estimates). After the failure of the project for the total conversion of Spanish Jewry, in what historian Jonathan I. Israel has called "the Jewish revolution of the sixteenth century",[2] Jews who specialized in various activities – farmers, artisans, doctors, bankers, traders, rabbis, men of culture – headed for Portugal, towards north African countries (Morocco, Tunisia, Algeria), to the Balkans and to other dominions of the immense Ottoman Empire where they found favorable conditions, and then on in the direction Eastern Europe and Poland.

The story of Portugal was paradoxical. The majority of the refugees from Spain arrived there in 1492, but they were expelled by royal decree just a few years later, in 1496. Importantly, shortly after the expulsion and in violation of the edict itself, Jews were prevented from leaving via the ports and were subjected to a forced mass baptism, which according to some historians involved around 70,000 Jews.[3] Here is where a true "Portuguese question" arises, which had a determining role in the subsequent history of the Jewish community in Europe, as we have seen, due to the vitality of the crypto-Judaic tradition and marranism. The resilience of crypto-Judaism in Portugal – as opposed to in Spain – can be explained by the Inquisition's absence there until 1536 (it became fully functioning only later). This lack of surveillance for part of the first half of the 1500s made it possible to practice marrano religiosity, based on concealing a clandestine and domestic Judaism. Moreover, the Portuguese converts were mainly Spanish Jews who had preferred exile to conversion, and were therefore much more motivated by and faithful to their heritage than those who had remained in Spain.[4]

Over time, however, the problem of controlling the religious behavior of the new Christians also became more urgent in Portugal. The arrival in the country of the mysterious Jew David Reubenì in 1525, the self-proclaimed ambassador of a Jewish king of Arabia, who had been invited to Europe – even to Rome – to press the Christian powers to ally with them against the Turks, filled new Christians with hope. King João III, however, suspected that his true mission was returning the converts to Judaism.[5] While Portugal began its long and complex negotiations with Rome for instituting the Inquisition, the climate grew increasingly serious for the new Christians. Thus, many Jews who had been forced into apostasy took any opportunity to leave Portugal and return to Judaism, especially after the institution of the inquisitorial court of faith in 1536, which acted with particular severity against such suspects. In any case, the phenomenon of marranism assumed an important role in Portugal. But everywhere the marranos went, their religion was based on secret transmission at the individual and family level, which with the passage of time ended up producing a specific culture and a strong group identity. Their identity was so strong that in Europe they were called "the men of the Nation" (*homens de Nação*). Over time, even the term "Portuguese" became equated with "new Christian" and "marrano".

The Arrivals in Italy

A strong current of Iberian migrants arrived in Italy and settled at Rome, at Venice, in the Este lands and in Tuscany. Consequently, Sephardic Jews (Spanish and Portuguese) on the peninsula found themselves living together with Ashkenazic (German) and Italiani Jews, that is, longtime residents of the area. However, this basic typology is a bit simplified. Other distinctions must also be taken into account: there were Levantine Jews, who arrived in Italy from the Ottoman Empire after various wanderings, Ponentine Jews, as refugees from the Iberian Peninsula were called, new Christians and judaizing marranos, the latter being mainly Portuguese, and finally Jews who had returned to Judaism after a more or less forced baptism. Coexistence of these "national" groups was common, and often not easy. The city of Ferrara, for example, had a multiethnic community in which all three of the components cited above were present.[6] The community of Ancona, where conflicts were not rare, was made up of Italiani, Portuguese (Sephardim), and Levantines.[7] There were some communities, such as Treviso or Pavia, which instead consisted solely of German Jews; this population had begun migrating to Italy as early as the 13th century following expulsions and persecutions to the North, in particular after the great plague of 1348.

Customs, culture, and behavior could also be very different among the three main groups of Jews in Italy. For example, a type of *condotta* which can be defined as Ashkenazic has been identified, different than those granted to the Italian Jews of the central-northern regions at the time: the statutes agreed to by the Ashkenazim back in the Middle Ages with the cities of central-northern Italy reflect their mentalities and the specific circumstances they had left behind.[8] We have already seen the differences between Sephardim and Ashkenazim regarding the practices of Levirate marriage and bigamy. However, the true problem of coexistence was triggered by the mass arrival of the Sephardim from the Iberian Peninsula.

Clashes, Contention, Hostility

The arrival and settlement of the Sephardic refugees represented a genuine trauma for the Jews that already lived in Italy, and across the peninsula conflicts and mistrust multiplied and grew between the various Jewish nations. On one hand, relations between the Italian Jews and the Sephardim, who poured into Italy from the Iberian Peninsula in successive waves starting in 1492 – some of whom had remained Jews, while some were new Christians or even marranos – were marked by strong rivalry, misunderstanding, and reciprocal hostility. On the other hand, the cultural, linguistic, and social differences between the groups were pronounced.[9]

These strong sentiments were both economically and socially motivated. The local Jews feared the financial and commercial competition from the wealthy new arrivals. Then, there were questions of mentality, connected to the refugees' sense of cultural superiority, arrogance, and their "Spanish" pride, which corresponded to the Italians' distrust of Jews who reeked of tepid religious ambiguity.[10] There was certainly no lack of concern on the part of the Italian Jews about the arrival of the marranos, that is, converted Jews who were secretly practicing Judaism. They were bearers of trouble, as already demonstrated by the *auto da fé* of 233 Spanish marranos conducted in Rome in 1498, and successively by the even more severe *auto da fé* of the Portuguese marranos in Ancona in 1556, which ended with them burning at the stake. As mentioned earlier, "marrano" is a word and a concept that refers to a negative connotation and perception, both for Jews and for Christians. The Sephardim and the Italian Jews thus constituted two different realities, and their encounters were marked by conflicts around identity, cultural clashes and differences, and reciprocal stereotypes. The two groups would soon be forced to live even more closely together, side by side in the ghettos.

In Ancona, the incident of the marranos being burned at the stake caused further animosities between Italian and Portuguese Jews, who accused the former of having betrayed and sold them out.[11] There were also tensions in Genoa, despite the fact that for most refugees, the port city was only a stopover and a base for travel, particularly in the direction of the Ottoman Empire. Although they were accommodated in a sort of ghetto, which in reality was just a special area set aside for them, the exiles were subject to many abuses, mainly from Christians, as is vividly related by the chronicler Joseph Ha-Cohen, an exile who arrived in Genoa with his family. His *Valle del pianto* (*Vale of Tears*) narrates cruelty, theft, and the kidnapping of children for sale into slavery.[12] However, the Jews who already lived in the city showed little solidarity with the new arrivals.[13]

We see the same phenomenon in the Piedmont. When Emanuele Filiberto released his list of privileges to attract Portuguese Jewish merchants to the State in 1572, the local Jewish community reacted with hostility, fearing the strong economic competition of the wealthy Sephardim. In 1573, the papal nuncio at Turin wrote to the Secretary of State of the Holy See that "the Jews who normally stay in Turin are against the aforementioned marranos" and wanted their expulsion.[14] In Venice, relations between local Jews and the Iberian Jews, mainly the Portuguese, were also tense, and the former sought to prevent the permanent residence of the latter in the city and in the ghetto.[15] A convert's testimony before the Inquisition in Venice in 1580 portrayed the Portuguese marranos as follows:

> The Portuguese of this sort are neither Christians nor Jews nor Turks nor Moors, but they live in their own way. And when they go to synagogue, they bring a Christian style book in the Portuguese language and are hated by the other Jews, who do not bring more than the Jewish turban.[16]

The phenomenon was therefore extensive and generalized, just as the negative image of the Sephardic Jew, in particular Portuguese, was present and active in the mindset of the Italian Jew. Here too arose the stereotype, which we hear from another witness in Venice, of the marrano as "a traitor and a man that cannot be trusted, and I don't take him either as a Christian nor as a Jew, but as a man without religion".[17]

The reception offered to the newcomers by their coreligionists was particularly bad in the case of Rome, the city that was home to the most ancient and populous Jewish community in Italy. At the beginning of the 1500s, in fact, just before the Sack of Rome in 1527, the Jewish population, which already included many immigrants, numbered 1772 (3.2%), out of a total Roman population of over 53,000 individuals.[18] A chronicler of the time, Solomon Ibn Verga, recounts that the Roman Jews, upon learning of the arrival of the Sephardic refugees in 1493 – a group of roughly 400 people camped on via Appia, pressing at the gates of the city[19] – asked Pope Alessandro VI Borgia, who was Spanish, to turn them away, and tried to prevent their entry into Rome, even offering the pope a large gift of cash. It is worth citing this passage of the story, although many scholars challenge its factual validity:

> some of the (*Iberian*) Jews, who had reached the port of Genoa, were forced to leave due to the rampant hunger, and they moved from there to Rome. But the Jews of Rome gathered and took counsel to prevent the strangers from mixing in among them and bringing serious harm to their economic activities. They then immediately put together a thousand *fiorini*, which they offered as a gift to the pope, so that he would not welcome them in his lands. When this was reported to the pope, he reacted by saying: "For me this is something really new. Until now I knew that it was typical for the Jews to close ranks around each other, and instead they behave without compassion! I have therefore decided that these too (*that is the Roman Jews*) are expelled from my lands and it is no longer legal for them to live here". Then the Jews of Rome were forced to collect another two thousand gold *scudi* to offer to the pope so that he would leave them in peace, and at the same time they resigned themselves to the arrival of the foreigners (*that is the Iberian Jews*) in the city. Thus the poor refugees could partake of the good of this land.[20]

Solomon ibn Verga was a Spanish Jew, and his account, even if unlikely, still reflects certain truths: the Sephardic Jews' negative perception of the Roman Jews, described as hostile and unkind, as well as the desire to separate the responsibility for the incident and exonerate the Spanish pontiff. There has been much discussion regarding the interpretation of this story. Although it is not true, it is an eloquent sign of the reciprocal mistrust and hostile attitudes that existed. Roman diarist Stefano Infessura, another chronicler of the time, confirmed the refugees' troubled entrance to the city, relating how the Jews were blocked outside the walls and made to wait on via Appia due to the fear that they would introduce plague.[21]

A significant series of problems arose from this encounter between different Jewish groups, provoked by the Roman Jews' difficulty in accepting the Sephardim. This difficulty had numerous and complex causes, but was essentially related to the fact that the new arrivals were considerably wealthier, well set up in the credit sector and more educated: for example, they had ideas about Kabbalah, which was little known in Italy. The Sephardic community, which began arriving in 1492, would become the most populous in Italy in the first half of the 16th century,[22] thus doubling the number of Jews in Rome. Conflicts between Roman, Italiani, and Spanish Jews would persist for all of the 16th century, exacerbated by the coexistence of different "national" *scole* or synagogues, which had reached 11 in number by 1518. There were not only Spanish synagogues – Catalan, Castillian, and Aragon – but also Sicilians, who had their own *scola* as well. A nucleus of refugees from the island formed after 1493, and especially after the expulsions from Naples ordered by the King of Naples in 1510–11, where they had first gone after Sicily.[23]

Conflicts, Agreements, Coexistence. The Emblematic Case of Rome

To better understand the types and modalities of conflicts which pitted the new immigrants against the Jews who already lived in Italy, along with the solutions that were found to foster coexistence among the various ethnic components, we should look closely at the case of Rome, which is certainly the most exemplary. Recent research clearly shows the evolution of the difficult relations between the Roman and Italian Jews and the *ultramontani* who came from over the Alps, to be joined by Jews arriving from southern Italy and Sicily.[24]

Since the 1400s, the *Universitas Iudaeorum in Urbe*, officially recognized by the popes, was meticulously organized, with five *scole* (synagogues) and a general council of adult Jews, which made appointments to the various governing bodies by a two thirds majority: the treasurer, who was elected for one year, and the governing council made up of three officers who represented executive power (*fattori*) whose terms lasted for four months. The *fattori* had the delicate tasks of dividing the tax burdens owed by the community, collecting taxes and overseeing internal order. Moreover, they constituted the official liaison with other Jewish communities, and particularly with the papal and city authorities.

However, in 1496, the *Communitas hebraeorum hispanorum in Urbe commorantium* arose alongside the original Roman community organization, and was clearly antagonistic to its predecessor. The Spanish community was trying, in fact, to avoid being governed by the Roman and Italian component, which had sole control over the most important offices – and meant to keep it that way, even in the new situation where they were now a minority. As early as 1501, however, the regional distinctions among the Spanish themselves gave rise to separate community bodies for Aragonese, Catalan, and Castillian Jews, with three different *scole* and three organizations for their "nations". There was also an analogous association of French and German Jews formed in 1505, with both groups together in one community; however, they too soon separated.

All of the community institutions organized by the foreign Jews, though without renouncing their own specificity, constituted the *Universitas hebraeorum forensium et ultramontanorum in Urbe existentium*, which was endowed with its own officials, a shared treasury and charitable institutions to provide assistance for the poor that were separate from those of the Romans. This presented a strong and united front against the institutions of the indigenous Jews. In 1505, they successfully petitioned Pope Julius II, who accepted the demands of the *ultramontani* and required the original Jewish community of Rome to name a foreign member to the trio of *fattori* who lead the general *Universitas hebraeorum in alma Urbe commorantium*. This primary body included all of the Jewish groups – Italiani and *ultramontani* – and was the only one whose officials were officially authorized by the papal authorities to act as representatives for the Jews living in Rome.[25]

The acrimony of the conflicts between the various "nations", clearly expressed by the proliferation of these separate bodies, and the tensions that dragged on for decades triggered a high rate of litigation between the foreigners and the Romans, and between the foreigners themselves for the designation of their *fattore*. Furthermore, the Sephardic Jews from the Iberian Peninsula were now not only the most numerous group but also the most solid financially, engaged in the credit sector with their available capital. In 1521, Pope Leo X authorized Jews to lend money at interest in the Urbe and in all the papal territories, ending a long period when Jewish residents of Rome were prohibited from practicing usury. Pope Leo was a Medici, a family of bankers, and a dynasty which recalls the well-known pro-Jewish policy the family practiced in Tuscany.[26] Naturally, the opening of lending banks in Rome favored the Sephardic Jews, who possessed greater capital: in fact, of the twenty banks authorized, a number of which were destined to grow over time, more than half were in their hands, and only a small portion belonged to the Roman Jews. In this way a hierarchy and social stratification not only became increasingly clear in the Roman Jewish community – which saw banker-lenders in a prominent position – but also had ethnic connotations, given that the Sephardim occupied the highest social positions and economically dominated the old indigenous group.[27]

The infinite controversies which continued to tear apart the group of Jews in Rome during the first two decades of the 16th century, especially regarding community offices and the division of taxes led Pope Clement VII in 1524 to seek a mediated agreement, meant to be an act of intercommunal reconciliation between the different "national" groups. The disputes revolved around the Roman Jews' desire to maintain control over the administration of the *Università*, and therefore over the division of the tax contributions at the expense of the immigrants, who were excluded from the institutions. However, those immigrants also represented the strongest faction economically, as mentioned, and had more bankers in their ranks. Another cause of conflict was the division of the entire community into economic groups linked to a social and power hierarchy, at the top of which was unquestionably the bankers, who held the real power. Below the bankers were the *ricchi*, who were merely wealthy, but were over the *mediocri*, people of modest means. The poor and the destitute were naturally excluded from internal offices, which were reserved only for those who paid taxes.

Coexistence between the Roman community and the Spanish had thus become so difficult that in 1524, due to the high tensions, the task of organizing their relations was entrusted to an outsider, Daniel da Pisa. He was a member of an important family of Roman bankers that had relocated to Tuscany, and a personality who was known and respected in Rome both by the Jews and by the papal Curia. He was very close to the Medici family, which included Clement VII, for whom he was the trusted banker. He was therefore called upon to settle the issue like a sort of Justice of the Peace. He compiled a series of *Capitoli*, which were approved by the pope in December of the same year. The new statute sought to correct the preponderance of the Italian Jews in management positions by establishing a more balanced presence among the different Roman and *ultramontani* components within the leadership bodies of the community. Here, the subject of ethnic membership as a criterion for division of the offices returned to the fore. In the preamble of the *Capitoli*, Daniel da Pisa states that the goal of the reform was to put an "end to the infinite disorder and to eradicate the bitter fruit of litigious Men, disturbing to all, who have been impediments and a poisonous offence according to everyone who has seen and heard them".[28]

The *Capitoli* respected the pre-existing ethnic and class divisions, but attributed power to each group more equitably. So, the three *fattori* now consisted of one foreigner and two Italians, and in particular the *Capitoli* established equal representation in the Congregation of Sixty, the legislative council of the Roman community and its main administrative body. The sixty members, who were nominated for life, had to be chosen through an equal division of Italians and *ultramontani*, and transversally in equal numbers according to economic and social differences: twenty *banchieri*, twenty *ricchi*, and twenty *mediocri*. All the other offices were for the most part assigned half to Italians and half to the *ultramontani*. The Congregation of Sixty, as the major governing body, had to decide all the most important questions, such as the appointment of the numerous different internal offices, settling on a general plan of taxation, and authorizing expenses. Deliberations were approved by a two-thirds majority. Five defenders of the *Capitoli* – three Italians and two foreigners – had the responsibility of supervising compliance with the institutional regulations. Executive power was still entrusted to the three *fattori*, who held office for one year, and maintained relations with the ecclesiastic authorities and the pope himself. Then, there were many other offices and roles, acceptance of which was obligatory. The *scole* or synagogues continued to be autonomous, with their own rules and liturgies.[29]

The *Capitoli* of Daniel da Pisa did not end the various conflicts and disputes – political, social and economic, or quotidian – among the different *scole* and factions. But by balancing responsibilities among the nations and social groups, it succeeded in its intent of building an adequately stable system and creating integration among the diverse nuclei of immigrants and natives, fostered both by the common residence in the same quarter and by a shared language, the Roman *volgare*. The statute's considerable success is demonstrated by the fact that the *Capitoli* were left unchanged until 1870, despite the relatively serious and increasingly unsupportable problem of the ecclesiastical authorities holding the *fattori* personally and jointly responsible for the serious failings of others.

Despite the disruption it caused, it's worth noting that the arrival of Iberian refugees at Rome did not just contribute to strong demographic growth – in the Roman census of 1591, the Jewish population had already risen to 3,500 individuals, compared to 1,772 before the sack of Rome in 1527 – nor did it only cause controversies and clashes. In fact, their arrival also had positive effects, as it led to a resumption of Jewish economic activity after a phase of depression and stasis, with the development of Jewish moneylending in the city and an increase in the number of banks. Thus, while Leo X granted the first authorization to practice moneylending in Rome to 20 Jewish bankers in 1521, half of which were "Spanish", the number rose to 40 with Julius III in 1552 and to 55 under Gregory XIII, until reaching the number of 70 in the 17th century.[30] To compete with the exponential growth of the Jewish banks, and in response to this worrying phenomenon for Christian society, a *Monte di Pietà* was also founded in Rome in 1539, meant to curb the phenomenon of Jewish moneylending by providing credit at a lower interest rate. The Jewish banks were closed in 1682 by order of Pope Innocent XI, in a further demonstration of the hardening of the papacy's anti-Jewish policy.[31]

The issue of the presence of Spanish *conversos* and judaizing marranos, the former wrongly or rightly often being identified with the latter, in Rome during the late 1400s – early 1500s was also significant for realities other than Rome. As early as 1498, the powerful Bishop Pedro de Aranda, master of the Sacro Palazzo of Alessandro VI, the pope who had accepted the Sephardic refugees into the city, was tried in Rome for marranism. In the same year, again in Rome, a grandiose *auto da fé* ceremony was held, at which 233 Spanish marranos denounced themselves as judaizers and were publicly reconciled, that is, absolved.[32] Certainly, the motivations in this case of mass abjuration, which involved working class people, appear more religious and political, meant to purify a potentially contaminating presence through the ceremony of absolution. However, the trials that involved wealthy and important figures such as Aranda lead us to suspect, as in fact contemporaneous witnesses also suspected, that the prosecution of Spanish *conversos* with the accusation of marranism was a way to obtain large payments from wealthy defendants.

In any case, research has revealed the presence in Rome at until least the mid-1500s of Portuguese new Christians who had already been investigated as judaizers by the Inquisition in their home country and had taken refuge in the pontifical city. There in Rome, acting as official agents of the Portuguese new Christians, they tried to enter the negotiations between the Holy See and Portugal to prevent papal legitimization of the Portuguese court of

the Inquisition. The interesting issue of the presence of crypto-Jews and judaizers in the city of the pope still remains to be explored. However, Rome's
constant attention on the marranos should be emphasized, along with the
attempt to control their activities and movements, keeping a particularly
close eye on the overly complacent policies of Venice, on one hand, and of
Pisa and Livorno on the other.

Marranos in Rome. Pedro Furtado and Jacome de Fonseca

The unexpected role that emerges for Rome in the itineraries of marranos in
Italy has been overlooked, and is little known compared to the roles played
by Venice, Ferrara, Pisa, and Livorno.[33] In fact, in the mid-1500s, various
representatives of the Portuguese new Christians lived in Rome, part of a
vast international network intent on obstructing the functioning of the Inquisition in Portugal and defending the new converts who had remained
at home. In Rome, which at the time was the center of the discussions and
negotiations taking place between the Portuguese Crown and the pope concerning the establishment of a court of faith in Portugal, men like Pedro
Furtado and Jacome de Fonseca tried to insert themselves in the diplomatic
talks and to influence papal policy, working to help their friends who had
remained in the home country. Both men were originally from Lamego, in
the north of Portugal, and they arrived in Rome at the same time, in 1543.

Furtado, a medical doctor of some fame and leader of a group of new
Christians from Lamego, survived a trial for judaization with his family.
Freed by the intercession of the papal nuncio in Portugal, he first took refuge
in Tuscany, taking advantage of the privileges conceded to new Christians
by Cosimo I de' Medici in 1549. He moved on to Rome, where he worked as
a procurator for new Christians. Shortly after his arrival in 1545, Fonseca,
driven by his desire to defend relatives and fellow citizens who were threatened by the Holy Office, but also by the desire for greater financial gains
was, like Furtado, also recognized by Paul III as a procurator and agent for
the Portuguese converts. He paid large sums of money to obtain papal briefs
that granted exemptions from the courts of the Inquisition, revoked sentences, and provided safe conduct for Portuguese who were in danger.[34] In
1551, Julius III also confirmed all of Furtado and Fonseca's privileges. Their
political activism did not interfere with their financial and trade activism,
because the two spheres did not conflict. Thus, Fonseca inserted himself
into the commercial fabric of the Urbe, recognized as a *mercator Portugal-
lensis Romanam curiam sequens*, that is, as a banker who could work at the
Roman Curia. Fonseca's activity in Rome as a creditor and procurator for
the Portuguese residents is evidence of the existence of a small community
of *conversos* in the city.

Jacome de Fonseca did not limit himself only to moneylending. The fact
that he bought a spice warehouse nearby the Church of Sant'Agostino, again
working together with Furtado, means that the two Lusitanians were also

involved in a trade that was widely practiced among Portuguese merchants, Jewish or otherwise, and which extended throughout the entire known world.[35] Portugal, starting with its discoveries and settlements in Africa and India at the end of the 15th century, had in the first decades of the following century become the undisputed master of the international spice trade. Via the Port of Lisbon, and for several decades also Antwerp, the Lusitanians had the almost exclusive rights over the sale and exchange of these products, which were becoming increasingly important in Europe.[36] One can suppose, therefore, that a Portuguese merchant such as Jacome de Fonseca had links with the international spice trade that gave him access to new and profitable business opportunities that were out of reach for most Roman merchants. This fact contributed to Fonseca's fortune in the Eternal City. Furtado, in turn, became a key figure in spreading the invitation issued in January 1549 by Cosimo I de' Medici to Portuguese new Christians to settle in Tuscany, where he himself, as has been said, was called by the grand duke to take up residence.

Jacome de Fonseca lived in Rome for over a decade, between 1543 and the first months of 1555, involved in the management of international trade, and often working in close contact with his brother António, who was in Lisbon. These were, among other things, decisive years for the fate of the Lusitanian converts, who witnessed the full and definitive establishment of a functioning Holy Office in Portugal in 1548. Perhaps sensing that the situation for the Portuguese new Christians at Rome and in the Papal States was completely changing, Jacome decided to abandon the city in the final days of the pontificate of Julius III, in March of 1555. He went to the Ottoman Empire where he apparently re-embraced the Jewish faith and changed his name. A few months later, the ghetto would be created in Rome, and the following year marranos would be burned at the stake in Ancona.

Towards Confinement

In other communities, just as had happened in Rome, the upheavals suffered by Jews across Italy from the end of the 15th century to the early decades of the 16th century led to fractures, tensions, splits, and the resulting administrative and organizational redefinitions. It was always a matter of economic and social conflicts, with the advance of the wealthy banker class, and ethnic differences between natives and foreigners. The bankers in Mantua actually organized themselves in a separate community in 1532. At Venice, Padua, and Livorno, the criteria for the choosing administrators were based on the country of origin. The internal organizational structure of the communities also varied. In Mantua, the highest authority rested with the *vicinia* or general assembly, composed of the heads of all taxpaying families, which made decisions about internal taxation, and from which were drawn members for the other two intermediate councils. In the place of the *fattori* there were *massari*, who starting in 1589 were required to be two Italians and one German.

The council assembly was an organ that was provided for in many other communities, accompanied by intermediate bodies. Obviously, one cannot speak of democratic participation, inasmuch as class factors related to the wealth and prestige of families often limited the number of those eligible to participate. Livorno operated with a particularly oligarchic system in which a council of twelve "seniors" governed, later increased to eighteen, who were elected for life. This council chose the forty community administrators – sixty after 1693 – who constituted the congress and were divided, as we saw in Rome, among three "classes" defined by wealth. They then nominated five *massari*. Membership in the congress was not for life, but it was transmittable by inheritance, a privilege that was abolished only in 1769. Until 1715, all of the Jewish community offices in that Tuscan city, the bastion of Spanish and Portuguese Jewry in Italy, were reserved only for Iberian natives.[37]

But now we are entering the age of the ghetto, the second trauma suffered by Italian Judaism, which we should analyze closely.

Notes

1 Israel, *Gli ebrei d'Europa*, 16.
2 Israel, *Gli ebrei d'Europa*, 42.
3 Marcocci, *I custodi dell'ortodossia*, 34–6. See also Paiva, *História da Inquisição Portuguesa*.
4 Israel, *Gli ebrei d'Europa*, 35–6.
5 Sestieri, *David Reubeni*.
6 Segre, "La formazione di una comunità"; Di Leone Leoni, *La nazione ebraica spagnola*.
7 Andreoni, *Una nazione in commercio*, 109–39.
8 Toaff, "Gli insediamenti askenaziti," 159–65.
9 Toaff, "Ebrei spagnoli e marrani," 47–60.
10 Toaff, "Ebrei spagnoli e marrani". An opposing argument is found in Stow, "Prossimità o distanza," 61–74 which unconvincingly dismisses the thesis of ethnic conflict. For Rome, cfr. Esposito, "Conflitti interni alla comunità ebraica," 66–80.
11 Toaff, "Ebrei spagnoli e marrani," 54–5.
12 Zazzu, *Sepharad addio*, 67. About Joseph Ha-Cohen, author of a chronological history of Jewish misfortunes, *The Vale of Tears*, see Bonfil, "Lo spazio culturale degli ebrei d'Italia," 452–3; Jacobs, "Joseph ha-Kohen," 67–85.
13 Zazzu, *Sepharad addio*.
14 Segre, *The Jews in Piedmont*, i, 509.
15 Pullan, *The Jews of Europe*, 192–3.
16 Ioly Zorattini, *Processi del S. Uffizio di Venezia*, 11, 117–8.
17 Ioly Zorattini, *Processi del S. Uffizio di Venezia*, 158.
18 Esposito, *Un' altra Roma*, 129.
19 Esposito, "The Sephardic Communities in Rome," 180.
20 Cited from Toaff, "Ebrei spagnoli e marrani," 48–9: the words in cursive in parentheses are those of Salomon Ibn Verga.
21 Foa, "Il nuovo e il vecchio," 20. Regarding the arrival of Spanish refugees in Rome, see Di Nepi, *Sopravvivere al ghetto*, 20–9.
22 From 500 to 1,000 individuals according to Toaff, "Ebrei spagnoli e marrani," 50.

23 Milano, *Storia degli ebrei*, 216–33; Esposito and Procaccia, "La 'schola Sicolorum de Urbe'"; Esposito, *Un' altra Roma*, 280–91.
24 Esposito, *Storia degli ebrei*, 384–91.
25 Esposito, *Storia degli ebrei*, 386.
26 Cfr. supra
27 Esposito, *Storia degli ebrei*, 387.
28 Milano, *Il ghetto di Roma*, 178.
29 For the text of the *Capitoli*, cfr. Milano, "I Capitoli di Daniel da Pisa," 324–38, 409–26; *Il ghetto di Roma*, 175–83. We do not yet have a specific and detailed study on the *Capitoli*.
30 Esposito, "Credito, ebrei, monte di pietà," 113–36.
31 Procaccia, "Banchieri ebrei a Roma".
32 Foa, "Un vescovo marrano," 533–51.
33 Novoa, "Portugal in Rome," 1–14.
34 On these two figures, cfr. Novoa and Bastos Mateus, "The case of New Christians in Lamego," 83–103; Bastos Mateus and Novoa, "De Lamego para a Toscana," 313–38.
35 Novoa, "Portugal in Rome," 5.
36 Regarding the Portuguese global trade market, there is a wide bibliography: cfr. Russell-Wood, *The Portuguese Empire*; Subrahmanyam, *The Portuguese Empire in Asia*; Naylor Pearson, *The Portuguese in India*.
37 Milano, *Storia degli ebrei*, 466–8.

Part Two
The Invention of the Ghettos

5 The Second Trauma. The Birth of the Ghettos

Geography and Chronology

Enclosures, *Seraglios*, and Cloisters for the Jews

The second trauma for the Italian Jews, after that of the mass arrival of Iberian refugees, was the birth of the ghetto. This event drastically altered the conditions Jews had lived under in the preceding centuries, even if not all Jews, as we have seen for Livorno and Pisa, lived within the confines of the *seraglios*.[1]

As far back as antiquity and through the Middle Ages Jews would concentrate their living spaces in particular areas of a city, varying in size from quarters to streets, even down to isolated houses. However, these clusters were mostly spontaneous and voluntarily, and responded to a variety of needs for economic, social, and religious solidarity and self-defense, not to mention the fact that on the Sabbath and other recurring holidays Jews were not allowed to walk beyond a certain distance to reach their place of worship.[2] The "paradox of the birth of the ghetto" – as it was defined by historian Michele Luzzati[3] – is that in certain cases where there was worsening anti-Jewish tension and violence, the Jews themselves could ask the local authorities to build a separate Jewish quarter for security and defense against the risks of aggression or even massacres. However, cases such as these were still not truly ghettos, even if over time the free choice of settlement in an area tended to transform into an obligation. Even if the concentration of Jews in a street or in a quarter was imposed by the Christian authorities, one could not speak of a ghetto in the true sense of the word because there were no physical barriers, no separating walls controlled from the outside, no entrance and exit gates, and no compulsory residence requirement. Other types of practices were at most used to separate the Jews from the Christian context, for example, the requirement for Jews to place an identifying sign on their clothing, the absolute prohibition on promiscuous and premarital sexual relations with Christians, the prohibition on Jewish doctors caring for gentile patients, and the ban on Christians working in the homes of the Jews as servants or wet nurses, and so on.

Forced segregations of Jews begin taking place in the last centuries of the Medieval period, first in Spain and then in France and Germany,

DOI: 10.4324/9781003188445-8

Figure 5.1 The principle Jewish communities in the age of the ghettos (drawn by the Author).

enclosing the minority in specific areas by means of physical barriers that offered few points of passage to the outside. From the end of the 14th century, worsening persecution and sacking, and the first mass expulsions led to a process of "ghettoization" on the whole Iberian Peninsula. In the German empire, the trend of segregation of the Jews began at Colonia in the 1300s and followed in many cities: in 1462, the *Judengasse* was instituted in Frankfort. In this phase, however, segregation – and also self-segregation – was accompanied by a series of exemptions thanks to which the wealthiest and most powerful Jews could continue to live outside the zone of forced settlement.

While it is difficult ascertain to what extent the establishment of a Jewish quarter physically separated from the rest of the city by walls took place at the request of the Jews themselves, for self-defense and the maintenance of their identity, or if instead it was imposed by the authorities, we do, however, know the official birth date of the ghetto: both the word and the thing.

The appearance of the real ghetto, understood as an area for the legally mandatory marginalization and segregation of the Jews, reserved only for them, considered permanent and physically isolated by a wall with entrances that were controlled in daylight and locked at night, when Jews were forbidden to leave,[4] took place at Venice in 1516. However, as we will immediately see, not even that city's institution of a closed quarter reserved for the Jews and named ghetto marked the definitive turning point. The circumstances connected to the war of the League of Cambrai had induced – as we have seen – the Venetian authorities to revoke the rigid prohibition on permanent Jewish settlement in the city of Venice itself. This decision provoked considerable and widespread immigration to various areas of the city. The resulting tensions led to the decision to isolate the Jews in an area located in the *sestiere* (neighborhood) of Cannaregio, in imitation of what had already happened in the Venetian colonies of the eastern Mediterranean. The new quarter was given the fateful name of "ghetto", a word destined to spread in every language and which to this day, by extension, is used to define every inhabited area where you find a concentration of marginalized groups that have specific characteristics in common (ethnic, religious, economic, and social), even without any restrictions, material impediments, and residential obligations.

The Ghetto Nuovo, the first closed and separate quarter set aside for the Jews, was established in 1516, when for the first time Venice permitted the permanent residence of Jewish moneylenders in the city, for the most part of German origin (Ashkenazim). Later, in 1541, when the Sephardic Jewish merchants arrived from the Ottoman Empire, the Venetian government offered these "Levantine" Jews their own area, the Ghetto Vecchio, which was connected to the Ghetto Nuovo by a bridge that crossed over a canal.[5]

The name "ghetto" came from the Venetian experience and was destined for future widespread use. Initially, however, it was used alongside other terms such as "*seraglio*", "cloister", or "enclosure" of the Jews. Historians have discussed the origin and significance of the word at length. Many scholars argue that the traditional and perhaps more certain origin and etymology are in fact Venetian, and derive from the activity of copper processing and smelting (*getus*, from the Latin *iactus*, is what smelting was called) which had taken place in the area then destined for the Jews. But according to another suggestive interpretation, the term assumes a much stronger symbolic significance. In fact, the word could originate from the Hebrew term *ghet*, the word for the document of separation and repudiation that a Jewish husband gave to his wife at the moment of divorce. With this association, the ghetto, which separated the Jews from Christian society, became the concrete symbol of "divorce" from the external majority society. The ghetto formalized the divorce between Jews and Christians, and made it clear and visible through physical separation. A further etymological derivation might refer to the terms *getto, molo*, or *banchina*, upon which Jewish refugees from Spain would have disembarked in the port of Genoa after 1492. But in actuality it fell to Venice to spread the word that represents segregation and discrimination around the world.

However, it was not the Venetian "invention" that paved the way for, or led to the general system of ghettos in Italy, which developed several decades after the prototype of Venice. The decisive turning point was the work of the papacy. First of all, it should be recalled that the popes had not adopted the Iberian strategy of expelling the Jews, eliminating them completely from the territories of their State. Papal policy, which was also the result of the theological position towards the Jews described previously,[6] tended to keep the Jewish presence in the State and then pressure them to convert through restrictions and limitations. The ghetto appeared functional for this choice of confinement, which was simultaneously a choice of inclusion and exclusion. Jews had to be excluded from Christian society, and physically separated from it by walls and gates that were closed at night to prevent them from contaminating the city; on the other hand, they were included in the city, though confined in the ghetto. Thus, the papacy's solution to the Jewish problem rejected Iberian style expulsion, instead adopting separation and segregation: this approach enabled and facilitated the most desirable outcome, the conversion of the Jews. The ghetto had to push towards conversion. It was also a politically realistic compromise solution that accounted for the practical needs of the Italian States, including the Papal States that permitted the extraction of financial and economic benefits and resources from the Jewish presence.

The direct intervention of the Church of Rome was therefore necessary in order for the system of ghettos and the ghetto model itself to be definitively established and generalized. As many Jewish historians have asserted,[7] and as the current historiographical vulgate mostly confirms, in reality not completely correctly, the papacy had frequently acted as a protector of the Jews in previous centuries. Over the course of the 16th century, however, papal policy was profoundly changed, especially concerning the anti-Protestant battle to which the papacy found itself committed. After all, in every era of crisis and severe difficulty for the Church and for the Catholic religion, the impulse to defend and reconsolidate internal forces has always triggered reactions of clearer exclusion and persecution of all forms of dissent and diversity, starting with the Jews. We will see this phenomenon in action in later critical periods and phases, such as the Age of Enlightenment and the French Revolution. But it is certain that in the 16th century, the struggle against the reformed "heresy", which was being pursued through the prosecution and execution of Christian dissidents, could not be conducted while continuing to offer guarantees to the "people of the deicide": to the enemy of Christianity par excellence. The Lutheran breakup of the unity of the Christian world thus led to guarding against all forms of otherness and their repression, and this involved the Jews.

Various signals and different stages suggested what the papacy's new direction would be. In 1543, the Casa dei Catecumeni was founded in Rome, an institution set up for the more or less free or forced conversion of Jews and other "infidels". This was followed a decade later by a sensational and threatening event: the public burning of the *Talmud* in 1553, which also happened in Rome – but subsequently took place in many other Italian cities – in the plaza of Campo de' Fiori, where Giordano Bruno would be burned alive in 1600. Two years later, the ghetto of Rome was born.

An "Absurd and Unseemly" Coexistence. The New Anti-Jewish Legislation

As with our review of the trauma of the arrival of the wave of Iberian Sephardic immigrants in Italy after 1492, the narration of the birth of the ghetto, and of the laws that supported it, cannot ignore the Roman situation. The Urbe was not only the home of the most numerous and important Jewish community in Italy but above all it constituted the heart of the temporal and spiritual power of the popes, who had always been the main authorities for producing legislation regarding the Jews.

The true instigator of the new papal policy was Paul IV (1555–59), the "great inquisitor", well known for his activity of harsh repression of all dissent and minorities. Immediately after his election to the papal throne, Paul IV issued the decisive bull *Cum nimis absurdum* on July 14, 1555. This articulated legislation launched a segregationist project that was destined to last, at least in Rome, until 1870. What was utterly absurd according to the pope? Paul IV declared that the fact of Jews and Christians living among one another was absurd and disgraceful. It is useful to cite the central passage of this document, which would regulate the condition of the Italian Jews for over two centuries:

> Since it is beyond absurd and disgraceful to the highest degree that the Jews, who by their own guilt have been condemned by God to eternal slavery, can, with the excuse of being protected by Christian love and tolerated in their cohabitation in our midst, show such ingratitude towards Christians as to insult them for their mercy and to expect dominion instead of submission; and since we have learned that, in Rome and in other locations subject to the Holy Roman Church, their effrontery has reached the point that they presume the right not only to live in the midst of Christians, but also in proximity to churches without distinguishing clothing, and they even rent homes in the main streets and piazzas, buying and owning real estate, hiring housekeepers, wet nurses and other Christian servants, and committing many other misdeeds to

the shame and contempt of the name Christian; [hence] considering that the Roman Church will tolerate these Jews as witnesses to the truth of the Christian faith and in order that they finally recognize their errors, moved by the mercy and benevolence of the Holy See, and making every effort to bring them to the true light of the Catholic faith and thus recognizing that they have been made slaves because of their own persistent errors, while Christians have been set free thanks to Jesus Christ, God and Our Lord, and therefore recognizing that it is unjust for the child of a free woman to be in the service of the child of a servant woman, desiring, with the help of God, to find a remedy for all of this, we establish, through this constitution which is valid forever, that for all future time, both the Urbe (Rome) as well as in any of the other cities, lands and places belonging to the Roman Church, that all the Jews must live in only one street, and if that did not suffice, in two or three, or however many are sufficient, being contiguous among them and completely separate from the homes of Christians to be designated by our hand in the Urbe and by the work of our magistrates in the other aforementioned cities, lands and places, which will be entered by a single entrance and exited via a single exit.[8]

The bull, or constitution of 1555 with which Paul IV instituted the ghettos in the Papal States, shines a light on the cornerstones of the papal and Catholic mentality towards the Jews. What was now stigmatized, and required imposing new, stricter rules, was the fact that Jews insolently and stubbornly continued to live among the Christians, often even close to churches, without wearing distinguishing clothing, carrying on with their traffic and trade and even employing nannies and other Christian servants in their homes. All this, wrote the pope, was in contradiction with the fact that the Church tolerated the Jews' presence only if they accepted their status as *slaves*, and only so they would have the opportunity to recognize their errors and, repenting, convert to the true faith of Jesus Christ. This prejudicial formulation reaffirmed the Jews' necessary condition of inferiority, in no way similar or comparable to that of other inhabitants. The papal decree followed with a whole series of prohibitions regarding work and movement, along with limitations on real estate ownership, set out in fourteen points incorporating a list packed with requirements and prohibitions.

The document is a sort of compendium of a great many ideas, representations, and stereotypes which had been widespread for centuries, but were now arranged in a complete and definitive narrative that would long influence the history of relations between Jews and Christians: the sin of deicide, the reduction to slavery as a punishment inflicted by God as a consequence of that sin, the ingratitude towards those who had accepted and tolerated them, the aspirations to dominance over Christians, and especially the insolent mixing with the latter, presuming to circulate without marks of identification – and exclusion – living among Christians and hiring them for

personal service. Moreover, the doctrinal explanation for Christian tolerance of the presence of Jews among them is explicitly reiterated. Jews were
tolerated solely by virtue of their being the witnesses to the truth of Christianity, and to facilitate their conversion.

The remedy for this mixing of Jews and Christians, once considered ordinary but now perceived as intolerable, consisted of concentrating and enclosing the Jews in a single area of residence in each papal city where they lived,
an area endowed with walls and gates. The cities in which Jews were permitted to live were subsequently reduced to two, Rome and Ancona. The Jews
had to sell all of their real estate and abandon any form of trade other than
the sale of used goods. The bull required them to wear an identifying mark
on their clothing that would visibly distinguish them from the Christian population. This was not an absolute novelty, given that the identifying mark
had origins in the Middle Ages; in Northern Europe, it consisted of a circle,
yellow or red in color, sewed on to the clothing. Hats, with their particular
shapes, a point or a turban, also constituted precise marks of identification
that were constantly present in the iconography aimed at delineating the figure of the Jew.[9] But even in this realm, special permissions and privileges
granted by the pontiff and by the authorities of other States could exempt the
most important people from the obligation of wearing the mark.

The ghetto was therefore the response to the choice between expulsion
and conversion: a response simultaneously aimed at keeping the Jews in the
State and pressuring them to convert, the true obsession of Catholicism.
They would be accepted and tolerated, especially in Rome, but a new form
of "temporary expulsion" of the Jews from the daily life of the city would
be instituted while awaiting their conversion. They were not permitted leave
their "*claustro*" at night. They all had to live together and work in a few poor
and meager occupations, keeping far away from Christians and their lives.

Thus, they were excluded. This could be the sum of a reflection on the relationship between the Jews and the urban space of Rome, and likewise with
the geographical spaces Jews occupied in the different cites that accepted
them, from the early modern age until the abolition of the last ghetto, which
in fact was the Roman ghetto, in 1870. However, in social practice, things
went much differently. The Jewish presence in the fabric of the city was not
really defined by just the small "enclosure" of the ghetto. It turns out to be
a widespread reality, present in various areas of the city, and therefore of
considerable mobility. We must speak of places, in the plural, and not of just
one place, because contrary to what we usually think about the isolation of
the communities in the ghettos, Jewish settlement in the city did not exist
only within the most obvious, restricted, and coerced space of the "enclosure", but instead refers to the existence of a plurality of "Jewish places" in
the city where they were accepted. In Rome, to use an example that relates
to the most important ghetto, space, as well as time, was punctuated by the
circulation of Jews in the urban and extra-urban territory at locations they
went to for trade. Their presence in the city was mainly divided among the

locations that were codified for the permanent residence of Jews, in particular at *rione* Sant'Angelo. That is where the ghetto was built in the modern age, replacing the previous ancient residential settlement in Trastevere; it was destined to endure for over three centuries. But, as we will see, there were also other sites in the city where the Jews could go for work and trade. They were therefore excluded, but also included in the urban fabric.

In fact, upon closer inspection, the entire Roman space was involved in the design of a "system" of Jewish visibility and mobility. This mobility inside and outside the city was also provided by the type of occupations they had to practice and their very structure, which required obtaining various permissions and licenses to attend fairs and markets in the provinces. In reality, if one were to only take account of the regulations, it would be hard to understand much of the Jews' actual role in the city. Social practices and behaviors were often quite different from the law, and were also capable of designing some forms of "inclusion" in the majority society.

Rome. Strategies for Survival and Freedom of Movement

So, Paul IV's decree came down on the Roman community in 1555, which formally defined the institution of a closed "quarter" set aside for the Jews, and established an extensive series of restrictions. In the space of just a few months, the Jews of Rome, accustomed to their settlements between the two banks of the Tiber in the ancient nucleus of *rione* Trastevere, by now greatly reduced in size, and in Sant'Angelo – where 62% of the Jewish population already lived – had to condense themselves into a few streets of the latter quarter. The surrounding wall was erected very quickly, with two gates. That number grew over time to five gates and then in the 1800s to eight; urban planning was entrusted to the pope's architect Giovanni Sallustio Peruzzi. Later, in 1589, it was the famous architect Domenico Fontana who oversaw the enlargement of the quarter towards the river.[10] In fact, the area given to the Jews, about three hectares in size, narrow and long, with a depth of only 150 meters, was perennially exposed to flooding from the Tiber and very unhealthy.

The imposition of the ghetto on a population that according to a rough estimate numbered 1,700–2,000 individuals at the time required the Jewish community to look for a new type of organization, and created numerous problems that had to be resolved: how should the closed space be configured? What were the regulations that defined its limits? Which of these would regulate internal relations? The ghetto represents the papal, counter-reformist, and thus the "Roman solution" to the Jewish question, which avoided the radical expulsion of the Spanish. As such, it is not easily found outside Italy, apart from some examples in Germany and at Avignon, which in fact was a papal possession. On the peninsula, in any case, the model of the ghetto that would be progressively followed in various local realities across Italy was the Roman model. The Venetian model from 1516 had somewhat different characteristics.

At first, the Jews of Rome were not fully cognizant of this radical change in their lives, which was likely seen as a transitory maneuver linked to Paul IV's intransigence. Together with Jews from Lazio and the provinces, they began to crowd into the place set aside for them, without offering any particular reactions. It was a limited number of streets and buildings on *rione* Sant'Angelo, a space delimited by walls with gates to the outside that were closed at night, and guarded by Christians who were paid by the Jews themselves. One could enter and exit from these gates only during the day. This solution was a very good representation of the ideological ambiguity of the papacy and of all Catholic theology concerning the Jews. The ghetto reflected, on one hand, the need for the Jews' presence as witnesses to the truth of Christianity, and on the other, their social degradation, which constituted decisive proof of their divine punishment for having denied Christ. In addition, this degradation would serve as an undeniable and material incentive for a quick and decisive conversion to Christianity.

The model of the Roman ghetto was gradually exported to all the cities of the Papal States, and to the other Italian States as well, in a process that would last until the 18th century, an indication of the long term continuity and persistence of the policy of exclusion towards the Jews: for example, the last ghettos in the Piedmont region were opened in 1723, while the final ghetto arose in 1782, at Correggio, in the current Emilia-Romagna. This policy, however, also had the paradoxical outcome of maintaining a culture, a language, and a core identity that, among various fluctuations, always remained substantially united.

The Roman Jews first reacted to the new decree with a certain disbelief, and then with a radical rethinking of their entire internal organization, which only recently had been developed by Daniel da Pisa. The number of *scole* was accordingly reduced from eleven to five and housed in one building, with great effort and at the cost of significant internal tensions, certainly not unwelcome to the ecclesiastical authorities. The system of governing based on the Congregation of Sixty and the three *fattori* was largely preserved. In this way, the Jews were able to maintain unity in a group that was seriously threatened by oppressive policies and efforts to sow disunity connected to the strategy of conversions.

Recent studies have focused on the series of adaptations implemented by the Jewish community to address the imposition of segregation and the novelties that this brought about, first and foremost on the institutional level. For example, although membership in the Congregation of Sixty and the offices of the three *fattori* had always been the exclusive prerogative of bankers, based on a principle of class, now the most important offices increasingly became occupied by rabbis, as representatives of the Law and doctrine. The change seemed to emphasize the transition from the predominance of economics to that of doctrinal skill, important for resolving the specific cases and problems provoked by the new situation. According to some historians who have explored the internal evolution of the community brought about by the new conditions of the ghetto, this process of the confessionalization of administrative management was very close to analogous processes that were also beginning within the Catholic Church after the Protestant Reformation.[11]

The condition of the Jews in Rome, however, and in the other cities with a ghetto was never strictly linked to just the reality of the closed "compound" or to the threat of conversion. Newer historiography has highlighted how the imposed separation and exclusion did not succeed in eliminating the connections and interactions with the life of the host city, nor the exchanges and relationships of friendship and affection between Jews and Christians. Encounters, conversations, and naturally disputes took place in shops, private homes, and even monasteries across Italy.[12] This new research has now set aside the usual schemes of victimization which have historically described the reality of the Jews as one of total confinement, closed, defensive, and turned exclusively in on itself, and out of contact with the outside world.

Staying with the Roman prototype, there were other places in the city outside the ghetto that were specifically delegated to the Jews: for example, the cemeteries located on Aventino, in the area of Porta Portese and Monteverde. There were also other spaces where Jews were constantly present, where meetings and exchanges with Christians were possible, and which constitute proof of Jews' freedom of movement in the city. These were less formal spaces than the ghetto, but were also used habitually because the Jews ran their businesses in the entire city, where they circulated as peddlers, or owned stalls and sold goods, even at the weekly market of Piazza Navona, or visited various hospitals as owners of the so-called "*fagotto*", that is, the right to purchase the clothing of the dead to resell in their trade as *straccivendoli* – secondhand goods sellers. They visited the shops and even the homes of converts and Christians, in spite of the severe prohibitions on doing so. Likewise, there were spaces for occasional meetings, such as the offices of the courts located in various districts, including the central ones, to which Jews were summoned or presented themselves spontaneously to sort out internal disputes or conflicts with Christians, and to answer for crimes. These primarily included the court of the *cardinal vicario*, near the basilica of San Giovanni in Laterano; the court of the Governor, first situated in via di Parione, then at palazzo Madama; and the court of the Holy Office, whose building, bestowed by Pius V, was and still is located to the left of Saint Peter's Basilica.

Furthermore, alongside the places of permanent and occasional presence, spaces that were connected to certain contingencies or situations, but which were also recognized and formalized should be included. Thus, we should also count the oratories where members of the Jewish community were called every Saturday to listen to the forced sermons, such as the *oratorio* of the Santissima Trinità dei Pellegrini and that of the Church of Santa Maria del Pianto. Sometimes, they also attended the preaching in churches – though in principle Jews were excluded from this activity to avoid desecration – such as Sant'Angelo in Pescheria, located in *rione* sant'Angelo. The Casa dei Catecumeni, along with the College of neophytes and the monastery of SS Annunziata for converts, buildings that were all located in the working class Monti neighborhood, which was characterized by great anti-Jewish hostility, and also the monastery of the Convertite al Corso, are also part of this Roman Jewish topography due to their particular characteristics as places meant to accommodate Jews and converted Jews.[13]

One can therefore reconstruct a map of the activity and presence of the Jews in their host city that is much broader and more extensive than what was believed in the past. The consistent participation of the Jews in urban ceremonies to which all components of the city were called to attend has been analyzed and documented. The cartography of the diffuse presence of the Jews in the urban fabric thus extends to ritual spaces, in which they also cyclically appear over time and acquire public visibility. Again in Rome, the community was an active presence in the lavish and articulated ceremony of papal "possession", the long procession which triumphantly brought the newly elected pontiff from the basilica of Saint Peter to that of Saint John. The Jews had the area of Tito's Arch, close to the Coliseum, "under contract" for the occasion, where they hung banners with more or less sincere celebratory writings in honor of the new pope.[14] They were present again, with their own delegation, at Palazzo dei Conservatori, for the installation of the city magistrates at Campidoglio; they were likewise protagonists, albeit unwilling, during the *Carnevale* games organized for all of the citizens, in the so-called *pallio degli ebrei*, the humiliating "racing of the Jews", and again in the infamous *giudiate*, which consisted of popular street theater featuring derisive representations of Jewish customs.

Jewish participation in city life remained lively even after the institution of the ghetto. It has been documented that until the mid-1800s and before the fall of the ghetto, Jews always owned shops and even homes outside ghetto despite the repeated prohibitions, for example, in the streets around today's Largo Argentina.[15] The Roman censuses of the 1700–1800s document the presence of many Jewish textile shop owners with Christian assistants, in violation of the strict rules that prohibited Jews from using the labor of non-Jewish hands. In sum, the exchanges between Jews and Christians in daily life never went away, creating reciprocal understanding, customs and even friendly invitations: for example, when Christians disregarded the prohibitions to attend the weddings of Jewish friends or acquaintances, or other Jewish festivals such as Purim.

The Geography and Chronology of the Ghettos in Italy

The bull of 1555 was also implemented in the rest of the Papal States. However, not all of the many cities and towns that had settlements of Jews went on to establish ghettos, as happened in Bologna, Ancona, Imola, and Recanati. Naturally, the Holy See pressured the Catholic rulers to follow

Rome's example. The Jews, who were already terrorized by the burning of the marranos at Ancona in 1556, in many cases reacted by converting or emigrating. After Paul IV's death in 1559, his successor Pius IV in 1562 authorized the Jews to keep some shops outside the area reserved for them in Rome, which for the first time is referred to by the name of "ghetto". But soon after, there was the papacy of Pius V, who prior to his election had been a severe inquisitor, much like Paul IV, whose heir he considered himself to be. His decrees of 1566 and 1569 aggravated the situation again by requiring the Jews to relocate to only two ghettos, at Rome and Ancona. These ghettos now had to accommodate all the refugees from the other sites that had in the meantime closed, such as the one in Bologna. Finally, in 1593, Clement VIII's bull *Caeca et obdurata Hebraeorum perfidia* definitively reduced the number of ghettos in which the Jews of the Papal States could live to only three: Rome, Ancona, and Avignon, which was outside the Italian territory. For those who would not accept this, the only option was expulsion. Many small, ancient communities, which had for centuries lived scattered in villages and towns, disappeared this way. However, as we will see, there was never a complete halt to the presence of Jews who, with licenses and trade permits, could leave a city with a ghetto and go to other locations to conduct their businesses.

Additionally, the devolution of several fiefdoms to the Church, such as Ferrara and Urbino, increased the number of "cloisters" in the ecclesiastic State. After the former Duchy of Este was annexed to the Papal States in 1598, the numerous Jews in residence were concentrated between 1624 and 1627 in Ferrara, where the Jewish population was very large and remained at about 1,500 people for the whole 17th century, and a little later also at Cento and Lugo. The Duchy of Urbino, which was made part of the Papal States in 1631, saw the rise of three ghettos in the 1630s: at Pesaro, with the biggest population, numbering 500 individuals, at Urbino and Senigallia. In Ancona, a long-time multi-ethnic city where religious minorities and many "national" groups – Jews, Turks, Greeks, Armenians – had settled, the Jews belonged to various nationalities, prominent among which were the Levantines and Portuguese. However, as we saw earlier, the latter's story came to a terrible end, with the burnings and dispersion.[16]

While the ghetto of Rome was created very quickly after the promulgation of the bull *Cum nimis absurdum*, the ghettoization of the rest of Italian Judaism was a rather lengthy process. Many ghettos were created only in the 1600s, such as at Mirandola in 1602, Padova in 1603, Mantova in 1612, Rovigo in 1615, Ferrara after 1624, Cento in 1635, and Lugo in 1639. Still others arose in the 18th century. The segregationist program gradually extended to the whole northern-central part of the peninsula, such that the 17th century, for the history of Italian Jewry – excluding Livorno – is characterized as the "century of the ghettos". While the weak Italian States accepted pressures from the Church for political as well as religious reasons, the phenomena itself of confining and marginalizing the religious

diversity of a minority clearly correspond to the contemporary and analogous process of confining all forms of marginality and deviance (the poor,
mentally ill, homeless, criminals, prostitutes) which developed in parallel
in European countries along with Italy, often called the "disciplinary process" by historians.[17]

The Church of the Counter-Reformation "could legitimately believe it
had launched a definitive solution to the problem of the Jewish presence
within the Catholic world".[18] The model proposed and created in the Papal
States, with its choice between expulsion and ghettoization, was successful, and was imitated throughout Italy. From the 16th century to the 18th
century, all of the Italian States that had not expelled the Jews from their
borders instead concentrated them in closed spaces. Between 1516 and 1797,
the number of ghettos with a population over 1,000 rose to seven: Torino,
Venezia, Mantua, Ferrara, Modena, Ancona, and naturally Rome.[19]

The ghetto was introduced in the Gonzaga Duchy of Mantua in 1612,
under direct pressure from the popes, in particular Clement VIII. The
Mantua community became one of the most numerous communities in
the Christian West, with around 2,300 Jews, for the most part Italians and
Germans, out of a total population of 50,000 residents; the number shrank
during the 1600s as, however, did the total population. In the 17th century,
the percentage of Jews became very high, reaching 8% of the total population, which as a whole was quite diminished.[20] As elsewhere, the Jews were
stuck with the high costs of setting up an area for the ghetto and for maintaining the guards at the gates. By order of Francis I in 1638, a ghetto was
also built in the Duchy of Modena, part of the Este holdings, in the quarter
already inhabited predominantly by the Jews, who were able to maintain
their trade and manufacturing businesses. The ghetto came much later to
Reggio Emilia, in 1669, by order of Laura Martinozzi, the widow of Duke
Alfonso IV d'Este, and ruler on behalf of her son Francesco II. In Tuscany,
the Grand Duke imposed two seraglios in Florence in 1571 and one at Siena
the following year. As we have seen, it was precisely in Tuscany where the
only free settlements of Jews in Italy arose, at Livorno and Pisa. Nevertheless, the fact that these examples were an exception, and had to remain so,
was demonstrated by the permanence of the ghettos at Florence and Siena,
and especially by the creation of others in small border cities, like Sorano,
Pitigliano, and Monte San Savino. Even Genoa, traditionally flexible towards the Jews, who were treated as de facto but not official legal residents,
ended up building a ghetto in 1660. The Republic of Venice, which, as we
have seen, had its "cloister" in the capital since 1516, allowed the creation of
other sites on the mainland; these, however, followed the Roman model and
not the Venetian. The City of Verona, under pressure from Cardinal Agostino Valier, the bishop of the city, was after various attempts able to pass a
resolution for the creation of a ghetto for around 400 people in the central
piazza delle Erbe. But it was actually built only several years later. In 1603,
Padua also had a ghetto that confined 900 Jews.

The concentration of "enclosures" for Jews in the region of Emilia-Romagna, where there were eleven real ghettos, was of particular importance: at Correggio, Guastalla, Reggio Emilia, Finale Emilia, Carpi, Modena, Bologna, Cento, Ferrara, Lugo, and Rimini. The institution of ghettos was articulated across the region in different ways between the mid-16th century and the end of the 18th century. The Bologna ghetto was the first, instituted in 1555 immediately after the promulgation of the papal bull *Cum nimis absurdum*, but it was also the first to be suppressed in 1593 with the definitive expulsion of the Jews from the city. The ghettos in Ferrara, Lugo, and Cento arose only in the wake of the political and administrative changes that resulted from the annexation of the Este territories to the Papal State. The Este family had inaugurated a series of "cloisters" in their territories with the ghetto of Mirandola, built in 1602. One was added at Modena in 1638 and then at Reggio in 1670, and later in Carpi, which got its ghetto in 1719, Finale in 1736, and at Correggio as late as 1782, on the eve of the French Revolutionary wave that would bring with it the brief interlude of the first Jewish emancipation.

The majority of the "enclosures" for Jews in Italy were set up in quarters where they already lived as a majority, and the strictness of the closure varied from location to location: in fact, Jews were often permitted to keep shops outside the ghetto (even at Rome) and to travel, with the proper licenses, for needs of trade. Moreover, despite the concentrations in the established quarters, various small groups of Jews resisted, living in places without a ghetto, especially in the countryside and small agricultural villages: this was particularly common in the rural centers of the northern-central duchies.

Though often believed to be medieval, the very "modern", origins of the ghetto are demonstrated, finally, by the emblematic case of the Savoy Duchy, and in particular of the Piedmont, where the era of the "cloisters" coincided precisely with the age of reforms and the Enlightenment, that is, with most of the 1700s. The first ghetto was instituted in 1679–80 at Torino and situated in the Ospedale della Carità, previously used for the segregation of the poor and ill; the last were those at Asti, Alessandria, and Nizza Monferrato, built in 1723 when the Duchy had become the Kingdom of Sardinia; others followed for the rest of the 18th century, involving twenty Piedmont localities, some very small.[21] In the second half of the 18th century, other small ghettos were created in the Republic of Venice, and in the Habsburg lands of the North-East, the ghettos were also set up late: they were established at the very end of the 1600s in Trieste[22] and Gorizia in 1696, and in the following century at Gradisca in 1762.[23]

Throughout this long process, between the 16th and 18th centuries, the ghettos became the only scene of daily life for the overwhelming majority of Italian Jews. In the 1700s, the number of ghettos rose from 29 to 41, gathering more than 75% of the Jewish population. In no other European country did the Church and Papacy manage to achieve a similar success.

The ghetto, which in other European realities was present in a much less systematic manner, can therefore be considered a typically Italian phenomenon, of Counter-reformation Italy, dominated by the quite particular relations that existed between the individual Italian regional States and the Papacy, and between the Papacy and the Jews. The latter's forced segregation represents the response given to the Jewish problem by the only area in Europe, North-Central Italy, where a total mass expulsion did not take place. It is also worth noting again that the segregationist "system" of the ghettos is a product of the modern world and not of the Middle Ages.

The turning point in papal policy in the mid-1500s was an important part of this result, as indicated by the fact that although the ghettos were removed, albeit temporarily, from the Italian urban panorama in the era of the first emancipation at the end of the 18th century and in the period of the Republics, and then definitively erased by the second emancipation in the 19th century, the Papal States resisted this process the whole time. Thus, the ghetto of Rome was permanently abolished only in 1870, and ended up becoming the very emblem of discrimination and the symbol par excellence of the physical and moral humiliation of the Italian Jews.

The Casa dei Catecumeni and the Conversion of the Jews

The ghetto system, oscillating between moments of relaxation and restriction, was always accompanied by a genuine "conversionist obsession", intended to produce those changes of faith that gradually eroded the Jewish communities, and should have eventually broken their unity and cohesion. An analysis of relationships with the "other" and the "different" in European societies of the modern age must also include the discussion of conversions, understood as the possible definitive solution to the problem of otherness.

The preoccupation with the conversion of Jews, Muslims, and other "infidels" dominated the Catholic Church for all of the modern age – the Protestant Churches much less so – and gave life to institutions that were specifically dedicated to the proselytizing mission. Central among these were the Case dei Catecumeni, in particular the one in Rome, which was founded by Pope Paul III in 1543 and was the first to be built, twelve years before the establishment of the ghetto. This institution took in and housed those who had more or less forcibly been induced to convert to the Catholic religion: this involved Jews, but also Muslims, who came from all over Italy and abroad, and some pagan idolaters. The institution developed considerably, including on the level of architecture and visibility in the urban space, and enjoyed the unconditional support of the popes. The building complex in Rome was improved by Urban VIII, who in 1634 united the various institutions that were connected with the Casa, such as the Collegio dei Neofiti for male converts and the Monastero della Santissima Annunziata for female converts. These disparate bodies were located in a single building that belonged to and was contiguous with the Chiesa della Madonna ai Monti, a fine 16th-century work by Giacomo Della Porta. Other Case dei Catecumeni based on the Roman model then arose in various cities of the

Papal States as well as in other regional Italian States. In the modern era, institutions for converts were densely distributed throughout most of the Italian territory: in Florence, Venice, Bologna, Ferrara, Torino, Modena, Pesaro, and Ancona. While they were much less common in the context of Catholic Europe, there were, however, Case dei Catecumeni at Halle, Lisbon, and Cracow.[24]

The Case de Catecumeni, as the centerpiece and engine of the conversion policy of the Counter-Reformation Church, turned their greatest care and attention to the Jews, who were considered the principal targets of their work. Acquisition of Jewish baptisms was much more important and significant for symbolic and apologetic value than that of Muslims and other "infidels". However, the number of baptized Muslims that emerges from the baptism registries is also significant, although there were few Italian institutions that concerned themselves with adherents of Islam. We must not, however, be misled by the examples of the Case in Rome and Venice, in which there were both Jews, in greater numbers, and Muslims. The institution was therefore a shelter for different categories of "others" from the confessional point of view as well as ethnic and geographic, and an intersection of confessional and religious mobility in the early modern age. It is paradoxical – but at the same time very indicative of who the preferred objects of conversion activity were – that the Jews in a city where a Casa was established had to financially support the institution. However, this situation is completely analogous to the fact that the Jews were always forced to pay the expenses for the ghetto gatekeepers, or, put another way, to keep their own jailers.

The Pia Casa dei Catecumeni e dei Neofiti of Rome, the first Casa and absolutely the most important and the best documented, thus accommodated Jews, Muslims, and pagans who had to begin, after religious instruction, the rite of passage and aggregation that was baptism. The Casa itself, being a place of accommodation, assistance, and residence, with all these minorities living together for considerable periods of time – converted or in the process of conversion, but also some who resisted – represented a microcosm of otherness and coexistence of cultural pluralisms. This reflected the phenomenon, which is partly known, but in reality still scarcely considered in terms of its consequences, of the widespread presence in Counter-Reformation Italy of various nuclei of diversity and religious minorities, of "foreigners", especially in the capital of the Catholic world itself. We will therefore look at the Casa dei Catecumeni of Rome in greater detail.

The Roman institution, which was entered by spontaneous request or by coercion, was endowed with accurate baptism registries which represent an invaluable source for the historian. From 1614 to 1797, there were 1958 Jews and 1,086 Muslims converted in the Roman Casa, for a total of 3,044 baptisms. The source allows analysis not only of the phenomenon of baptisms themselves but also the high degree of mobility, for reasons that were not exclusively religious, that constituted one of the main characteristics of the conversions. Moreover, it provides information about the degree of new converts' inclusion and assimilation in the city, whether they were local or had come from the outside.[25]

The catechumens were subject to strict surveillance inside the institution and to limitations on their movements outside. On the other hand, Jews were strictly prohibited from coming near the Casa due to the fear that they might convince some coreligionist who was housed there to renounce conversion. The neophytes received a rather mild catechism and were instructed in the new faith, often with the assistance of converted priests who knew the native languages of the "guests". Clearly, it was easier to take care of the doctrinal aspect of conversion, the catechism, and sermonizing, with those who had spontaneously requested baptism. But in the cases of those who had been forcibly confined to the Casa, a program of powerful moral and psychological pressure to accept baptism was employed over the course of a real imprisonment of forty or more days called a *quarantena*. The instruction of Jewish converts was often entrusted to the Dominican fathers who were in charge of the forced sermons to which the members of the community were subjected weekly.

Training, which lasted at least two months, generally included memorization of the fundamentals of the Christian doctrine, based on Roberto Bellarmino's catechism in Italian. Neophytes were taught prayers, the Credo, the commandments, and the sacraments, read the *Vita dei santi*, practiced the *Quarantore* devotion, participated in solemn festivals and learned to recite the rosary. Over time, the regulation and methods of doctrinal and behavioral instruction became stricter, also trying to keep those who had been baptized separate from those who had not. In any case, in order to prevent converts from fleeing Rome to engage in apostasy once they had obtained the subsidy that was now theirs along with their baptism, the rules prohibited them from leaving the city until three years after their ceremony, and imposed weekly attendance at Christian doctrine and spiritual exercises. Even the subsidy reserved for the convert, which often represented a strong motive for requesting baptism, was administered by the Casa, which invested the money in *Luoghi di Monte*, that is, in State bonds.

It is difficult to get at the deep motivations of someone who decided to convert, to reconstruct the intimate psychological experiences and individual interior paths, inasmuch as the stories and self-representations offered by the converts themselves do not always represent reliable sources, given their apologetic and often instrumental uses. On the other hand, it is certainly easy to find the most apparent and superficial economic and social reasons, but also the interpersonal and emotional motivations which may have led to this step. Poverty, isolation in the group of membership, escape from fractures in the family, a desire for redemption, and a step up in social status, matrimonial aspirations, strategies to evade justice for crimes committed, the desire for the freedom of a new identity that also provided a new name and surname, all of these constituted material and psychological incentives to conversion. They were also well known to the ecclesiastical authorities, however, who always suspected the sincerity of converts. The Roman documentation confirms the prevalence of poor, young males among converts, while the data showing only a small number of spontaneous conversions by women is striking. Certainly, the role of the Case dei Catecumeni as distributors of material as well as social and symbolic resources and privileges underlines the inevitable instrumentality of conversions. However, they were often also prompted by considerations that were not strictly utilitarian, but rather related to some crisis of relations between an individual and the community or family context. Put another way, conversions could represent a strategy for responding to moments of conflict within families around the unequal distribution of domestic resources among children, especially between male and female, given the latter's greater advantage. Conversion could also present opportunities for avoiding legal penalties or, again, for carrying out personal vendettas and retaliation within the community.[26] In any case, we should not underestimate the psychological complexity of motivations that are not simply reducible to material fact, nor the articulated dynamic that leads to the construction of a new identity. The stereotype of the "insincere convert", which historians have inherited from the sources they use, does not always turn out to be valid, given the difficulty of defining identities when speaking of minorities and confessional transitions. Only the study of individual stories can avoid the risk of generalizations. In many cases, for example, conversions are the result of genuine individual crises of conscience, or affectionate relations between Jews and Christians that lead to embracing the religion of the partner in order to gain access to the sacrament of matrimony. In any case, the majority of converts were from the most vulnerable social strata, although rabbis and wealthy merchants were also not lacking. There were fewer conversions of women, for reasons linked to the specific and particular role played by Jewish women within the family.

Forced Baptisms

The obsession with the conversion of the Jews had an eschatological doctrinal element, and was essentially based on the millenarian-messianic concept relating to the expectation of the second coming of Christ on earth, and so the beginning of 1,000 years of peace and happiness that would be achieved when the world was unified within the one faith.[27] The conversion of the Jewish people was seen as necessary in order to hasten this moment of liberation and universal unity, and so was to be encouraged in every way and by all means, for the salvation of the Jews themselves and of all of humanity. In any case, even outside of any knowledge of doctrine, the current and widespread idea even among the popular strata was that obtaining the baptism, and so the salvation, of a Jew was a good and meritorious act. Thus, when Christian wet nurses saw, or believed they saw, a Jewish child at risk of death they did not hesitate to summarily baptize him, often acting in good faith, but still contrary to every teaching of Thomas Aquinas that prohibited baptisms against the will of the parents. They would then report the baptism to the authorities, who would intervene to separate the child from its family. This happened frequently between the 16th and 19th centuries: in 1858, there was the sensational case – one of the last – of the kidnapping of the child Edgardo Mortara in Bologna, who was forcibly taken from his parents and brought to Rome after a Christian servant reported that she had secretly baptized him years earlier.[28]

In addition to these baptisms, which can be defined as "clandestine", there were other types of coercion, though certainly not practiced naively or in good faith as could be the case with the nannies. Forced baptisms could result from a report presented to the authorities by Christians or even Jews who gave sworn statements that they had heard a Jew say they wanted to convert. They could also be the result of so-called "offers", which derived from the "right" of converts to "offer" wives or children over whom they had guardianship, and even other more distant relatives for conversion to their new faith and Church. The ecclesiastical authorities always accepted these offers. Things reached the point where converts who were grandfathers or grandmothers were given the right of guardianship over their grandchildren, even in cases where the parents were still alive. This was allowed based on the principle of *favor fidei* ("in the interest of the faith"): a canonical principle which served to resolve all manner of difficulties, such as determining the rights for the guardianship of minors based on the needs of the religion, thus bypassing any obstacles posed by natural or common law, or even by canon law itself. It was believed that the interests of the Catholic religion coincided with those of the Jew who had been "offered", who was now under the direct protection and care of the Church. These interests prevailed over any sort of jurisprudence and led the ecclesiastical authorities to work around and manipulate legislation and natural laws, for example, those that offered protections for mothers, especially from the seizing of their children. These practices were even more onerous when the offered woman was pregnant and the offer also included the unborn child.[29]

While children were the primary victims of forced conversions, women were equally so, often having to follow the will of their husband or father, or embrace the faith of a baptized child to prevent being separated from them forever. Jewish women were therefore the preferred targets of this policy of conversion, and a large number of offers involved women. In fact, though women were less willing to convert compared to men, they were, however, the most coveted subjects along with children. One of the strongest reasons for the authorities' acceptance of denunciations and offers that involved women was connected to their reproductive ability: Jewish women who converted would give birth to Christian children (according to the Christians, but not according to the Jews). Converting a young Jewish woman thus meant ensuring Christian children. Widows in particular were primary victims of this practice, as their children could be stripped from them if offered by other converted relatives. An example of this happened in 1702, involving Grazia Anticoli of Rome: widowed by Giuseppe and named the guardian of their six children by the husband himself in his will, she saw them kidnapped after being offered by their paternal uncle, who had converted to the Christian religion.[30] However, once the mothers converted in order to follow their children, those bonds of affection constituted the best guarantee of their perseverance in the new faith and integration in their new community. This was true even more so if, as often happened, the neophyte married an original Christian and had other children with him.

This attention to female conversions explains the fury towards the young Anna del Monte, who left us a wonderful diary of her dramatic incarceration in the Casa dei Catecumeni of Rome in 1749.[31] Her confinement did not succeed at converting her, despite the powerful emotional and psychological pressures that were applied. But this was an exception. In fact, it was rare for even the strongest and most rebellious women to not end up giving in, especially when subjected to a *quarantena* that was often extended several times, or if they had children that were already baptized in the Casa.

Conversion, forced or spontaneous, culminated with the ceremonies of baptism and reconciliation, which were celebrated, especially in the most sensational cases, with triumphant pomp and the solemn public display of the baptized. This display constituted, above all else, a kind of performance that had great appeal to Christian society, with a strong favorable apologetic value for the Church and the Papacy. The higher the "quality" and social status of the convert, the greater was the glory derived from the conversion to the Church and to Rome. At the beginning of the 18th century, in 1704, great prominence was given through printed reports which were circulated among the public to the baptism of Angelo Vesino, a wealthy Jewish merchant from Livorno, and his entire family. The ceremony was celebrated at Rome and officiated by Pope Clement XI personally. Sponsors were chosen from among the most prestigious cardinals and the most important protagonists of the Roman Court, such as the former Queen of Poland, Maria Casimira Sobieska.[32]

The phenomenon of forced baptisms, which intensified during the 18th century and continued into the heart of the 19th century, was not without consequences and repercussions on later history, as the case of Edgardo Mortara demonstrates. Taking place in the midst of the Italian Risorgimento, the case had a very strong international resonance and serious political consequences for the Papal State, accelerating its downfall. It was an international scandal whose repercussions are felt within the Catholic Church even today, continuing to influence its relations with Jewish organizations. One thinks, for example, of the tensions triggered by the beatification of Pius IX, the protagonist of the Mortara affair, celebrated in the Jubilee year of 2000.

The practice of forced baptisms developed in parallel with the revival, between the 17th and 18th centuries, of centuries-old anti-Jewish stereotypes, including the more violent ones – such as the accusation that Jews practiced the ritual murder of Christian children – and with the virulent anti-Jewish polemic of reactionary Catholic Restoration publishing. As we will see, after the French Revolution, the Jews were branded as the standard bearers of modernity, the enemy of religion, and the leaders of an anti-Catholic conspiracy. The civil and political emancipation sanctioned during the revolutionary and Napoleonic decades would actually exacerbate growing Catholic antisemitism, which, developing and expanding on tones and themes already present in the 18th century, became a primary component of 19th–20th-century intransigent ideology, and opened the way to political antisemitism.

The Social and Symbolic Value of Jewish Converts

The study of the destinies of converts brings out the symbolic value of these figures as instruments of apology and glorification of the Counter-Reformation Church and Papacy, as well as their social relevance resulting from the substantial series of economic and legal advantages obtained everywhere with baptism. Among the privileges granted in Rome, the automatic attainment of citizenship rights and the advantage of being able to use, for legal issues, a particular or "private" judge were particularly significant. Furthermore, converts were exempted from the payment of some taxes paid by those who opened one or more shops, such as the road tax. Finally – and this was certainly not a minor concession in a "corporate" society like that of the Old Regime – they did not have observe the Statutes, the taxes, or the monopoly rules of the trade guilds. This allowed converts a productive and entrepreneurial freedom that was impractical for the majority of workers, including Christians. However, they did not escape the controls and surveillance required to demonstrate their fidelity to the new religion.

The complex dynamic between privileges and control is made evident by a very particular institution, which operated outside the substantially common structure of the assistance and devotional systems of the other confraternities; the confraternity of converts dedicated to St. John the Baptist and formed in 1620 "for the greater confirmation of the Neophytes in the Holy Faith". The association, formed in Rome, soon took the title of arch-confraternity, which placed it at the head of all similar factions that formed in the Catholic world. Membership, as well as attendance at functions and sermons, was required not only for all converts, but for their descendants up to four generations and even the husbands of converts, original Christians, and the spouses, also original Christians, of the converts' children. In exchange for this obligation, the Christian spouses enjoyed all of the privileges that the apostolic constitutions reserved for new converts. The Statutes then required the confraternity brothers to go to the oratory on every mandatory holiday to hear the sermon. As a result, converts and the native Christians related to them were all subjected to the same regime of suspicious control and to the same practice of forced preaching which was obligatory for the

Jews, a clear demonstration of the suspicion and mistrust harbored towards converts.

However, the cultural and social role of the converts was even more complex, inasmuch as they were liminal, borderline figures capable of playing a role of mediation and exchange, more or less conflictual, between different religious-cultural groups. The mediating function of converts was clear in the case of "illustrious" conversions, of rabbis and Jewish scholars who became ideal collaborators in the work of proselytization. They were often employed in the practice of forced sermons and polemics against the Jews, with the goal of motivating the conversions of their former coreligionists. They were also active in the censorship of Jewish books.[33]

Another phenomenon that clarifies the task assigned to this group is the encouragement by ecclesiastical institutions of marriages that we could call "mixed", that is, between native Christians and converts from different faiths. Although studies have just begun on this important aspect, we can say that the contribution of female converts in their function as a hinge between different worlds was central, and they were targets of ecclesiastical strategies for accelerating the integration of converts in Christian society. However, these matrimonial unions also presented other, more material and concrete implications. If the safest mechanism for strengthening, the faith of converts was to have them marry native Christians, for Christian men marriage to a female convert also represented an excellent investment because of the large dowries they were entitled to, along with the financial, tax and work privileges that automatically accrued with the union, in addition to the dowry.[34] Female converts represented considerable social and economic capital, and thus they entered the marriage market in a position of strength and absolute privilege. Moreover, the prohibition of marriage between converts, at least for those who had already been married as Jews, and the strong incentives for "mixed" marriages, including on the material level, and even when it meant breaking up pre-existing marriages, served to prevent possible remorse or return to Jewish practices. For this aspect, these instruments represented an absolutely central element of the ecclesiastic strategy for the religious and social integration of converts.

The social and symbolic value of female converts, who offered future husbands guarantees of honesty and good morals in addition to a secure dowry, leads us to reflect on the significant inclusion and absorption of converts, and especially female converts, into the fabric of Christian society and work without too many traumas. In short, contrary to what had happened in Spain between the 15th and 16th centuries, and to what would happen in the 20th century with the Italian racial laws of 1938, marriage totally integrated Jewish converts within Christian society and included them in the overall urban fabric. As a result, though the conversion of single individuals often appears instrumental, meant to obtain the betterment of one's own social and economic position via the possibility of entering a "good" marriage with Christians, it is also true that "mixed" marriage turned out to be the most efficient strategy for conversion as well as definitive and radical assimilation.

However, strategies of conversion do not always succeed. Rereading a very important historical document like the diary of the young Anna del Monte we mentioned earlier, it is possible to better understand the forms of sophisticated psychological pressure brought to bear in trying to convince her to accept catechism. Likewise, we see her reactions as an educated young woman, capable of responding to the tone of the sermons and refusing to be "sprinkled with water" – as she states, referring to baptism – against her will. "A Jewess I was born, and a Jewess I want to die", Anna courageously declared, until she obtained her release.[35]

Notes

1 Instead, Ravid, "'Cum nimis absurdum'," 85–100 disputes the thesis that the 1555 bull establishing the ghetto and other restrictions for Jews constituted a turning point in the history of the Jews on the peninsula, but with several inaccuracies, and only in reference to the case of Venice.
2 Luzzati, *Il ghetto ebraico*, 3.
3 Luzzati, *Il ghetto ebraico*, 10.
4 Luzzati, *Il ghetto ebraico*.
5 Regarding the Jews and the ghetto of Venice, cfr. Cozzi, *Gli ebrei a Venezia*; Calabi et al., *La città degli ebrei*; Calimani, *Storia del ghetto di Venezia*. However, there is a vast bibliography.
6 Cfr. Part One, Ch. I.
7 Israel, *Gli ebrei d'Europa*, 28 ss.
8 Cfr. *Bullarum Diplomatum et Privilegiorum Sanctorum Romanorum Pontificum* (1860), vi, 498–500. The translation from Latin to Italian is by the author, the translation from Italian to English by the translator. Part of the bull is published in Italian by Milano, *Storia degli ebrei in Italia*, 247.
9 Blumenkranz, *Il cappello a punta*; Ravid, "From Yellow to Red," 179–210. For the modern age, see Moretti, "'Glauci coloris'," 29–64; Capriotti, *Lo scorpione nel petto*.
10 See Milano, *Storia degli ebrei in Italia*, 188–9 for a precise description. Cfr. also Benocci and Guidoni, "Il Ghetto". Regarding the architectural structure of the Roman ghetto and its forced upward development, cfr. Ferrara, "La struttura architettonica," 3–22.
11 Di Nepi, *Sopravvivere al ghetto*.
12 Refer to Caffiero, *Legami pericolosi*, for these aspects.
13 Lirosi, "Monacare le ebree"; "Case pie e monasteri". On the variegated distribution of the Jewish presence in Rome, refer to Caffiero, "Spazi urbani e scene rituali," 3–22.
14 Concerning Jews' participation in the possession ceremony, cfr. Caffiero, "La maestà del papa". See also Di Castro, *Gli ebrei romani*.
15 Caffiero, "Le botteghe degli ebrei," 273–92.
16 On the Portuguese of Ancona, cfr. Segre, "La formazione di una comunità," 779–841; Cooperman, "Portuguese Conversos in Ancona," 297–352; Bonazzoli, "Una identità ricostruita," 9–38. For the Levantines, cfr. Bonazzoli, "Ebrei italiani, portoghesi e levantini," 727–70. But for Ancona and the Jews, now see Andreoni, *Una nazione in commercio*.
17 Foucault, *Storia della follia*.

18 Luzzati, *Il ghetto ebraico*, 20.
19 Harris, "La demografia del ghetto," 12.
20 Regarding the Jews at Mantua, cfr. Simonsohn, *The Jews in the Duchy of Mantua*; for the 18th century see Bernardini, *La sfida dell'eguaglianza*; Cavarocchi, *La comunità ebraica di Mantova*.
21 Segre, *The Jews in Piedmont*. On the ghetto of Torino, cfr. Allegra, *Identità in bilico*.
22 Dubin, *The Port Jews of Habsburg Trieste*.
23 Del Bianco Cotrozzi, "Tolleranza giuseppina," 689–726.
24 The better known Case dei Catecumeni and the first to be studied are that in Turin, about which cfr. Allegra, *Identità in bilico*, and the one in Rome, about which refer to Rocciolo, "Documenti sui catecumeni," 391–452; Caffiero, *Battesimi forzati*. For Ancona, cfr. Andreoni, "La Casa dei catecumeni di Ancona," 155–210. For Venice, cfr. Ioly Zorattini, *I nomi degli altri*. For Modena and Florence now see Al Kalak, "Convertire e sostenere," 71–105; Marconcini, "La Pia Casa dei catecumeni," 107–27; *Per amor del cielo*. For Bologna, cfr. Campanini, "L'identità coatta," 155–76. A rich bibliography on the Case dei Catecumeni can now be found in Caffiero, "Tra due fuochi".
25 The numerical data for Rome, provided based on the baptism registries, are in Rudt De Collenberg, "Le baptême de juifs de Rome," 24, 91–231; 25, 105–261; 26, 119–294.
26 Allegra, "Modelli di conversione," 901–15.
27 On the millennial myth of the final conversion of the Jews, cfr. Caffiero, *La nuova era*.
28 Kertzer, *Prigioniero del papa Re*. Significantly, the original 1997 publication uses the word 'kidnapping' in the title, *The Kidnapping of Edgardo Mortara*, a term that is not used in the Italian version.
29 Regarding the various aspects of the phenomenon of conversions and forced baptisms, and on the importance of converting women and children, see Caffiero, *Battesimi forzati*; for the English version see *Forced Baptisms*.
30 Caffiero, *Forced Baptisms*, 81–2.
31 Caffiero, *Rubare le anime*.
32 For a description of the grandiose ceremony, cfr. Caffiero, *Forced Baptisms*, 214–21.
33 Cfr. Caffiero, *Legami pericolosi*.
34 Caffiero, "Le doti della conversione".
35 Caffiero, "Non farsi rapire l'anima," 54.

6   Jewish Culture and Christian Culture

Jewish Culture and Books: The Holocaust of the *Talmud*

Notwithstanding the limits and humiliations imposed by the process of ghettoization, with the growing population crowded into cramped spaces and prohibited from practicing the majority of occupations, culture and education continued to flourish among the Jews. The traditional areas of Jewish culture related to the exegesis and interpretation of the Law or Kabbalah continued to be practiced within a highly literate society. It has been noted that the fundamental difference between Judaism and Catholicism with respect to the practice of reading lies in the Jewish perception of study as a "religious ritual" and as an obligation.[1] What was defined as the "sacralization of the book" in medieval times, but also later, made it an object whose contents, and their communication, were secondary to the book's supernatural, magical-religious charge as a sacred relic.[2] Naturally, it was precisely this character of sanctity, which for example led the Jews to insistently ask for the return of the volumes that had been confiscated by the Inquisition, which made their books very dangerous in the eyes of Christians. The Jews read, including the women, who although they received more limited instruction, were at least able to read the prayers in Hebrew.[3] It should be noted, moreover, that for a long time Jewish books that were aimed at the general public, for example at women, were in the Italian language, but written with Hebrew characters, a type of linguistic hybridism in which Hebrew and the Italian language were mixed.[4]

Although physically separated from Christians, Jews did not live isolated from the surrounding culture. The regular and continuous intertwining of reciprocal communication and relationships between the two worlds not only refutes, as we have said, the most common interpretive paradigm of separation and inability to communicate between the two groups but also refers to a system of daily interactions, of negotiated relations and mutual knowledge of their respective religions. Books could be the most influential intermediaries in these contacts, which the Christian authorities feared and wished to prevent. So, between the 16th and the 18th centuries, the Inquisition oversaw the compilation of two *Indici* (Indexes) composed exclusively

DOI: 10.4324/9781003188445-9

of Hebrew books to be banned and eventually destroyed, entrusting the task to converted Jewish scholars, for the most part former rabbis.[5] Standing out among them all, naturally, was the dangerous and hated *Talmud*. Confiscation, censorship, and revision of Jewish books were fully part of the Christian view of the need for re-examination and correction of the Jewish scriptural tradition. This corresponded to the constantly reiterated belief that the Jews actively falsified sacred texts, and that there was a need for Christians to intervene and purge Jewish studies in the field of Mosaic Law itself, that is, of their own doctrine, of those misunderstood and interpreted out of malice and ignorance. The censoring of books thus served to protect not only the Christian religion but also paradoxically Judaism too: or, at least, the Jewish religion as it should have been according to the Christians, who also remained the sole true interpreters of the Jewish textual tradition.

However, censorship also served another, perhaps more essential goal, which was that of conversion. Not by chance, the total ban on the *Talmud* and on other so-called rabbinic texts was aimed at getting what were considered the greatest and most powerful obstacles to their conversion out of Jews' hands: books themselves. An expert auditor of their volumes wrote in 1731 that the Jews were not converting "as they too comfortable, they have books, all of which should be seized in conformity with the Holy Apostolic Constitutions".[6]

But what was represented by the *Talmud*, one of Judaism's sacred texts which contains discussion and commentary on the Law given by Moses and expressed in the *Torah*?[7] The definitive inclusion of the Jews in the category of heretics, and as such prosecutable by the court of the Inquisition, was preceded in the early modern age by the formal act of condemnation and destruction of the *Talmud* and other books defined as unquestionably heretical, blasphemous, and dangerous, as had in fact already happened in the Middle Ages.[8] Even before the institution of the ghetto of Rome in 1555, the popes promulgated various censorship measures reconfirming prohibitions that had been gradually established in the Middle Ages, and reviving the burning of banned books. On September 12, 1553, a decree *De combustione Talmud*, which significantly was issued by the newly formed Congregation of the Roman Inquisition and not by the current pope Julius III, sent a message that the Congregation was not only responsible for eliminating heresy but also for policing the Jews. The latter are portrayed as not content with living mixing among Christians like chaff – "*sicut zizania*" – and their access to the Sacred Scriptures, but instead in the habit of studying superstitious books full of empty fables and blasphemy, filled with hateful insults towards Christ and curses against Christians, "called *Talmud*".[9] The hunt for "heretical" books went hand in hand with that for Jewish books, and illustrates the connection that the Catholic mentality had formed between the two phenomena, Judaism and Reform.[10]

To eradicate this evil at the roots, the Inquisition's decree ordered the seizure of books in the synagogues and in the homes of community members in Rome and throughout the State, to examine and then burn the books and *Talmudic* codices. These books, published in whole or in part, contained open and ungodly blasphemies against God and against the Mosaic Law, which the Jews also prided themselves on following, as well as expressions contrary to natural law and the Catholic religion. All the Christian Princes were invited to do the same in their States. Just three days prior to the Inquisitorial edict, on September 9 – a holiday for the Jews as it was the first day of the New Year – at Piazza Campo de' Fiori in Rome and in front of a large crowd, the executioner publicly burned a huge number of copies of the *Talmud* that had been seized from the homes of the Jews of the city. All the Jews living in the Papal States were ordered to spontaneously turn over volumes of the cursed book, under penalty of confiscation of their goods, a quarter of which would go to informers.[11] Similar measures were adopted in Bologna, Ravenna, Pesaro, Cremona, Mantua and Ferrara, and also in Venice, where in that same year of 1553, the book burning mentioned earlier took place.

It is worth noting the fact that the control and repression of books anticipated the personal restrictive measures, that is, the decision to enclose the Jews in a specific quarter and to increase control over them. Analysis of the chronology of events clearly shows the unfolding of this repressive process. The centuries-old prohibition of the *Talmud* that was reiterated by the court of the Holy Office in 1553, and the mass book burning that took place in Campo de' Fiori were followed by the brief *Cum sicut nuper* of May 29, 1554, issued by Julius III *"contra hebreos retinentes libros in quibus aliquid contra Fidem Catholicam notetur vel scribatur"*. This decree again ordered the ecclesiastic authorities to demand that Jewish communities hand over, within four months of being notified, books that had been identified as containing blasphemy or other injuries to the name of Jesus. Those who disobeyed would be subject to very severe penalties, up to death.[12] The provision, which classified Jews who owned such books as apostates, and therefore heretics, only granted them that short period of time in which to carry out self-censoring revisions of all of their texts. The term was then extended at the request of the Jews themselves. All of this happened just before the institution of the ghetto in 1555, and demonstrates how at the time control was mostly being exercised over books, and how it later transferred from books to individuals. So, it was rabbinical books first and foremost which were considered dangerous inasmuch as they suggested beliefs, precepts, and behaviors to individuals. These teachings ended up being considered as deviant and heretical compared to the "pure" biblical text, which the Jews also had to observe. Another and different problem, naturally, was related to who should present and interpret the Old Testament in its "purity", and how.

Destroying the *Talmud* and the rabbinic writings which preserved Jewish tradition and its very identity, as well as the rules for guiding behaviors, meant removing the main obstacle that stood in the way of the real and definitive solution to the problem of the existence of the Jews: that is, their conversion. The fasts and prayers of the Roman Jews to save their books through divine intervention were of no use. Indeed, this blow was also interpreted in the highest ecclesiastical spheres as a sign of divine approval for having taken away the book that was the main impediment to conversion. The powerful Cardinal Guglielmo Sirleto wrote sarcastically to the future Pope Marcello Cervini, on the same day as the burning in Campo de' Fiori, that "the Jews have fasted many days with prayers to God to keep this book, but God answered them with having it lifted from them today which is the first day of their year, and certainly a great impediment to their conversion has been lifted in having seized this book from them".[13]

It is therefore the problem of books that opened the difficult and often ambiguous relationship between the Inquisition and the Jews, and from then on the possession of prohibited texts was one of the most frequent charges in cases brought by the court against them.

The famous pyre of Campo de' Fiori of 1553 – called "the holocaust of the *Talmud*" by contemporaries[14] – was then followed, at the pope's invitation, by confiscations and burnings in many other cities of the Papal States and the rest of Italy, with a destruction of considerable dimensions. In 1559, in Cremona, according to the story told by Sisto Senese, who was tasked by Paul IV with burning the "superstitious, and directly contrary to the Christian Faith" *Talmudic* books, 14,000 volumes were destroyed, even though Sisto wanted to save the Kabbalistic books. In May of 1557, when the ghetto of Rome had been in existence for only two years, a decree by Paul IV himself repeated the order for requisition of all of the Jews' books in the lands of the Papal States, making an exception for the Bible.

The fact that the issue of the prohibition of the *Talmud* was absolutely central in the war against dangerous books is made clear by the role that it occupied during the drafting of the various *Indici* of prohibited books through the 16th century, which continually oscillate with respect to the dilemma of expurgation or destruction. The first of the *Indici*, published in 1559, in 1564, and in 1590, vacillated between total and strict prohibition and acceptance of censored editions. However, at the end of the century the inquisitorial hard line prevailed, advocating the material destruction of the *Talmud*. Thus, the book was the focus of a very harsh clash that continued even into the following decades.

In 1593, the constitution by Clement VIII, *Cum Hebraeorum malitia*, definitively finalized the strictest and most detailed decree, which guided law for at least two centuries on the subject of the censorship of Jewish books, and more generally regarding oversight of the Jews. In addition to the books they owned, the law was especially concerned with the magical practices and witchcraft that Jews supposedly practiced, which would have been taught in precisely these texts.[15] The bull, which condemned the *Talmud*, Kabbalistic books and commentaries to being burned without appeal, was requested of the pope by the Holy Office and the powerful Cardinal Giulio AntonioSantori, the strict and severe "supreme inquisitor" who was its author.[16] This represented not only a victory for the Inquisition, but above all a milestone in anti-Jewish law.

The constitution *Cum Hebraeorum militia* was promulgated on February 28, 1593, meaning only three days after the renewal of the order for the expulsion of the Jews from the Papal States, excluding Rome, Ancona, and Avignon, imposed by another anti-Jewish bull, *Caeca et obdurata Hebraeorum perfidia*, also inspired and written by Santori. The two decrees, so close in time, tried to resolve two problems: the question of the Jewish presence in the Papal States, and, once again, the longstanding issue of the *Talmud*.[17] In this direction, the *Cum Hebraeorum malitia* referred to the decrees of predecessors on the matter. In particular, it explicitly pointed to the fact that the first prohibition and destruction of the *Talmud* had been imposed by Innocent IV with the constitution *Impia Iudaeorum perfidia* of 1244 as an important precedent. And naturally, it should be noted that all of these pontifical decrees, for the most part dictated by the Inquisition, employ a specific lexicon that was applied to the Jews and destined to have a long and successful history, from the first words of the document headings and throughout the text, using terms such as *improbitas, malitia* and *perfidia*.[18]

But what did Clement's constitution *Cum Hebraeorum militia* establish in more detail? First and foremost, as has been said, it prohibited in perpetuity and condemned to be burned "ungodly *Talmudic* and Kabbalistic books and codices, and others that are dangerous". To these were added all the works, commentaries, writings, or treatises, either in Hebrew or other languages, already printed or to be printed in the future, that tacitly or expressly contained heresies and errors, or insults, impieties, and blasphemies against the Old and New Testaments. These offenses were carefully listed in the document, following a precise hierarchy of importance in descending order, as those directed against God, the Trinity, Jesus Christ and the Christian faith, the virgin Mary, the angels, the patriarchs, the prophets, the apostles and all the other saints, the Cross, the sacraments, the sacred images, the Catholic Church, the Holy See, Christian believers, and, in particular, bishops, priests, neophytes, and converts.[19] Any exception or license regarding such books was revoked, and their owners had to deliver them within ten days to the Holy Office of Rome or to local inquisitors: serious corporal and spiritual penalties, up to excommunication, were established for violators, be they Christians, reformed "heretics", or Jews. The Inquisition was furthermore responsible for procedures against Jews who had committed blasphemy either against Christian belief (*contemptus fidei*), or against beliefs shared by Jews and Christians: it was a very wide field, naturally, that likewise extended the Holy Office's sphere of competence, intervention, and control over the Jews. On the other hand, the connection between heretical books and individual behaviors that were also heretical, and therefore prosecutable, was found in the same thing: the Jews studied – and taught – doctrine, beliefs, and practices from books, which were widely read and written. The *Talmud* was considered heretical because it contained heresies that are contrary not only to the Evangelist and Christian beliefs, but contrary to the Old Testament itself, which the Jews should have defended, but instead interpreted in a false and deceptive way. Hence, the best expurgation was burning.

The bull of 1593 concerning the *Talmud* and other Jewish books derived from it, and thus considered completely heretical, just as those who read them were also considered heretics, strongly influenced the drafting of Clement VIII's *Indice* of 1596. Driven as always by Santori, this *Indice* definitively condemned *Talmudic* and Kabbalistic books, without any chance of appeal and "in perpetuity", due to the impossibility of their ever really being expurgated. From then on, those who kept and read the heretical *Talmud* would be considered heretics and treated as such. The bull of 1593 and the *Indice* of 1596, both promulgated by the same pontiff, Clement VIII, formed the final ban of the *Talmud*, which has never been revoked since then, and the cessation of all reprinting of the volume in Italy.[20]

The measure was reintroduced in full again two centuries later on February 2, 1733, just two years after the large seizure of Jewish books in all of the Papal States that took place in 1731; it was repeated in 1751, as always accompanied by seizures, and was finally repeated again, at the height of the Enlightenment, with the edict concerning the Jews dated April 5, 1775, declared by the newly elected Pius VI. It is very significant that these 18th-century edicts, which were strict and restrictive regarding many aspects of the Jews' lives, also started by immediately addressing the subject of books and renewing prohibitions and punishments. This demonstrates the extent to which this problem was a core concern for the ecclesiastical authorities, who identified books as the most dangerous instruments in the hands of the Jews. Even the periodic searches that were carried out in the community aimed at seizing texts, and the Inquisition's failure to return the volumes to their owners were part of the "book hunt".[21]

As we have seen, in the papal bulls that definitively condemn Jewish books, there was almost always a reference to Kabbalistic books. Although the indication was often generic, and there had furthermore never been a formal condemnation of Kabbalah by the Congregation of the Holy Office,[22] the condemnation of texts to be burned without appeal also involved these texts and their contents. We should therefore take a closer look at this important aspect of Jewish culture.

The Kabbalah

An important element of Jewish culture transmitted through books was the Kabbalah, which arrived in Europe with the Jewish refugees from Spain. In the new framework created by Isaac Luria (1534–72) and his student Chayyim Vital (1543–1620), Kabbalistic mysticism presents itself as the cultural reaction to the material and spiritual catastrophe that followed the exile from Spain and the shock of expulsion.[23] In particular, metempsychosis gained an immense popularity then, since it focused on the different stages of the exile of the soul, suggestive of the tragic fate of an entire exiled people and the expiation of sins until liberation.[24] The theory of reincarnation is defined in the Jewish esotericism of the 16th century and in mystical theology. Chayyim Vital condensed these in *Sefer ha-Gilgulim* ("The Book of the Transmigration of the Soul") presenting it as a universal law that also applies to animals, plants, and stones. It was believed that every man carried with him secret traces of his own soul's peregrinations in the lines of the face and hands and in the aura that radiates from the body.[25] The doctrine of transmigration, at first limited to restricted scholarly circles, increasingly spread beginning in the mid-1500s and for all of the 1600s, fully entering the popular beliefs and culture of the Jews.

It is no surprise, therefore, that all of Isaac Luria's work was included in the *Indici* of Jewish books to be absolutely prohibited. The main charge against it was the doctrine of transmigration of souls, in particular the idea that the souls of sinners could become demons or evil spirits, capable of entering human bodies and completely dominating them.[26] The problem, therefore, was the Kabbalistic derivation of these theories. In Rome, for example, the affirmation of a somewhat more rational Judaism had emerged within the Jewish universe since the 16th century.[27] Subsequently, at the height of the Counter-Reformation, the official and repeated condemnation of magical, Kabbalistic, and esoteric arts, which were quite popular in the Renaissance, even among Christians, certainly had an influence on pushing the Jews in more prudent directions. The bull *Coeli et Terrae Creator* by Sixtus V in 1586, and the one that followed, *Inscrutabilis* by Urban VIII in 1631, threatened very severe penalties including the death sentence for anyone, Christian or Jew, who practiced divinatory and magical arts.[28] However, it is still the case that Kabbalistic doctrines and rites, though suspect and dangerous, continued to be professed and practiced by the Jews, and not only by them. For example, with the doctrine of metempsychosis, while it referred to the Jewish belief according to which the spirit of a dead person, the *dibbuk*, could take possession of someone living,[29] it also explicitly echoed the phenomenon of diabolical possession that had long tormented the Christian world. The doctrine, therefore being very close to witchcraft, raised the suspicions of the inquisitors and the bishops.[30]

The Kabbalah, spread through Europe by Iberian Jewish refugees, became increasingly widespread starting in the mid-1500s thanks to the availability of a fundamental work, the *Zohar*. This book was published in Italy in two different editions, one in Mantua in 1558 and one in Cremona in 1560, both printed for foreign markets and destined to circulate in all of Jewish Europe. Between the 16th and 17th centuries, Kabbalah, albeit in different ways and with ups and downs, became a fundamental piece of Jewish culture both in the Ashkenazi communities of Eastern Europe as well as in the Sephardic communities that were settled in strategic European centers, such as Amsterdam and the Ottoman Empire, including in the land of Israel and Safed, the quintessential center of Kabbalah.

This great cultural wave also included Italy. As we have seen, the *Universitates iudaeorum* of the Italian cities had more or less unwillingly accepted the Spanish refugees and their culture. Indeed, according to studies by cultural historians Kabbalah was already widespread in Italy by the end of the 15th century, although only among the most cultured strata and the Italian rabbinate who were more inclined towards mysticism. Not by chance, Giovanni Pico della Mirandola and the other Christian Hebraists, fascinated by the interpretive methods and the open possibilities of Kabbalah, all had Italian Jewish instructors.[31] The arrival of the Spanish exiles, with their books and their traditions, merely reinforced a trend that was already underway. The real novelty is that this brought it outside the very restricted intellectual circles. Within a century, Kabbalistic readings and practices had penetrated so deeply into the cultural space of the Italian Jews that it led to significant changes in the liturgy, culture, and common practices, spreading in many settings. Kabbalah, however, is a very complex and varied form of knowledge, meant for interpretation as much as for intervention in creation. According to scholars such as Gershom Scholem, Moshe Idel, and Roberto Bonfil, it established itself in Italy between the 16th and 17th centuries, supplanting the now insufficient Scholasticism.[32] The establishment of Kabbalah took place, therefore, during the crucial years of the institution of the ghettos, namely in the very critical years in which, following the Roman model ordered and established by Paul IV in 1555, Italian cities embarked on a new form of exclusion-inclusion of their Jews, who were relegated to a quarter/prison, closed at night, and open only during the day.

It is in this climate that Kabbalah established itself in the ghettos, where the perception of the Jews as an integral part of the local social fabric began to fade, and where, although they had not been expelled as had happened on the Iberian Peninsula, Jews participated in daily municipal life as guests, more or less welcome, but always guests, foreign, different, and certainly not citizens. These are also the years, however, in which the anti-dissent, standardizing, and normalizing turn imposed by the Council of Trent and the Counter-Reformation led Christian Kabbalah, the science so loved by the humanists and Platonists of the Renaissance, to lose its status as high philosophy. It progressively became a trifling magical practice appropriate for sorcerers and witches, and therefore for the ecclesiastical hierarchy a "superstition" to be fought at all costs. As a result, it ceased to be an opportunity for encounters between Jewish and Christian scholars, and returned to being a tradition that was exclusively and typically Jewish, and precisely because of this became even more suspect.

However, the ire and the intervention of the Holy Office were feared even among the Jews within the enclosure of the ghettos. The last Jewish astrologer to serve a pope, the rabbi and doctor Bonetto de Lattes, wrote his predictions between the end of the 15th century and the first years of the

16th century, but was very careful to scientifically legitimize the practice of astrology with respect to Jewish and rabbinic culture as well as Christian culture.[33] The subsequent birth of the Holy Congregation of the Inquisition and its surveillance led to even greater caution. In fact, although the Jews could not be heretics, inasmuch as they were not baptized, the Holy Office had jurisdiction still over them, as they did over other "infidels", in cases where they attacked the Catholic faith and abused the sacraments and "sacred objects", and especially regarding doctrinal matters in common with Christians, thus falling into heresy. Certainly, the evocations of demons as well as divinatory and magical ceremonies were fully included among the expected cases. In this way, a long series of Kabbalistic rituals meant to unite creation and man with the supernal spheres became absolutely synonymous with magical-diabolical rites. Additionally, the Italian Jews themselves, long divided between a rationalist tradition and adherence to the Kabbalistic doctrines, tended to keep their distance from the more esoteric side of Kabbalah, at least officially, to avoid the suspicions and accusations of the ecclesiastical authorities. It was no accident that in the 17th century, scholarly rabbis like Leon Modena refuted its more extreme derivations, even if often only in writings destined for the public.

The Lurianic Kabbalah, which was the most "magical" and connected, for example, to the Prague myth of the *golem*,[34] was also present in Italy, as demonstrated by the high number of active Italian Kabbalists in various cities who were often intercepted by the Inquisition, such as in Livorno, Venice, Mantua – one of the most important Italian centers of Jewish mysticism – and Reggio. This is what happened, in the midst of the 18th century, to the noted Kabbalist rabbi of Mantua, Salomone Basilea, who was interrogated for heresy in the years 1733–38, and even tortured. His crime was possession of amulets, writings suspected of superstition, prohibited books, among which was the *Talmud*, and for having practiced sorcery and the evoking of demons.[35] Sensational trials like this, which were not infrequent, contradicted the rationalist Leon Modena, to whom we will return later, who claimed in public, but not in private, that rabbis were against or distanced from the world of magic and superstition. This idea is repeated defensively in much of the historiography that followed. Mystical phenomena such as revelations and the appearance of angels, for example, were also widespread among educated Jews between the 16th and 18th centuries, and showed affinities and similarities to contemporary Christian mysticism.[36]

Similarly, magic and sorcery were also widespread and common in both worlds. During the modern age, the entire population, whether Jewish or Christian, often recited formulae in Hebrew or in a Latin mixed with an incomprehensible pseudo-Hebrew; they practiced magic, divination, and exorcism, independently of their membership in a specific social class. One only needs to read the edicts of the Holy Office in the cases opened against Jews for magic and witchcraft, which are very numerous in the archives, to notice how in these centuries, as the witch hunt ended, the connection between Judaism and witchcraft advanced.

Judaism and Magic

The image of the Jewish sorcerer and the legend of Jewish witchcraft were very widespread, and referred back to Christian perceptions of the "strange" rituals and customs of the Jews. Jews were considered to be magicians and necromancers par excellence and, not too paradoxically, precisely because of this reputation Christians turned to them when they needed experts and intermediaries in magic. Christians also used Jewish doctors, who often were also rabbis, because of their reputation as being highly skilled, and to do so were willing to violate the Church's prohibitions on making use of their services constantly reiterated by the popes, and to ignore the rumors and fears of being poisoned by them.[37]

So what type of magic was involved? It was mainly the type of magic that was predominant, the kind useful for resolving the troubles and small problems of daily life. It was a practice of ordinary magic and "superstition", of spells and rituals or prayer formulae aimed at the retrieval of objects or supposed treasures, the making of love potions and amulets, the practice of folk medicine, or the divination of future events. However, there were also formulae and ceremonies meant to protect from the temptation of conversion, or that derived from the diffusion of certain beliefs, all of Kabbalistic origin, in dreams, demons, angels, and the transmigration of souls. Thus, these were practices and doctrines that were highly suspect to the Christian authorities, and which referred to a universe of objects, books, and Kabbalistic prayer formulae that were not at all foreign to the Italian Jews.

Since the 16th century, there have been reports of cases of Jewish sorcerers who counted many Christians and even clerics among their visitors and clients. Christians and Jews performed sorcery and magic spells together, fully sharing the same culture, and demonstrating another context in which the reality of exclusion and repression did not prevent exchanges, relationships, and networks of contacts from developing. The old tradition of the Jews' specialization and superiority in the field of magic persisted and was actively fed by the peculiarity and mysterious exoticism of the Hebrew language. It was the language in which Scripture had been written, and according to some exegetes, the only one that the angels understood. It was an incomprehensible idiom, believed to be very effective for magical formulae precisely because of its characteristics of obscurity and secrecy, and the fact that it was often mangled in pronunciation, making its meaning all the more unclear. The grammar of the occult sciences was written in Hebrew characters, whether real or imaginary.[38]

Among the books confiscated from the Jews, and within the minutes of interrogations conducted in inquisitorial trials, we find angels and demons, amulets, protective papers full of strange signs and incomprehensible characters, dreams, invocations of devils, and well-known booklets such as the *Clavicula Salomonis*.[39] The presence of these elements evokes a universe of magic, and not only folk magic, characterized by a cultural mingling with the Jewish world which appeared very dangerous and suspicious to the ecclesiastic authorities. Perhaps, this mixture should not be overlooked when interpreting the phenomenon of magic in general, without reducing it to an innocuous popular remnant. In fact, we can ask ourselves if the persistent attention of the Roman Inquisition towards the magic-ritual dimension should be ascribed to the perception of Jewish magic as diabolical, and the fear of a dangerous alliance. The widespread and continual representation over time of the Jew as sorcerer constitutes a new node and point of view for interpreting the phenomenon of magic and witchcraft as a whole, including that of non-Jews. The history of the Jews is therefore essential for the understanding of general history, even in the area of witchcraft.

The long survival of demonological beliefs, well beyond the 16th century and at least into the heart of the age of Enlightenment, by which time the activity of witchcraft repression – the witch hunt – had waned (starting to relax, in fact, as early as the end of the 16th century), and the careful control that the Roman Inquisition maintained over these beliefs, among both Jews and Christians, pose some historiographical and methodological questions that should be pointed out. On one hand, the chronological relationship of how the end of the obsession with witchcraft coincides with the revival of a more virulent anti-Judaism emerges, making it possible to think that the shift from repression of witchcraft to that of sorcery and divination represented a crucial passage for the persecution of the Jews, as they became the sole target of the fears and anxieties of society; on the other hand, the wide circulation of the Jews' culture of magic and esoterica in the Christian world concerned the religious authorities, and increasingly pushed them towards the demonization of Jewish diversity, reinforcing the vicious circle of Jew-sorcerer-devil. Magical practices and Jewish magic in particular were not considered marginal, trivial phenomena in the modern age. The courts did not underestimate the episodes and cases upon which it had to rule, as demonstrated by the trials prosecuted. Even the judges, all good Catholics, not only obviously believed in the existence of the devil, as the practice of exorcism demonstrated, but they also thought that the Jews were more capable of evoking him, and of teaching others how to do so.

The attention that the inquisitorial courts gave to Jewish magical practices and rituals carried out in complicity with Christians must therefore be related to the contemporary, harsh writings about the superstitions and diabolical rites practiced by the Jews, and with the mounting of anti-Jewish legislation, in particular that which tried to prevent all relations with Christians. Ultimately, based on the representation of the Jewish universe as witchcraft, we can ask ourselves if the condemnation and repression of magical phenomena, divination, and sorcery ordered in papal bulls – such as those of Sixtus V in 1586 and Urban VIII in 1631 – also had something to do with the suspicion of judaizing or pernicious Jewish influence on Christians, considering that Hebrew names, practices, amulets, and terminology occupied an important place both in trials conducted against Christians and in their books of magic. Furthermore, we can ask how and to what extent the insistence of the anti-Jewish polemicists on the Jews' greater experience and skill in magic was used in the service of demonizing religious diversity and generalizing it as heresy. Ultimately, it was used for the ends of a growing anti-Judaism in the modern age.[40]

In any case, the nexus of sorcery-Judaism, common, and natural for Christians, led to two opposing results. On one hand, Christians themselves made use of Jewish magic, which they believed to be very effective; on the other hand, however, theologians and polemicists used this belief to accuse the Jews of "superstition", and above all to demonize them.

This demonization of Jewish traditions, customs, and rites went on for all of the 18th century and even beyond, and showed how the condemnation of Jews for their rituals anticipated a new cultural climate dominated by representations meant to foment hostility, from evoking accusations of ritual murder and anti-Catholic conspiracies to the focus on the "physical" and "moral" characteristics of the Jew, who was anthropologically and biologically different. This climate foreshadowed the great revival of early biological and racial stereotypes and their religious, secular, and iconographic representations in the 19th and 20th centuries. In sum, as we will see later, the century of the Enlightenment represented an important turning point in relations between Jews and Christians, and in the representations of the former by the latter; a turning point that was in no way positive or reassuring, which incorporated the stereotype of the evil sorcerer within a more generic accusation of "superstition". As a result, through this belief relating to the demonic imprint of the Jewish universe, which was still dominant in the midst of the 18th century, Jewish rituality was perceived as a dangerous threat aimed directly at hurting the world of Christians.

The World of Culture

There is a common and widespread notion that once Jews were closed in the ghettos they lost the ability to interact with Christians, along with the will to produce independent intellectual works, sometimes detached from the dominant traditional Jewish culture, and even capable of having influence outside the Jewish circle: however, this idea does not correspond with reality. Contrary to what has long been believed, despite the limitations and constrictions placed on the community by the process of ghettoization, Jewish thought and culture were not too negatively affected by the consequences of the new situation, and managed to interact independently with the Christian culture. Thus, there was a "ghetto culture" which should be understood not only as a self-representation of the new Jewish identity produced by the enclosure but should also be considered from the outside point of view of non-Jews, inasmuch as it had a significant effect on the relations and exchanges between the two groups.

According to some interpreters, Kabbalah was the dominant culture among the Italian Jews for all of the 17th century, with beliefs and practices that involved both the elite and the popular strata.[41] The medieval form of Jewish mysticism expressed in Kabbalistic knowledge continued to be transmitted as a mode of esoteric wisdom in the 1500s. In the early modern age, a confluence of factors, among which were the mass emigrations of Jews from the Iberian Peninsula, the printing of Kabbalistic books, and the interest of major Renaissance intellectuals, contributed to the diffusion and also a redefinition of Kabbalah, understood as an esoteric aspect of Jewish thought and behaviors. There also were internal voices raised that were critical of Kabbalah as being contrary to reason and the nature of tradition, such as the harsher voice of Leon Modena (1571–1648), or the more moderate voice of the *rabbino* of Ancona, Sansone (Simson) Morpurgo (1681–1740). There was no lack of intellectual tension and strong debate on the subject within the Jewish world, which indicates a discussion that went beyond Kabbalah for a broader examination of the nature of Judaism and its religious tradition. So, while the confinement and separation of the ghetto did not affect the traditional areas of study, *Halakhah* (the Law) and Kabbalah, other fields of knowledge were also able to flourish in confinement.

Although they were physically separated from Christians when it came to living spaces, we have already seen how the Jews did not exist in a condition of cultural isolation with respect to their neighbors. Exchanges, encounters, relationships, and conversations were frequent and possible in many situations, and especially in workplaces. Recent studies about Italian Judaism, which tend to focus on the interpretive perspective of social and cultural intermixture, have disproven the idea that the two worlds were completely separate with no communication between them. This also holds true regarding the intellectual dimension and the social exchange of ideas; what has emerged is that there was a high degree of Jewish interaction with the gentile culture, which did not, however, compromise the Jews' ability to maintain their independence and defend their own identity.[42] This perspective allows us to shed light on the history of Jewish thought between the early Baroque Age and the end of the 18th century and its intertwining with Christian thought, such that it is possible to speak of Jewish-Italian intellectual production over the span of almost two centuries, and not only in the sense of the use of the Italian language, but of a genuine process of acculturation. For example, studies have increasingly highlighted the presence in Italy of a strong Jewish rationalist current between the 17th and 18th centuries. As a result, today we are witnessing a parallel historiographic and interpretive process which considers as inadequate and to be overcome, within a symmetrical reconsideration of both worlds, both the image of Italian culture in the age of the Counter-Reformation and the image of Jewish culture in the age of the ghettos, which have each long been represented in clearly negative terms.

Jews cultivated theater, music, literature, and science in Hebrew, Ladino, and Italian, demonstrating the high level of acculturation and the extensive cultural exchange between Jews and Christians, at least among the elites. Leon Modena, the famous rabbi and intellectual of the 17th century, says in his autobiography that many Christians of high rank attended the synagogues to hear the rabbis' sermons, including his own.[43] Modena also wrote poetry and panegyrics in Italian for his friends and Christian protectors. His most famous work, the *Historia de' Riti Hebraici*, published in Italian at Paris in 1637, and at Venice in 1638, was dedicated to the French ambassador to Venice and edited by the scholar Jacques Gaffarell, librarian to Richelieu: the Italian edition of 1638 was dedicated to him and again to the French Ambassador. Between the 16th and 17th centuries, the figures of several Jewish intellectuals, men and women, though a small group, were therefore indicators of a change in mentality that was underway in Jewish society, marked by the desire for dialog with the outside and with the dominant culture, and by a growing distinction between sacred and profane.[44] These trends were emphasized in the realm of language with the Jews' adoption of Italian, leaving Hebrew confined to only the domain of religion. Above all, the accentuation of the rationalist and modern character of one's ideas meant maintaining a certain distance, sometimes in contradictory and ambiguous ways, from mystical and Kabbalistic religiosity, which survived in Italy at least until the 19th century, and to engage with European culture.[45] However, Kabbalah's resilience also raises the problem of its relationship with modernity.[46]

In fact, again in the 1700s, personalities who were much different from each other, such as the Roman rabbi and doctor Tranquillo Vita Corcos (1660–1730) and Mosè Vita Luzzatto (Ramhal) (1707–47), confirm the coexistence of different inspirations, in which a rationalist dimension could live with a view linked to the Kabbalah and the philosophical mysticism of the Kabbalists. But we will see this better further ahead.

Leon Modena/Jehudah, a Double Personality

Venice was certainly the center of this renewed Jewish cultural presence, as well as the effort to open the educated society of the ghetto to external influences and dialog with Christian culture. From this perspective, the role of Rabbi Leon Modena (Jehudah Arieh mi-Modena, 1571–1648) was important. Celebrated preacher, an extraordinary scholar of Jewish and non-Jewish culture, Modena authored numerous works in Hebrew, Latin, and Italian, as well as translations and books of poetry.[47] He also, among other things, composed poetry in Hebrew and Italian, and wrote polysemantic verses in which each word had a meaning in both languages. Known and appreciated in Italy and abroad, where he enjoyed various and prestigious relations within the Christian world, Modena taught Giulio Morosini, the famous Venetian convert who then became a vigorous anti-Jewish polemicist, and was a friend of Samuel Luzzatto and Sara Copio Sullam, the woman of great culture and celebrated poet in the world of Jewish Venice, on whom we shall focus later.

Modena's publishing output, vast and multifaceted, displays a fruitful exchange between the Jewish culture to which he belonged and the classical-humanistic legacy of which he felt a part. His fame is mainly connected to the *Historia de' Riti Hebraici*,[48] which was written in Italian, in which he described the ceremonies and customs of the Jews. In the *Proemio* to the Italian edition, he stated that various Christian scholars, among whom were some prelates, wanted to "have knowledge" of the rituals of the Jews, and had asked him to write on the subject. He asserted that in doing so, he had tried to be a "simple, and neutral reporter", and to forget about being Jewish in order to avoid the impression he was writing apologetics. He said that he aimed only "to report and not to persuade", and certainly not to "defend them [the Jewish ceremonies] and support them".[49] Beyond these rhetorical statements, clearly meant to obtain the approval of the gentiles and to protect himself from any ecclesiastic attack or accusation of attempted proselytism, his stated goal was to push back against widespread distortions and denigrations of Jewish religious practices, explaining and interpreting them in a moderate, anti-superstitious, and rationalist key, thus meeting the expectations of the many Christian scholars with whom he was in contact.

Modena had been asked to write the brief treatise some years earlier, in 1614–15, by the English ambassador to Venice, Henry Wotton, who wanted to offer King James I a report on the rituals and customs of the Jews. As such, the *Riti* had already circulated widely among English scholars in manuscript form before its publication. We are therefore not far from the time when the William Shakespeare staged his demonizing representation of the Venetian Jews through the figure of Shylock in *The Merchant of Venice*, a drama published in 1600, but composed prior to 1598. As Natalie Zemon David has rightly noted,[50] if the English playwright, who died in 1616, had been able to read Modena's text, which was circulating among scholars in his country, he may have revised the figure of the Jew he had sketched. Thus, Leon, who dedicated his *Dizionario hebraico-italiano* to the Patriarch of Aquileia, Ermolao Barbaro, who in turn accepted it "with affection",[51] played an integral part in the literary Republic, and became part of a European network of scholars, within which there was a lively interest in Jewish culture and the Hebrew language itself, for which Leon, with his translations from Hebrew to Italian and his *Dizionario*, represented an important mediator and informant.

In his brief, *Historia de' Riti Hebraici* Leon Modena fought and denied Jewish Kabbalistic tendencies, opposing a conception of the universe that was widespread among his coreligionists. This conception was founded on the belief in a "middle world" which is neither wholly material nor completely spiritual, and is populated by thousands of demons and angels who function as intermediaries for magical powers.[52] In reality, not even the scholarly circles of his time were exempt from demonological beliefs and practices. Nevertheless, in the brief chapter entitled *De Auguri, Divinazioni, e Magie*, Modena instead insisted on a rational, anti-superstitious, and anti-magical representation of his people's culture. He emphasized that for the Jews "putting faith in all and any sort of *Auguri* (Fortunetellers), *Giudiziaria* (Astrological predictions), all Witchcraft, Geomancy, Chiromancy, and all similar forms of divination, are a serious sin".[53] Added to this list were necromancy, magic, and making "*Prestigij* (Spells), incantations to Demons or to Angels, seeking responses from the Dead, and all such activities".

The insistence with which the rabbis condemned all superstitions and magical beliefs may indicate their fears that the Jewish religion could be seen and accused by gentiles in ways that were not only denigrating, but also susceptible to inquisitorial interventions, which were common enough. Neither should we overlook the fact that Leon Modena's little book on Jewish rituals was published about the same time that Urban VIII promulgated the bull *Inscrutabilis* (March 31, 1631), prohibiting any type of magical or divinatory arts as diabolical works, under penalty of very severe punishments.[54] Leon wanted, above all, to oppose the beliefs of many Jewish Kabbalists and at the same time to reassure Christians, not without dissimulation and ambiguity, as we will see. The following year in Venice, in 1639, Modena composed a treatise of criticism of Kabbalah entitled *Ari Nohem* ("The Lion Roars"), in a word play on his own name, which remained unpublished until 1840. With this text, he argued in favor of a return to the rationalism of Maimonides, beginning a debate among the Jews between Kabbalists and their critics that would endure for a long time, even into the following centuries.[55] The treatise remained in manuscript form for a long time, but it circulated widely: as was the case with many of Modena's works, especially those that were controversial, it was not published. The reasons for not passing from manuscript to print were numerous: fear of censorship, threats of persecution, a desire for closer proximity to the reader. Modena knew that he could not completely control the press as a means of communication; he certainly intended to get his ideas in circulation, but not too loudly. In the end, the treatise offers a notable Hebrew example of the marriage between textual criticism and religious dissent that characterized a large part of European intellectual life in that period. In those decades, scholars submitted almost all certainties – religious, theological and scientific – to the light of criticism, but often incurring censorship and self-censorship.

For Leon, as well as for other Jewish intellectuals who were open to the outside world, cultural and social integration did not help avoid trouble in the community stemming from cultural proposals not aligned with the prevailing directions in the ghetto, or harassment from the Inquisition. To address the criticisms of their coreligionists, these intellectuals were pushed to conceal rationalist or even skeptical positions, as in the case of Simone

Luzzatto. Regarding his attitude towards the court of the Holy Office, in his autobiography, which he signed with the Hebrew name, Jehudah, Leon recounts his fear of falling into the clutches of the Venetian Inquisition because of the manuscript on Jewish rituals, and that this is why he did not want to publish it in Italy in the first place. He anticipated the charges and so made a spontaneous confession before the Inquisition, leaving, he says, totally absolved,[56] but not without having to excise some parts of his work. The censors' criticisms were directed at the doctrine of metempsychosis and the denial of divine incarnation.

On the other hand, if his public figure presented Leon Modena as a modern and rational scholar, completely in line with the contemporary gentile culture, it was also true that a much different image of Leon/Jehudah emerged in his autobiography. Destined to remain a private document, in this autobiography, we find a man involved with magical beliefs and practices, and experimenting with alchemy. In fact, in the private life revealed by his secret autobiography, Leon/Jehudah completely abandoned the rhetorical self-representation meant solely for the Christian public. Here, he described himself as dedicated to the interpretation of dreams, requesting horoscopes from Jewish and Christian astrologers, teaching others how to make spells and amulets, writing and selling books on witchcraft, to Christians as well, with which he earned a living, rounding off his income, which was constantly eaten away by his gambling habit.[57] He tells of going to four astrologers, two Jews and two Christians, to have his own horoscope read, and how he believed in the messages of dreams, which he carefully wrote down. The rational and Cartesian image of the rituals of the Jews that Leon intended to convey in his Italian treatise ends up completely overturned by his Hebrew autobiography, which was destined to remain secret and private. The latter revealed a troubled man, haunted by the demon of gambling, which was also prohibited by the rabbis, and the resulting sense of guilt. Dreams, spells, magical and alchemical beliefs and practices, astrology, heavenly signs, horoscopes, and prophecies occupied positions of great importance for him, and even an economic role, revealing an obsession and an anxiety for reassurance that accompanied his tragic sense of life.

Leon, author of a serious and rigorous treatise on Jewish rituals aimed at a Christian public, appears to us as very different than the Jehudah who wrote his autobiography, which remained closed off in the private family sphere, inaccessible to gentiles; here, he could write with the total freedom to reveal himself and his thoughts.[58] His two names, the Christianized Leon and the Hebrew Jehudah, are the most effective representations of his ambiguous identity and the difficult process of interaction between the two cultures. However, as we will see, while these apparent contradictions were common in the culture of the time, there are other figures that lived in subsequent eras who also presented this coexistence of different inspirations.

Simone Luzzatto, a Rationalist Skeptic

In the same years that Leon Modena was working there was another important Jewish intellectual active in Venice. Venetian rabbi Simone (Simcha)
Luzzatto (1580?–1663) certainly represents a figure of great importance on
not just the Jewish but also the European cultural scene. We have seen that
there were similar characters who were his contemporaries, such as Leon
Modena, with whom Luzzatto also had relations. In the lives and work of
both men, and especially that of Luzzatto, himself a rational spirit par excellence, it is possible to detect the intense dialog with the gentile culture,
the use of Italian and the full integration in the social and cultural life of
the host city. These elements clearly reveal the wholly unique situation of
Venice as a cultural hub for exchanging ideas and acquaintances.

Luzzatto, with his baroque Italian – full of comparisons, similes and rhetorical figures which are not found in Leon Modena – certainly stands out for
the stature of his political and philosophical thought and for his boundless
scholarship in the area of Judaism, as well as in the classics and Christianity.
He was author of the important *Discorso circa lo Stato degli Hebrei et in particolar dimoranti nell'inclita città di Venezia* – published in Venice in 1638, in
the same year and by the same publisher as the Italian edition of the *Historia
de' Riti Hebraici* by Modena – and of a philosophical work written in Italian, *Socrate overo dell'Humano sapere*, also printed in Venice in 1641, which
included skeptical positions, albeit masked. The *Discorso* initiated a literary
current of reflection on the relations of the ghetto with the rest of the local
population, which would culminate in the late 18th-century considerations
of Giovanni Battista Gherardo D'Arco (*Sull'influenza del ghetto nello Stato*,
1778), and finally with *Interdizioni israelitiche* by Carlo Cattaneo (1835). This
was an essential current of self-representation of the ghetto's Jewish identity
– and of external representations of it – which offers the possibility of observ-
ing the evolution of the majority society itself and the renewed interaction of
the Jews with the outside world, even in the era of ghettoization. That was
certainly not without risks, as demonstrated by the attention the Inquisition
turned on both Leon Modena and Luzzatto, and the serious accusations directed at Sara Copio Sullam. Moreover, with regard to the methodological
aspect, the *Discorso* fits completely with findings in recent studies on Italian
Judaism which, as we have said, tend to focus on the interpretive perspective of the social and cultural relations and intertwining between the two
worlds. In fact, in his works, Luzzatto already focused, and not just oppor-
tunistically, on more than just the limitations and repressive rules imposed
on the Jews, but also on the networks of exchanges, on tolerance, integration,
on friendship with the common people and on the charity of the Venetian
government. He himself, after all, was living proof of this by his use of the
instrument of communication par excellence, that is, the Italian language.

The *Discorso* is constructed in two parts.[59] The first addresses the economy and the function of the Jews in Venice; the second refutes traditional

accusations directed at Jews since the classical era, in particular emphasizing the "lies" and falsifications of Tacitus. This second part culminates in two important final considerations, the first on the subject of tolerance towards the Jews, and the second relating to the cause of their diaspora, throughout which, however, they had always preserved their faith and culture. Both parts respond to a clear apologetic and political objective: praise of the Venetian Republic for its tolerance and protection towards the Jews. Venice occupied a determining role in Jewish political thought in the modern age, which has yet to be fully investigated, as demonstrated well before Luzzatto's writings by the work of doctor David de Pomis, who moved to Venice in the mid-1500s from papal Umbria. De Pomis was author of a *Discorso*, composed in the 1570s, in which he referred to similar theses by the famous Isaac Abravanel (1437–1508), another refugee from Spain who had come to Venice, comparing the institutions of the ancient Jewish State with those of the Republic, demonstrating their accordance and therefore their divine legitimacy.[60] The Venetian State fully responded to the model of republican State desired by God. And at this point, we could ask to what extent this Jewish-Venetian treatise contributed to building the "myth of Venice", which flourished between the 15th and 16th centuries in the Christian world and was passed down by historiography even after the fall of the Republic, up to present day.

Returning to Luzzatto, his work is focused on the idea of the full integration of the community in the context of the city and the Republic, on the economic as well as cultural level. The Jews were part of the "common" people of Venice, although they represented only a small part of them. To illustrate this, Luzzatto made a comparison with Democritean atoms, thus evoking modern corpuscular and atomist physics. These were theories that were severely prosecuted by the Church in those same years, as we are reminded by the case of Galileo Galilei, and which were particularly widespread at the University of Padua, a hotbed of suspect philosophical ideas. We still do not know why Luzzatto included such a risky comparison in his work. In any case, it is very indicative of how at the time corpuscular philosophy and the controversy with Aristotelian physics constituted a "transversal" doctrine, which united innovators of all religious denominations in a shared anti-Aristotelianism that crossed confessional boundaries. One might then think that the Jewish world, in its diverse cultural aspects, was also involved in this new vision of physics, and that perhaps its scriptural and religious tradition made it particularly receptive to it. We might further ask ourselves if this element of Jewish involvement could also have represented an additional factor in the ecclesiastical condemnation of these doctrines.

It should be emphasized how modern some of Luzzatto's arguments are. For example, his insistence on the usefulness of the Jews to society and the State, to which they contributed taxes and payments deriving from their commercial activities, tracing an entirely secular history of trade as the foundation of peace between peoples, and above all of the history of the Jews themselves. Or, when he states that the Jews "are in the State", of which they are an integral part, here citing the very modern idea of citizenship. And, beyond the apologetic praise, the statement that "the major attraction for business [of commercial traffic] is the freedom to live, and the safety for the possession of one's assets" is certainly modern, and was exactly what happened in Venice.[61]

But the essential point is his method of historical analysis. Here, a uniquely secular, political, and historical dimension emerges in the explanation of past events, in particular of the expulsion of the Jews from Spain in 1492, in which theological, providential, messianic, and thus religious considerations play no part at all, unlike what was typical in previous Jewish histories. In a famous book by Yosef Hayim Yerushalmi on the relationship of history and memory in the Jewish world, the author emphasizes the problematic nature of Jews' relationship with their past, and recalls how historiography as a record of historical events was in no way "the principal means through which the collective memory of the Jewish people was stimulated to awaken".[62] For all of the Middle Ages, and up to the 16th century, there were other preferred channels of Jewish memory, different from the writings of history: rituals and liturgy, holidays that celebrated long ago events to commemorate and transmit to new generations, but also chronicles with accounts of persecution, perhaps to be read in synagogue.

Significantly, it was precisely the trauma of the expulsion between the end of the 15th century and the 16th century that determined a "need" for history and a profound change in the models of transmission of past memory, with a vast flourishing of studies. Different chronicles appeared – a dozen – dedicated to the events that had marked the history of the Jewish people, from the two destructions of the Temple until the epochal catastrophes of 1492 and 1496–97 in Spain and Portugal. These included the chronicle by Joseph Ha-Cohen (who was mentioned in Chapter 4), and that of Abraham Zacuto, both from the 16th century.[63] As a result the 16th century has been considered a genuine "golden age of Jewish historiography", which Yerushalmi has compared to the Italian Renaissance, arguing that the flourishing of studies following the crisis at the end of the 15th century is comparable to the link between the birth of the Italian historiography of Humanism and the collapse of republican structures in the City-States on the peninsula.[64] Thus, we see among the assumption of models that were foreign to the tradition and typical of the majority society, even though in the 18th century Jewish historiographical culture then seemed to return to tradition. Modern Jewish historiography arose only in the 19th century with the *Wissenschaft des Judenthums*, the German science of Judaism, and its scientific and critical method of approaching history. In Luzzatto's text, there is still an echo of the phase of transition towards a new way of doing history, with which even Jewish tradition – as would happen primarily starting from the 1700s – was turning to a modern, secular, worldly, and scientific conception of history. So, the explanation offered by Luzzatto for the Jewish specialization in moneylending, that it was a necessary fact owed to precise historical contingencies, along with the prohibition on working in most professions and owning real estate, is part of a purely secular analysis.[65]

On the other hand, one notes a certain embarrassment or disparagement on Luzzatto's part when he deals with Kabbalah, which he claims to be not be very widespread, found mainly in the Levant and in Poland, and about which he emphasized both the "extravagant" aspect of the combination of letters, numbers, and figures,[66] and the more theoretical part which, similar to Platonism, was focused on the soul and punishments after death. Here, the reference to the doctrine of the transmigration of the soul from one body to another, dangerous in the Christian context, is fleeting and perfunctory. This embarrassment also seems to be found in the long and severe refutation of the accusation of superstition directed at the Jews from Tacitus on, in which he is eager to disprove charges of magic and necromancy. These he rejects as "abuses and excrement of true religion", which were, according to him, widespread common beliefs, even among the ancients. It is not difficult to think, in addition to a controversy with Jews who were adherents of Kabbalah, of an implicit response to accusations current among Christians, for whom, as we have seen, the connection between Judaism and magic was still deeply rooted and taken for granted.[67]

Ultimately, what should be noted is that the works of Leon Modena and Simone Luzzatto offer a rational, historical, and political explanation of the practices and customs of the Jews, clearing them of any suspicion of irrationality, and most of all of superstition. Leon declared in his *Proemio* to the *Historia de' Riti Hebraici* that he had tried to remain objective and neutral in order to avoid producing a work of apologetics. He wanted only "to refer and not persuade", with the goal of pushing back on denigrations of the Jewish religion by explaining its rites in a moderate and rationalist key. Beyond the goals of self-defense and the representation of a Jewish world that was closer to the Christian world than what was generally thought, and thus beyond the purposes of legitimizing that world and those rituals, what emerges from the works of these authors – and of subsequent authors, who we will examine – is a real need for openness to the external culture and acceptance of its intellectual demands, with the possibility of establishing exchanges and encounters. A century later, in 1736, the converted Jew Paolo Sebastiano Medici would publish a refutation of Leon Modena's book with the significant title of *Riti, e costumi degli ebrei confutati*, in which, with extremely violent and denigrating tones, he openly accused Leon of having misrepresented and watered down the superstitious practices of the Jews. A century had passed, and now the question of rituals and their negative, heretical implications was becoming increasingly pressing and controversial. This is really where another story begins, that of the turbulent relations between Jews and Christians in the 18th century, with a doctrinal hardening that led to the radicalization of the inter-religious conflict in the 19th century.

Debora Ascarelli, the "Clever Bee"

While the works of Luzzatto and Modena constituted an extraordinary contribution to the history of Italian Judaism between the Baroque era and the late Enlightenment, as well as more generally to the intellectual history of Europe and Italian social and cultural history, there were also important female figures who should not be overlooked. Did a cultural role exist for women, and if so what was it, both within the quintessential minority religion and also in the Christian context? More educated than average Christian women, Jewish women received an education, albeit not necessarily equal to that of the men, considering that literacy was required for them to read texts and prayer formularies as well as the liturgy.

Two Jewish women who lived and worked between the 16th and 17th centuries, a Roman and again a Venetian, distinguished themselves for their poetic and literary abilities, which they expressed in Italian: Debora Ascarelli and Sara Copio Sullam. Debora, who lived between the second half of the 16th century and the beginning of the 17th, was a Jewish "aristocrat", well educated, and wife of a leading member of the Spanish community that had recently arrived in Rome, a city that had recently resolved, at least formally, the controversies that had opposed the "native" Jews against *ultramontani* Jews over the administration of the *Universitas hebraeorum*. While we know little or nothing about her life, we do know the texts she left behind.[68] These are almost exclusively translations, and a few original verses.

A woman who was a minority within a minority, inasmuch as she was part of the group of Spanish Jews that took refuge in Rome after the expulsion from Spain, the poetess and translator fits completely within the climate and more general literary options of 16th-century Italy, demonstrating the full adherence of at least a part of Jewish culture to the general context. Her fame is connected mostly to her activity as a translator. And, considering the moment in time, this does not appear to be by chance. After the discussions for the first half of the century on the issue of the Italian language, the second half of the Italian 16th century is an age of great translators, as demonstrated by famous cases like the translation of the *Aeneid* by Annibal Caro, or the Italian version of the complete works of Tacitus by Bernardo Davanzati. The world of Italian Jewish culture did not escape this climate: towards the end of the 16th century, the Jews began a bilingual path in their literary production, which would include texts with alternating lines in Hebrew and Italian, translations into Italian written with Hebrew characters, and even linguistic games between Italian and Hebrew, such as those created by Leon Modena with his polysemantic virtuosity.

The introduction of printing is the vehicle for greater knowledge of non-Jewish production, which was brought into Jewish libraries, especially those belonging to the ruling class of which Debora was a part.[69] Works written in a now ennobled Italian were especially directed at women, in the form of collections of precepts and prayer formulas. In this atmosphere of openness and exchanges, in which translation seems to represent the ideal tool for mediation, Debora translates and publishes, at Venice in 1601, a text by Mosè da Rieti, *Abitacolo degli oranti* (The Abode of the Supplicants), an imitation of Dante's poem written in Hebrew tercets, and composed in the 15th century. Translating these verses, Debora finds a way to clearly expose the themes of the Jewish world that were dear to her: the oneness of God, the reaffirmation of Jewish identity, the sense of guilt, and the plea for forgiveness.

Debora's translations from Hebrew to Italian did not only make these texts accessible specifically to other Jewish women. Produced a few decades after the institution of the Roman ghetto in 1555, they also took the form of a dual cultural mediator: between Jewish culture and Italian culture, but also between the different Jewish identities among the "national" groups of different origins and histories that, by love or by force, had to find unity and coexistence in the ghetto. In this way, beyond the theological subjects that Debora addressed with wisdom, what emerges from her activity as an original and independent poetess – which is linked to religious subjects and is in many ways comparable to the poetry of Vittoria Colonna – is a sort of political-cultural project aimed both at encouraging, through the use of the Italian language, Jewish self-perception as constituting a united and unified group, as well as promoting a climate of unity among Jews of different origins who had been forced into an unavoidable coexistence and solidarity in the restricted space of the ghetto.

It was now an inescapable fact that all the Jews of the city were forced to act in a way that was certainly more united than in the past in order to confront an external and hostile authority, common to all; more and more they were forced to *think of themselves* as a whole unit with only one destiny and inevitably shared interests. Debora, who was part of the Spanish group – which constituted the community's elite from the social, economic and cultural point of view – sensed this atmosphere and reacted with her intellectual tools, offering her own personal contribution to the need for mutual understanding and coexistence, in addition to culturally elaborating on the new and difficult situation. But, significantly, the instrument of this project is the exchange between the majority Christian culture and the culture of the Jewish minority, which remained active for all of the modern age; an exchange that once again highlights the permeability of the two worlds, capable of overcoming the wall of separation. And the preferred vehicle for this exchange is the common language, Italian: the Roman poetess thus seems to have precociously skipped the initial phase of bilingualism among the Italian Jews, characterized by the use of only spoken Italian. Debora, the "clever bee" as she was called by an admirer playing a word game with her name – Debora means "bee" in Hebrew[70] – should therefore be included as a protagonist of this interaction, just as she should be entered into the canon of Italian literature and the rich vein of 16th-century Italian women's poetry.

Sara Copio Sullam, "the Beautiful Jewess"

Sara Copio Sullam, the cultured and beautiful Venetian poetess, lived a life that was far more unconventional and vibrant than Debora's. Recalled by Giorgio Bassani in a passage of *Il giardino dei Finzi Contini*, she is described as "A great woman, in conclusion: the honor and pride of Italian Judaism at the height of the Counter-reformation".[71] Sara (circa 1592–1641) was a true protagonist in Venetian cultural life, and not only Jewish culture. Her father, Simone Copio, a well-educated, prominent member of the community, wanted Sara to receive instruction that was out of the ordinary, in both Hebrew and Italian. She learned Greek, Latin, studied the Old and New Testament, the works of Aristotle and of Giuseppe Flavio, philosophy, theology, music, and poetry. She began writing in Italian at a very young age and continued to do so for all her life. Even after her marriage to wealthy trader Jacob Sullam, she continued to hold a literary salon at her home in the Ghetto Vecchio, which became a meeting place where discussions included theology; guests included artists, writers, intellectuals, and clerics from both faiths. Sara was also a student and friend of Leon Modena, who dedicated *L'Ester Tragedia tratta dalla Sacra Scrittura*, published at Venice in 1619, to her; it was also he who dictated the epitaph on her tombstone, where he calls her "a woman of high intelligence".[72]

Sara was eager to establish herself in the literary world, and to open dialog and contacts with intellectuals outside the ghetto and the non-Jewish culture. In 1618, after having read *La Reina Esther*, a drama published at Geneva in 1615 by the then famed Genovese poet Ansaldo Cebà (1565–1623), a Tasso imitator who was twenty-seven years older than her, she took the initiative, fairly uncommon at the time, to write to him to express her admiration.[73] Thus began a correspondence that lasted four years, accompanied by exchanges of gifts, poems, and portraits; it was an affectionate, almost loving relationship, but strictly platonic, given that the two never met each other. Cebà's intent to convert Sara was clear and explicit: "I did not refuse to make love to her soul, to improve the condition of my own". The poet wrote to her, exhorting: "My love is so pure and true/that I ask and plead with you/to leave the ranks of Jews".[74]

The exchange of letters ended when it became clear to Cebà that Sara, proud of her own identity and faith, which she claimed with rational arguments that revealed great understanding, would refuse to convert. Cebà's letters were published after his death in 1623.[75] We do not have Sara's letters, but it is clear from these documents that, while Cebà emphasized the theme of the immortality of the soul to be reached through conversion, Sara responded by juxtaposing her desire for immortality gained through literary fame. Leon Modena also was involved in this struggle between the waters of Parnassus and those of baptism. His play *L'Ester*, dedicated to Sara, seems to reveal the rabbi's concern about the relationship with Cebà. The biblical story of Queen Ester was therefore used by the two – Cebà and Modena – to wage a type of battle within the soul of Sara/Ester. So, while the poem by Cebà presented the biblical heroine in a pre-Christian light and as a sort of saint, Modena's *L'Ester* built a prototype of a virtuous woman that was closer to the traditional Jewish model which, at the time, was spread in the Venetian community by Italian handbooks for women's instruction such as *Precetti da hesser imparati dalle donne ebree.*[76]

The battle around Sara's soul reached a crescendo with the public accusation of heresy directed at her by an attendee of her salon, the priest Bartolomeo Bonifacio, who was destined to become the Bishop of Capodistria, and who was also interested in securing her conversion. His booklet entitled *Dell'immortalità dell'anima* (1621) was meant to demonstrate that Sara did not believe in this dogma, the immortality of the soul, obligatory for Jews and Christians. She responded to this accusation, particularly dangerous in the context of the era, both within the community and especially outside it, with the *Manifesto di Sarra Copia Sullam Hebrea*, printed in Venice in 1621.[77] This was a cutting self-defense from which the accuser emerges discredited and demeaned, and with which the poetess demonstrated theological preparation, dialectic ability and a strong awareness of self and of her own intelligence, as well as her faith.[78]

Thus, Sara found herself the focus of all sorts of efforts by various Christian intellectuals to induce her to convert, men who were quite aware of how the baptism of a well-known Jewish woman would have meant personal affirmation and prestige for whoever secured it. Paradoxically, these efforts contributed to the spread of the writer's fame and therefore to the realization of her intellectual aspirations and ambitions, and to the self-construction of her own myth. There was no lack of conflict and sometimes violent criticism, accusations of plagiarism, and even plots against her, as well as disappointments with respect to the trust that she had nurtured to be able to engage in free intellectual relationships, regardless of faith. The inherent difficulties in the interaction of Jewish society with Christian society, even when it came to the intellectual elite and cultural mediators, emerge in this story. But while it all ended by conferring upon Sara the fame that she sought and her permanent inclusion, as a woman and a Jew, in the Parnassus of 17th-century Italy, her story, like that of Leon Modena, Simone Luzzatto, Debora Ascarelli, and other intellectuals we will meet ahead, reveals the search for a new definition of Jewish culture and the need for the recognition of an autonomous identity and actual value.

Souls, Demons, Reincarnations

The study of the self-representation of Jewish identity in the ghetto and its changes over time, which arose from contact with the Christian culture as well, outlines new dynamics of interrelationship with the outside between the 17th and 18th centuries, but with broad characteristics of autonomy.

The controversy about the immortality of the soul that broke out between Sara Copio Sullam and her Christian accuser must be placed in the context of the exchanges and discussions between Jews and Gentiles that involved both scholars and common people. Belief in the immortality of the soul, in fact, was identified as a matter of faith common to Christians and Jews who, based precisely on this shared doctrine, were considered heretics or apostates in the event they departed from it.[79]

As we have seen, in his *Discorso*, Simone Luzzatto resorted to a comparison with Democritean atoms, evoking the dangerous and suspect corpuscular and atomistic physics with a risky appeal. However, this is very indicative of the extent to which conceptions relative to the soul and its destiny occupied an important role in the exchanges between Jews and Christians, even those who were less educated. It was a very delicate subject, since it questioned the dogma of the immortality of the soul and its fate of punishments and rewards after death, the existence of the inferno and purgatory, and the final resurrection. In short, the risk was that of falling into a materialist vision that conceived of the soul as mortal, a vision that was undoubtedly, and generically, defined as "Epicurean" by the ecclesiastical authorities. The modern atomist theories posed more than a few problems around the scholastic conception of the soul upon which Catholic dogma was based. With the denial of the Aristotelian doctrine of eternal incorruptible celestial matter, abysses opened up here for faith. What actually became of the immortal soul?

These ideas were not limited to just the restricted educated circles. An example of this can be seen in a proceeding opened in 1658 by the inquisitor in Mantua against Simone Loria, a Jew from Padua, who had been reported by a coreligionist for having stated "during a discussion about eternity, that after the body dies and the soul dies, there is nothing more".[80] The accused stood up to the interrogation, first denying that he had spoken the incriminating phrase, but then adding that in any case, "it did not seem to him that he had committed any error that should be punished by this Holy Office, inasmuch as he was not required to believe in the immortality of the soul, as this article is not expressly found in the five books of Moses (the Pentateuch), which contain the law of God" and neither was it mentioned in the Holy Scriptures. Another witness to the conversation added that Loria had also said that "there was nothing after death, and that there was no need to do either good or bad". The accusation therefore took on a serious and heretical nature. This materialistic vision of the soul not only implied its mortality but also contemplated disregard for "works" – one's good or bad behavior – because there were no rewards or punishments after death. While the devaluation of works for individual salvation and the denial of purgatory could immediately evoke the ideas of the Reform and "heretics", another possible line of derivation for these ideas appeared highly suspicious. The hypothesis of some influence by Democritean, epicurean, or Lucretian atomism, all rejected and condemned by the Church, was in fact quite strong.

However, the rationalist or even skeptical tendencies within Jewish culture, such as those of Luzzatto, had not erased mystical and Kabbalistic beliefs. Even an educated woman like Sara Copio Sullam, after all, could be fooled by her Christian friends, who hatched a scheme to steal from her by taking advantage of her readiness to believe in the existence of spirits capable of intervening in daily life. And so we must ask ourselves if these apparent contradictions were common in the culture of the age, given that different inspirations also coexisted in other figures who we will discuss later – such as Tranquillo Vita Corcos in Rome and particularly Mosè Vita Luzzatto (Ramhal) in Padua – for whom a rationalist dimension was able to coexist with a vision linked to the philosophical mysticism of the Kabbalists.

The fact that the fascination of the Kabbalah still endured and would for a long time is demonstrated by the belief in demons, which was common to the faith of both Christians and Jews, and which moreover was connected to belief in the soul's fate, since it too referred to the existence of inferno and purgatory. The extent to which the modalities of Jewish beliefs in demons were of interest to Christians, as well as to the judges of the Holy Office, is confirmed by a proceeding brought against Rabbi Mosè Zamat at Ancona in 1607. From this trial, which was immediately transmitted to Rome, there emerges an interesting comparison between the respective beliefs of Jews and Christians and their mutual perceptions on the matter of angels and demons.[81] The Jew had been investigated and imprisoned for various statements, all suspected of heresy: he had argued that demons did not exist, and that for the Jews believing in their existence did not constitute an article of faith, that God did not permit evil and did not grant power to those who used it improperly, or to bad people or things, that Job had denied the intervention of divine providence on things in the lower world, and that the Holy Scripture could be interpreted "figuratively" and according to anyone's opinion. Finally, he had denied the resurrection of the dead. The inquisitor at Ancona turned to the Holy Office in Rome to ask the court if the existence of demons was or was not part of the common beliefs between Jews and Christians, because it was a requirement of faith for Christians to believe in the existence of demons. If this was also so for the Jews, the rabbi would be considered a heretic and be severely punished as such. In Rome, the cardinals ruled that all of the rabbi's statements were contrary to the Holy Scripture, and were heretical not only for Christians but also for Jews. They also required the addition of a clause to the sentencing decree expressly stating that the existence of demons constituted a matter of faith, belief in which was obligatory for both Christians and Jews. Inferno, resurrection, demons, and angels: they were all very delicate points, as they related directly to the belief in the immortality of the soul. Denying these points or misrepresenting them meant subscribing to a material idea of the soul, or rather denying its immortality.

However, the affair also troubled and interested the Inquisition from another point of view. If the rabbis themselves began to completely deny the existence of demons and to doubt a series of doctrines that were also established for the Jews – that the inferno existed, that God allowed evil and intervened in the things of this world – one could no longer fear just the superstitious and heretical results of their beliefs, but also another sort of dangerous consequence: that is, the dangerous infiltration among the Jews of a certain "modern" tendency, more rational and less linked to the mythological cosmology. And what consequences would this have had with regard to the beliefs of the Christian faithful? Thus, it was imperative that the Jews continued believing in demons, albeit in the "correct" way established by Christians.

The inquisitors were interested in Jewish beliefs about angels and demons because they knew of their *Talmudic* and Kabbalistic derivation, their "superstitious" charge and the uses made of them in magical arts, often in complicity with Christians; special amulets were made and sold to ward off demons, just as Leon Modena writes about doing. After all, the belief in the ability of King Solomon to evoke or repel demons, as described in the popular booklet *Clavicula Salomonis* and similar writings was common to both groups. Due to concerns for their safety, the Jews, in turn, often tried to downplay the importance of angelology and demonology without denying them, and to make them as close as possible to those of the Christians.

There was another Jewish belief of *Talmudic* and Kabbalistic origin that worried the inquisitors, and led them to intervene in the fear that it might take root among Christians: the doctrine of the transmigration of the soul, an idea of Pythagorean origin which, moreover, had already been condemned in Giordano Bruno's works, as well as in the authors of Renaissance Naturalism and those who followed.

A trial that took place between Modena and Rome in 1620 shows us the extent to which this belief was thought to be serious and dangerous, and especially the extent to which it was reputed to be an integral and characteristic part of Jewish doctrine. Following a complaint presented to the local inquisitor about the Jew Ezechiel Fintio, who was accused of blasphemy against Christ, a search of his home was carried out, in the course of which were found writings full of "errors about human souls, that is that they pass from one body to another". Questioned about these papers, he responded that these doctrines were written in the books of the Jews and that he, as a Jew, believed they were true. The trial was sent to Rome. From here came the order that Fintio be subjected to torture, and be required to confess to having believed in the false doctrine of the transmigration of souls from one body to another, and in their creation at the beginning of the world according to the *Talmudic* doctrine of the preexistence of souls,[82] and finally to abjure and be punished accordingly. Therefore, this was no minor accusation, all the more so because it involved the demonological doctrine which claimed that demons took possession of human bodies and souls.

Other trials demonstrate how sensitive this accusation was and how the Jews, who knew it, attempted to deny any involvement with the subject; however, they also demonstrate how well informed Christians were about

Jewish beliefs. Christians talked about them with Jews, only to later report them. That is what happened in 1612, at Lugo, to a certain Zaccaria, who was questioned for having said in public that "when a Christian or a Jew dies, the Soul goes inside an Animal, that is, in a dog, or in a goose, or in a pig, or another Animal". The good Christians who were present naturally had reproached and even mocked him, arguing that if this was so, then one could not even kill a bug, never mind chickens for the table, because there could be a Jewish soul confined within. Significantly for the historians of today, Zaccaria told the judges that Christians constantly questioned him on this subject, which clearly intrigued and disturbed them, but that he had always replied correctly that it was an opinion, and not an obligatory point of faith.

Towards the Age of the Enlightenment. Tranquillo Vita Corcos and the Amulets

Regarding these delicate matters, we have the testimony of a famous doctor-rabbi from the early 18th century. Tranquillo Vita Corcos (1660–1730), member of a family of Spanish origin, was the true leader of Roman and perhaps Italian Judaism from the end of the 1600s until the 1730s. Highly educated in the sacred and the secular, he was considered the top rabbinic authority; the Jews turned to him for consultation and decisions on a variety of issues, as did the Christian authorities, which whom his relations were frequent and trusted, in accordance with the political line of conciliation and pacification he always pursued. A rabbi since 1712, he was the author of a philosophical treatise on the holiday of *Purim*, and therefore on the story – very dear to Jews for its symbolic aspects – of Queen Ester.[83] He also published speeches within the *Accademia* he himself founded in Rome, which he wrote in Italian, proof of his attempt to begin a cultural opening within the Roman community, working for reform and renewal in a moderate and rational sense.

This desire for exchange and good relations with the external majority world was emphasized by the dedications of his writings to prominent Christian figures. As further confirmation of this, we must mention the decision made around 1719 to use Italian as the official language in the minutes and resolutions of the Council, whose formal documents had until that time been drafted in Hebrew. Moreover, following his request to the Roman authorities, the sale of meat in the ghetto was regulated, with the unusual concession that Jews were permitted to sell the parts of the meat that were prohibited for them to Gentiles. This was *sciattata* meat, however, that is, meat that was treated according to the Jewish *kashruth* procedure, and thus strictly forbidden for Christians. In 1723, the rabbi managed to get a Christian butcher who sold kosher meat to work in the ghetto of Rome. A tireless defender of the community's rights, Corcos produced a large number of written interventions addressed to the ecclesiastical authorities. In one example, he wrote in 1699 defending the right of Jews to make wills, over and against the objections of others who feared that converts would be disinherited. He managed to avert an accusation of ritual murder, which in 1705 had led to the arrest of five Jews at Viterbo. He composed two briefs addressed to the Christian authorities in which he demonstrated that the accusation was unfounded and produced a series of historical documents related to this slander. He also worked with Jewish books, drawing up a brief on the subject for the Holy Office in 1727.

His most significant works, however, were those written in response to attacks by the convert Paolo Sebastiano Medici, who at the time was a leading protagonist of the most violent anti-Jewish preaching and publishing in various Italian cities: at Livorno, Pisa, Florence, Bologna, and in territories subject to the Church.[84] Acting as the spokesman for the vigorous protests of the Italian communities, Corcos managed to block the publication of Medici's fiercely anti-Jewish work *Riti, e costumi degli ebrei confutati* (1736) for at least thirty years. In 1697, he presented a brief of strong protest to the Holy Office, which was printed by the printing house of the Apostolic Chamber that same year: this is not a trivial element, indicative as it is of the close and positive relations between the ecclesiastical authorities and the leading exponents of Judaism.[85] In his brief, the rabbi argued the bold thesis that Judaism and Christianity diverge on only one doctrinal point, that concerning the coming of the Messiah. But most of all, he responded to and refuted, point by point, the representation advanced by Medici of Jewish rituality as superstitious and the fruit of demonic inspiration,[86] with a clear concern for presenting a version of the rites and customs of the Jews as reasonable and acceptable, not superstitious. Thus, he was a rational and open Jewish intellectual.

In 1713, Corcos published *Spiegazione ovvero Riflessione sopra l'uso delle Pergamene scritte con Caratteri Hebraici* in Rimini, written, as he himself states, at the request of the Dominican Giuseppe Maria Tabaglia, commissioner general of the Holy Inquisition. The inquisitor, to whom the text was dedicated, had asked Corcos to translate and explain for him the contents of a parchment written in Hebrew language and characters which he considered suspect of being superstition. In this brief treatise, little known until today, Corcos again addressed the subject of Jewish rituals to clarify their essence as not superstitious, advancing a demonological and angelogical theory that revealed his adherence to the Kabbalah of Isaac Luria. This is further confirmation of the ambiguous coexistence of different inspirations and dimensions, the rationalist and the mystical-Kabbalistic, within the same personalities.[87]

Two elements of this text must be noted, as they are indicative of the ongoing relations between Jewish culture and Christian culture. The first is the fact that – in a phase when the Holy Office's interest in magical or "superstitious" practices in general, and in those of the Jews in particular had been growing – the sacred tribunal did not hesitate to consult the most

learned rabbi in circulation, so he could tell them if the incriminating Hebrew paper did or did not contain superstitious beliefs, and so if it should
be condemned. In the second place, it is worth noting his effort – typical in
all of Corcos' texts and naturally instrumental, but nevertheless indicative
of an open, conciliatory and modern mentality – to demonstrate how the
beliefs of Jews and Christians were really quite similar, and basically not far
from each other, responding to common needs. The effort was pursued even
in the case of a document, such as the one he had been called to evaluate,
which objectively related to the more typically Jewish apotropaic and Kabbalistic practices and beliefs.

Corcos' argumentation, in fact, was also Kabbalistic, based on the tech-
nique of numerology – which refers to the Tetragrammaton, the name of
God with its numerical value – the inversion or exchange of letters and
words, and the power of names in prayers and invocations, following the
teachings of Luria and his disciple Chayyim Vital. The written parchment
he had been hired to examine, which the Jews preserved with devotion and
veneration, contained the names of God and the angels to whom prayers
were addressed to obtain a grace. Thus, it had nothing to do with superstitions, emphasized the rabbi, but only orations based on the Jewish tradition;
he also added that angelology was not, after all, only a Jewish belief, but
a doctrine shared by Christians. Corcos, after reporting the oration in its
entirety, concluded his discourse by asserting, falsely in fact, that the use of
these parchments was not very common among the Jews, and that they still
had to be written by learned men who were competent with sacred objects,
and most of all who were devoted, virtuous and just. As a result, he stated,
"in these parts you find hardly anybody who is involved in writing them".[88]

But what was this parchment really, with all of its signs, numbers, and
words? It was actually an amulet, a *camì*, a paper with many Hebrew texts,
invocations of God, scriptural passages, and verses of the Psalms written on
it, which Jews closest to Kabbalah used to wear for apotropaic purposes, to
protect from and keep away dangers and misfortunes, and, most importantly,
to guard against the temptation of conversion.[89] The use of these amulets
was prohibited by the Christian authorities both because they were believed
to be superstitious, and also because they referred to practices of sorcery
and abuse of sacred things for magical purposes, in particular the name of
God and sacred texts. In fact, quite to the contrary of Corcos' claims, they
were very common. It is not by chance that the previously mentioned trial
against Rabbi Salomone Basilea of Mantua, which took place between 1733
and 1738, revolved around the fabrication and distribution of these amulets.
Basilea's defense lawyer actually produced Corcos' *Spiegazione* in his client's
defense, claiming that the illustrious Roman rabbi, known and esteemed by
all, had demonstrated that there was nothing at all superstitious in these customs. Significantly, however, the inquisitor rejected the twenty year old text.
What is interesting to note here is that Corcos' entire discussion, aimed at
avoiding any malicious interpretation of the parchment in the magical and

diabolical sense, was centered on the distinction between superstition and religion, according to which the practices it described had a purely religious, and therefore acceptable sense, and were supported by sacred texts that were shared by Christians. But in reality, the text's emphasis on the "mysterious significance" of the signs and words it analyzed and on the secret and arcane was clear and emphatic, continuously alluding to a universe that was not very rational and entirely to be deciphered in its highly symbolic connotation.

The most important Italian Kabbalist was the rabbi of Padua, Mosè Vita Luzzatto, who was called Ramhal.[90] Almost contemporaneous with Corcos, but a little younger, he was a poet and mystic who received revelations from a celestial being, the *maggid*, which were the inspiration for his many works on Kabbalah. Ramhal was one of the last followers of the pseudo-Messiah Sabbatai Zevi (or Shabbetay Tzevi, 1626–76), who brought great upheaval to 17th-century Jewish Europe, and his life was much more difficult and controversial than that of the Roman rabbi, who had been much less inclined to reveal his personal beliefs. But the times had changed. The Jewish Enlightenment (the *Haskalah*) began to spread in Europe, and Ramhal was isolated within his own community precisely because of his mystical inspiration; he had to leave Padua for Amsterdam, while rabbinical authorities across Europe banned his works. In the end, he headed for the Holy Land, where he died from a plague at Acco between 1746 and 1747. His tomb remains a destination for pilgrimage to this day.

During the 1700s, the cultural climate of the Enlightenment began, despite the fundamental hostility of Catholic culture, to penetrate even Rome and the ecclesiastic world, leading at least some minority groups to more rational and open positions compared to the age of the Counter-reformation. In this environment, the idea that a whole world of superstitions persisted, to be fought and eradicated, took on urgency in the name of a rational and regulated piety such as that supported by Lodovico Antonio Muratori. This battle for an "enlightened" and modern religion that was against superstition focused precisely on the Jews, targeting their customs, beliefs, and rituals. On the other hand, in the midst of the then current return to a strongly anti-Jewish climate, it was no longer possible for Catholicism to accept dismissing the magical practices of the Jews as unimportant or harmless. The efforts of the Venetian Leon Modena in the previous century and the Roman Tranquillo Vita Corcos in the early 1700s were no longer credible; both of them had tried to offer a rational, anti-superstitious, and anti-magical representation of Jewish culture and customs, in an attempt to remove any suspicion from them of contact and a pact with the devil.

Notes

1 Bonfil, "La lettura nelle comunità ebraiche," 172–3.
2 Bonfil, "La lettura nelle comunità ebraiche," 156–7.
3 Bonfil, "La lettura nelle comunità ebraiche," 179.

4 Bonfil, "La lettura nelle comunità ebraiche," 180.

5 On the 16th- and 18th-century *Indici* of Jewish books and the periodic searches in the ghettos, cfr. Caffiero, *Legami pericolosi*, 28–77.

6 Bonfil, "La lettura nelle comunità ebraiche," 29.

7 The *Talmud* represents the first oral, then written transmission and discussion of the *Torah*, the Law revealed on Mount Sinai to Moses. It was set down in writing only with the destruction of the second Temple in Jerusalem (70 CE), when the Jews feared that the religious foundations of Israel could disappear with the overturning of the related social and legal norms. The *Talmud* consists of a collection of discussions that took place between sages around the significance and applications of passages in the *Torah* and on behavior and practical decisions; it incorporates rules, traditions, and rituals. There are two versions, the Jerusalem *Talmud*, written between the 4th and 6th centuries, and the Babylonian *Talmud*, written between the 5th and 7th centuries in Babylon.

8 Parente, "L'Église et le Talmud," 233–394. Regarding the Christian reception of the *Talmud*, see also Tollet, *Les Églises et le Talmud*.

9 On this decree, often mistakenly called a bull and so attributed to the pontiff, see indications by Parente, "L'Église et le Talmud," 307.

10 On the *Talmud* as a heretical text according to canonical law, and therefore on the pope's right to intervene on the book as well as the Jews who read it, see Parente, "L'Église et le Talmud," 362–6. Cfr. also Caffiero, *Legami pericolosi*, 5–20.

11 Parente, "L'Église et le Talmud," 308.

12 Caffiero, *Legami pericolosi*, 9.

13 Caffiero, *Legami pericolosi*, 10.

14 Caffiero, *Legami pericolosi*.

15 Caffiero, *Legami pericolosi*, 12.

16 Ricci, *Il sommo inquisitore*.

17 Parente, "L'Église et le Talmud," 324.

18 Regarding Jewish "perfidy" cfr. Caffiero, *Legami pericolosi*, 296–330.

19 On the condemnation of the *Talmud* and the following publication of the *Indice* of Clement VIII, cfr. Parente, "The Index, The Holy Office," 164–94.

20 Parente, "L'Église et le Talmud," 360.

21 On the periodic requisitions of Jews' books, cfr. Caffiero, *Legami pericolosi*, 30–43.

22 Parente, "Cabbala," 239–40.

23 On Luria and Vital, and the center of Kabbalah at Safed, cfr. Chajes, *Posseduti ed esorcisti*. Of course also see Scholem, *Kabbalah*; *La Kabbalah e il suo simbolismo*; *Le grandi correnti*.

24 Scholem, *Le grandi correnti*; cfr. also Goetschel, *La Cabbalà*.

25 Scholem, *Le grandi correnti*, 301.

26 Cfr. Chajes, *Posseduti ed esorcisti* also for beliefs in demons and possessions.

27 Di Nepi, "Dall'astrologia agli Astrologo," 41–70.

28 Ernst, "L'astrologia tra natura," 255–79.

29 This is the belief, particularly widespread in the Judaism of Eastern Europe, that gave rise to the myth of the *dibbuk*, the soul that returns from the afterlife to incarnate and which must be exorcized like a demon by expert rabbis. According to Scholem, *Kabbalah*, 349–50 the term, of Yiddish origins, appears at the end of the 17th century in Volhynia. This is a version of the doctrine of transmigration of souls (*gilgul*). The difference from *gilgul* is that while it is a soul that reincarnates, the *dibbuk* in Jewish folklore is a spirit from beyond that enters a living person and speaks from his mouth, maintaining a separate personality.

30 Cfr. Romeo, *Inquisitori, esorcisti e streghe*; *Esorcisti, confessori e sessualità*; Lavenia, "Esorcismi e censura," 129–71; "La lunga possessione," 213–42.

31 Concerning the Christian reception of Kabbalah, cfr. Secret, *Les kabbalistes chrétiens*; Yates, *Cabbala e occultismo*; Garin, "L'umanesimo italiano," 361–83; Dan, *The Christian Kabbalah*; Idel, *Kabbalah in Italy*.
32 On the use and the fortunes of Kabbalah among Italian Jews, cfr. Idel, "Major currents in Italian Kabbalah," 242–62; "Magical and Neoplatonic Interpretation," 186–242; Bonfil, "Lo spazio culturale degli ebrei," 433–8; Ruderman, *Essential Papers on Jewish Culture*; and naturally Scholem, *Le grandi correnti*.
33 Esposito and Procaccia, "La 'schola Sicolorum de Urbe'," 92–106.
34 The Kabbalistic myth of the golem, the artificial anthropoid defender of the Jews, was born in Prague. According to the tradition, which originated in the 18th–19th centuries, around 1580 Rabbi Loew, in order to defend the community of the city from the racist and superstitious accusations hurled at them, created the first *golem* out of clay following a complex magical procedure, called him Joseph, made him a servant and tasked him with protecting the Jews of the city. The ritual of fabrication – and then of deactivation – of the *golem* is a typical example of Kabbalistic ritual based on speech and writing. About this myth, in addition to the well-known novel by Meyrink, *Il Golem*; cfr. Scholem, "La rappresentazione del golem," in *La Kabbalah e il suo simbolismo*; Idel, *Golem*.
35 Regarding the trial of Rabbi Basilea, cfr. Caffiero, *Legami pericolosi*, 156–66. On Basilea, a scholarly Kabbalist and author of important works, see Guetta "Qabbalah e razionalismo," 50 ss.
36 Lattes, "Il Maggid di Ramhal," 209–18.
37 On rabbi/doctors, cfr. Silvera, *Momenti di storia*. On Jewish magic, see the still very useful Trachtenberg, *Jewish Magic and Superstition*.
38 Concerning the nexus of Judaism-magic-witchcraft, cfr. Caffiero, *Legami pericolosi*, 121–80.
39 Barbierato, *Nella stanza dei circoli*.
40 For all of these aspects, see Caffiero, *Legami pericolosi*, 78–180.
41 Guetta, "Qabbalah e razionalismo," 44.
42 Regarding cultural exchange, cfr. Bonfil, "Lo spazio culturale degli ebrei," 415 ss.; on the lack of separation between Jews and Christians, see Caffiero, *Legami pericolosi*.
43 Rossi Artom et al., *Vita di Jehudà*. The autobiography was written in Hebrew. About Leon Modena, cfr. Bonfil and Malkiel, *The Lion Shall Roar*. About the autobiography, see Zemon Davis, "Fama e riservatezza".
44 Bonfil, "Lo spazio culturale degli ebrei," 419 ss.
45 Guetta, "Qabbalah e razionalismo," 43.
46 Weinstein, *Kabbalah and Jewish Modernity*.
47 See the extensive list of his works in Rossi Artom et al., *Vita di Jehudà*, 82–6. On Leon Modena, cfr. Ioly Zorattini and Morelli, "Modena, Leon," 193–200.
48 Modena, *Historia de' Riti Hebraici*.
49 Modena, *Historia de' Riti Hebraici*, 304–5.
50 Zemon Davis, "Fama e riservatezza," 39–60 especially 51.
51 Rossi Artom et al., *Vita di Jehudà*, 68. See also Modena, *Novo Dittionario hebraico et italiano*.
52 Trachtenberg, *Jewish Magic and Superstition*; *The Devil and the Jews*.
53 Modena, *Historia de' Riti Hebraici*, 572.
54 Cfr. *supra*
55 Regarding Leon Modena and his criticism of the Kabbalah, cfr. Dweck, *The Scandal of Kabbalah*.
56 Modena, *Historia de' Riti Hebraici*, 103–4.
57 Rossi Artom, et al., *Vita di Jehudà*, 116 and 120.
58 About the specific characteristics of Jewish autobiography, cfr. Zemon Davis, "Fama e riservatezza"; for women, "Glikl bas Yehudah Leib," 7–66. An example

of an Italian Jewish woman's diary is that of young Anna del Monte from the mid-1700s: see Caffiero, *Rubare le anime.*

59 Luzzatto, "Discorso circa lo Stato degli Hebrei," 3–106. On Luzzatto, see Veltri, *Filosofo e rabbino.*

60 Bartolucci, "Venezia nel pensiero politico ebraico," 225–47.

61 Luzzatto, "Discorso circa lo Stato degli Hebrei," 24.

62 Yerushalmi, *Zakhor,* 40.

63 Yerushalmi, "Clio and the Jews," 608.

64 Yerushalmi, "Clio and the Jews"; *Zakhor,* 94. Bonfil, "Jewish Historiography," 78–102 does not agree with this interpretation, however, claiming that 16th-century historiography is the successor of medieval Jewish historiography.

65 Luzzatto, "Discorso circa lo Stato degli Hebrei," 64.

66 Luzzatto, "Discorso circa lo Stato degli Hebrei," 92.

67 Caffiero, *Legami pericolosi.*

68 For this portrait of Debora I refer to Procaccia, "L''ape ingegnosa'," 355–67.

69 Bonfil, "Lo spazio culturale degli ebrei," 412–73.

70 Procaccia, "L''ape ingegnosa'," 366.

71 Bassani, *Il giardino dei Finzi Contini,* 182 where Sara appears with a different name (Sara Enriquez Avigdòr).

72 Fortis, *La "bella ebrea",* 19. About her see also Cavarocchi Arbib, "Rivisitando la biblica Esther," 143–57; Da Fonseca-Wollheim, "Acque del Parnaso," 159–70; Busetto, "Copio Sullam, Sara".

73 On Cebà, cfr. Mutini, "Cebà, Ansaldo," 184–6.

74 Fortis, *La "bella ebrea",* 56. On the Cebà-Sullam correspondence, see Caffiero, "Amor platonico tra conversione e immortalità".

75 Cebà, *Lettere d'Ansaldo Cebà.*

76 Published in 1616, and reprinted many times. The book, translated from Yiddish into Italian by Jacob Halpron, circulated widely and was condemned by the Roman Holy Office only in 1732. Cfr. Settimi, *La donna e le sue regole.*

77 Boccato, "Il Manifesto sull'immortalità dell'anima," 633–46.

78 Copio Sullam, *Manifesto.*

79 Caffiero, *Legami pericolosi,* 180 ss.

80 Caffiero, *Legami pericolosi,* 181–3.

81 On beliefs in demons and angels among Jews and Christians, cfr. Caffiero, *Legami pericolosi,* 93–111; see the case of Mosè Zamat on 173–7.

82 J. Trachtenberg, *Jewish Magic and Superstition,* 50 connects the doctrine of the transmigration of souls to metempsychosis and the possession of bodies by demons. Cfr. also Caffiero, *Legami pericolosi,* 98–9, 181–9.

83 Corcos, *Discorso accademico.*

84 On Corcos, cfr. Milano, *Il ghetto di Roma,* 391–3; Caffiero, *Battesimi forzati,* 31–48 and notes. For an overall profile of Corcos now see Caffiero, *Il grande mediatore.* On the neophyte P. S. Medici, cfr. Caffiero, *Legami pericolosi,* 80–3, 90–3, 109–17 and notes.

85 On the *memoriale* of 1697, cfr. Caffiero, *Legami pericolosi,* 111–7; *Il grande mediatore.*

86 Medici, *Riti, e costumi degli ebrei.*

87 Caffiero, "Il rabbino, il convertito"; *Il grande mediatore.*

88 Corcos, *Spiegazione ovvero Riflessione,* 19.

89 Caffiero, *Legami pericolosi,* 155.

90 See the contributions in Luzzatto Voghera and Perani, *Ramhal,* many of which also highlight the openness of the mystic towards European rationalist philosophy.

The Age of Emancipation

Part Three
The Age of Emancipation

7   The Turning Point of the 18th Century

The Paradoxes of the Age of Emancipation

The second important turning point for the history of Italian and European Jews should be identified with the age of emancipation and assimilation in the 18th century, after the first that took place between the 15th and 16th centuries, which as we have seen was characterized by expulsions, more or less forced conversions, and the birth of the ghettos. Historian Yosef Hayim Yerushalmi has established a parallel between the two time frames, not only because they both represent historic breaks with the past, but especially because during both periods the part of Christian society where Jews had a presence manifested the most acute reactions of hostility and rejection. These reactions were inspired by an already racial hatred, which first gained acceptance without the official sanction of the States, but which ended up being institutionalized by law. In both cases, the decisive and final element is the appearance of a biological and racial conception of the Jews. For Jews in the 18th century, furthermore, the embrace of the new culture and participation in the intellectual life of the Enlightenment, theorized by exponents of the Jewish Enlightenment (*Haskalah*), produced a growing secularization. Internally, this process involved the introduction of the ideas of modern culture and the growing distinction between individuals and community, and externally on the demand for equal rights in civil society. The parallel established between the two phases has been advanced by some historians to the point of asserting that the assimilated Jew of the 1700s, with his ambiguous identity and destabilizing oscillation between integration and marginality, acceptance and rejection, would present characteristics very similar to those of the Iberian marranos of the preceding centuries. Assimilated and emancipated Jews would therefore be the new, modern marranos.[1]

Over the course of the century in Italy, while the atmosphere and the cultural themes of the Enlightenment began to enter even Catholic intellectual circles, there is a resumption of a general climate that is strongly anti-Jewish.[2] There were many active expressions of this growing anti-Judaism, and not only in the realm of Catholicism. First of all, it was expressed in the demonization of Jewish traditions, customs, and rituals, as we find for example in

DOI: 10.4324/9781003188445-11

the previously cited 1736 treatise by convert Paolo Sebastiano Medici, *Riti, e costume degli ebrei confutati*, which was successful, reprinted, and widely distributed for all of the 18th and 19th centuries. The violently polemical arguments and propaganda employed by the convert Medici demonstrated how accusations against the Jews that related to their customs and rituals went well beyond the generic charge of "superstition". However, while such accusations would continue to characterize conservative Catholic culture, they were also shared by the secular culture of the Enlightenment, which, though it wanted to emancipate the Jews, blamed them for being superstitious and for not assimilating, renouncing their identity.

These arguments manifested a cultural perception that was perhaps not new, but was certainly deeply hostile and diffuse. It was dominated by negative and denigrating representations, by new evocations of ancient accusations of ritual murder and conspiracy against Christianity, by an insistence on the "physical" and "moral" type of the Jews and their innate characteristics, seen as biologically and anthropologically different. The new climate anticipated the great revival of racial stereotypes and their iconographic, religious, and secular representations in the 1800s and 1900s. In short, the Enlightenment and universal rights represent a decisive turning point in the history of relations between Jews and Christians, and of the representations of the former by the latter, a turning point charged with repercussions for the future, in which the paradoxes of Enlightenment regarding the Jews were also at work: the recognition of equal rights did not actually include the right to diversity.

Through the belief in the demonic imprint of the Jewish universe that was part of traditionalist Catholic culture, which remained dominant until the heart of the 18th century, Jewish ritual was perceived as being aimed directly at attacking the world of Christians, as threatening and dangerous. Obviously, the increasing insistence on these dangers, in addition to the reinforcement of the negative and frightening image of the Jews, attributing distinctive moral and physical, eternal, "natural", and biological traits to them, responded to the purpose of discouraging the numerous forms of communication and exchange which constituted a normal part of daily life for Jews and Christians. So, the "blood libel", that is, the accusation of ritual murder, far from being a memory out of the distant medieval past, menacingly resurfaced in different contexts for all of the 18th century, whenever the state and ecclesiastical authorities deemed that the game of political dynamics required an anti-Jewish crackdown. In 1761, in Venice, Giovanni Pietro Vitti published the book *Memorie storico-cronologiche di vari bambini ed altri fanciulli martirizzati in odio alla nostra fede dagli ebrei*, which listed all the cases of ritual murder recorded by history and presented them as events that had really happened. In 1775, a booklet by the Rector of the Casa dei Catecumeni of Rome, Francesco Rovira Bonet, revived the legend of little Simon, the child whose violent death three centuries earlier in 1475 was blamed on the Jews of Trento, who were severely punished.[3]

In the second place, in order to contextualize this growing anti-Judaism, which was mostly, but not only, Catholic, we must recall the policy of conversion which had been launched by the papacy at least two centuries earlier, and which in the 18th century still retained its symbolic and apologetic value as well as its ideological and political role. The Catholic Church's increasing anti-Jewish rigidity over the course of the century clearly appears in the debate over and practice of forced baptisms. In reality, these had been carried out by the Catholic authorities for centuries, but in the 18th century, the practice achieved doctrinal accommodation and theoretical legitimization from Pope Benedict XIV: a pope who is revealed to be, at least in this area, quite far from the traditional image attributed to him as a tolerant and enlightened pontiff.[4] In the Papal States, the conversionist revival and the anti-Jewish hardening happened during the crucial phases of the conflict with the modern world, with the culture of the Enlightenment, and later with the Revolution. Hence, the growing anti-Jewish pressures in the 18th century must be seen in direct relationship to the external affairs of the Church.

The Jews began to be identified as accomplices, as well as beneficiaries, of the anti-Catholic conspiracy hatched by modern culture and the secularized policies of the States. Only two months after his election on February 15, 1775, Pope Pius VI marked a break with past policy, opening his papacy with a very significant act: he revived a harsh anti-Jewish law which responded to the idea that only the rejection of diversity and affirmation of religious unity could guarantee the cohesion of Christian society. The edict of April 5, 1775, *Fra le pastorali sollecitudini*, which in forty-four articles restored old prohibitions for the Jews (on occupations, books, living spaces, contacts and exchanges with Christians) and evoked the danger of subversion represented by these "enemies within", became the point of reference for successive papal anti-Jewish policy. The political and ideological break was confirmed by the new pope's second act, which was closely connected to his anti-Jewish decree, when Pius V issued an official condemnation of Enlightenment culture with his first encyclical, *Inscrutabile divinae sapientiae* on Christmas Day 1775. With this document, the pope very severely censured the ideas of the century of the Enlightenment, which are presented as the work of the devil and a conspiracy directed against civil coexistence. Modern thought was accused *in toto*, with almost apocalyptic tones, of spreading atheism and of wanting to sweep away the traditional harmony between the Church and the States: something that would have dissolved any form of civil society.

It was to this considerably hostile pope that the Jews of Rome sent a quite provocative and certainly bold *Memoriale* in 1789. In this document, they first recalled the privileges and exemptions extended to the Jews by the rulers of different Italian States based on common law and natural law.[5] The dispositions that are mentioned – almost all recently granted – regarded the Duchy of Parma and Piacenza, the Republic of Genova, the imperial cities of Mantua and Trieste, the Grand Duchy of Tuscany and the Duchy of Modena. These measures – wrote the authors of the *Memoriale* – equated the Jews with other subjects and citizens, considering the former equal to the latter.[6]

The expressions used in this document of protest are striking, first of all because they evoke, in that fateful year of 1789 and in the heart of Catholicism itself, concepts of citizenship and equality that would soon become established despite the bitter opposition of the ecclesiastical hierarchy, also extending to the Jews in a large part of Europe. In addition, it is striking that they came from the Roman community, whose condition of economic and cultural decay is a matter of agreement among historians – in reality, wrongly – and which, in any case, was also perceived to be the closest and most connected to ecclesiastical power. Finally, the Roman protests also reflect and describe with concise efficiency changes that on the one hand had been underway for some time in the area of policy towards the Jews in many Italian States, and on the other hand, the differences that set apart local situations, which were by no means homogenous. In fact, in the list mentioned above, while the ecclesiastic State is obviously not mentioned, the Republic of Venice and the Savoy Kingdom don't appear either: that is, those states that, during the 18th century, were not only the most opposed to any sort of emancipation of the Jews, but would instead, especially starting from the 1770s, further harden their positions within a reaffirmed Catholic orthodoxy. The polarity between those that have been defined as "old" States and "new" States, identified by historiography of the 18th century in reference to their lesser or greater openness to reforms and modernization of the State, is thus also reproduced with the Jewish question.

The 1780s and 1790s thus represent a chronological watershed of great importance for the history of the Jews in Italy, even before the turning point of the Revolution and the ruptures that occurred at the end of the century.[7] Therefore, we must examine the consequences of 18th-century reforms and ideas on the condition of the Jews and their relations with the rest of society, and place them in the context of the great differences that characterized individual situations and local relations, even those that seem more alike. The differing evolutions of the regional States' attitudes towards the Jews were reflected in different rhythms and internal timeframes that led, in the same time period, to contradictory provisions. For example, on one hand, there was the novelty of the gates of the Trieste ghetto being opened in 1784, making it possible for the local Jews to live alongside citizens of other faiths, while on the other hand, Correggio saw the institution of the last ghetto in 1782. Furthermore, as we have seen in discussing Jewish culture between the 17th and 18th centuries, it appears that the story of 18th-century Italian Judaism cannot be interpreted as a process of continuous and irreversible cultural and economic decline which, according to the accusations of secular and religious anti-Judaism, loomed over the closed, impermeable system of the ghettos, causing internal cultural and social deterioration and preventing exchanges with the outside. This negative vision of the story of the

Italian Jews in the 1700s, which cannot be supported based on recent studies and documentation, has nevertheless long influenced historiography, Jewish and otherwise.[8]

In order to reflect on the nodes of interaction and relations between the minority reality and dominant society in the century of the Enlightenment, it seems that we must focus on two coordinates in particular. First of all, in an era in which the processes of secularization are advancing, the Jewish question occupies a primary role in relations between State and Church, where it is used, more or less instrumentally, by the two parties as part of the political and jurisdictional conflict. On the other hand, the conflict itself recalls the problem of the strengthening of the State which, in the age of enlightened absolutism and centralizing reforms, tries to assert itself against particular bodies, separate powers, and acquired autonomies. The State, therefore, also tends to include the "body" of Jews as part of the process of unification, not without ambiguity, which produces tensions and crises within that body. So, let's examine the subject of the relationship between the State and the Church in relation to the problem of the Jews.

A Three-Way Relationship: The States, the Church, and the Jews

As said earlier, the condition, the very quantitative consistency and role of the Jews in Italy between the age of Enlightenment and the Revolution seem to depend first and foremost on the situation and evolution of relations between the various regional States and the Church. During the 18th century, the structures established during the Counter-Reformation era collapsed, and the substantial agreement historically maintained between civil powers and ecclesiastical authorities was broken, within a gradual process of disengaging the State from the control of the Church. The growing conflicts between the two spheres, and the new balances of power established from time to time had powerful repercussions in the Jewish world, which became an instrument – and a victim – of this dialectic. Indeed, if we look closely, the Jewish question became increasingly important in the context of this conflict precisely because of it political uses by both parties. However, it is not a coincidence that discussion about this issue was accentuated in the second half of the century, which sees an acceleration of jurisdictionalist and anti-Roman politics in many Italian and European States that is also a consequence of the influence of the new Enlightenment culture, and at least theoretically the bearer of greater tolerance. On the other hand, the opposing side of the Church symmetrically reignites virulent Catholic anti-Judaism in a defensive response to the process of nationalization and secularization that recovered and rehabilitated the Jews precisely in an anti-Roman function. An example of this "use" of the Jewish question in the relations between Rome and the States is offered by the latter's conversion policies, milder and more permissive in some phases, stricter in others, according to the politics of the moment. This oscillation confirms how state policy towards the Jews was functional for broader policies, especially for conflicts or alliances with Rome, and was always located within the claim of its own prerogatives.

In this perspective of the relations between State and Church, the problem of the relationship between the Jewish question and Enlightenment era reforms much remains to be clarified, as there were different levels in play. First of all, we must ask how, and how much, 18th-century reformism influenced the condition of the Italian Jews, considering the backlash it provoked in the Jewish world itself, causing conflict between conservatives and innovators, and between different social groups. The negative reaction provoked in the Catholic context by the new and more tolerant policies of many Italian States towards the Jews is also an important problem. Thus, the Jewish question constituted an important indicator of the level of conflict between Church and State, and of the former's capacity to resist the reforming forces of the State. An effective example of the fact that the Jews were pawns of a broader policy and conflict is offered by the unfortunate outcome of the attempt to readmit them to the Kingdom of Napoli, begun in 1740 by the new King, Charles of Bourbon.

Recalling the Jews to the Kingdom was part of Charles' reformist and mercantilist policy, in the context of a series of initiatives aimed at the economic revitalization of the State. The now widespread economic paradigm of "usefulness" suggested offering a series of privileges that quickly attracted 121 Jews to Naples alone, for the most part from Rome, Livorno, and also Holland. However, despite the positive opinions of educated and open Catholics, who appealed as much to the principles of tolerance found in "true" Christianity as to the ideas of "enlightened men", the initiative immediately encountered the protests of Christian merchants and strong hostility from the clergy and the general population, and with Rome's able and severe intervention rapidly failed. While anti-Jewish pamphlets and rumors about the fraudulent circumcision and conversion to Judaism of young Catholics reawakened the stereotype of the Jews as the mortal enemies of Christians, Rome also inserted the question into the ongoing negotiations for a concordat with the newly formed and weak Kingdom of Napoli. In this way, the Holy See obtained first the modification and finally the revocation of the Bourbon decree in 1746. The Jews were expelled again, by a King who was terrified both by the clerical threat that he would not have sons because of his decree, and by the connections made between that decree and the plague of Messina. The readmission of the Jews into the Kingdom became a test case for the new reformist policy, which rested on Enlightenment ideas. However, in this case concerning the Jews, the reforming party was defeated, and the failure must be ascribed to the powerful pressures personally exerted by the pope: again, the same Benedict XIV that historiography has constantly praised for his tolerance, while it is precisely to him that we owe a meticulous, continuous, and harsh legislative action towards the Jews.

The case of the Savoy State also confirms the extent to which the dialectic between the two powers and the standoff between the State and the Church of Rome played on these pawns – the Jews – and conditioned the community's situation, a demonstration of the historiographic thesis of antisemitism as a political resource.[9] In the Piedmont, however, we find a different situation. Here, the growing cultural and ideological influence of the Church on the State reinforced the isolation of the Jews and their separation from the Christian world over the course of the century, while the ecclesiastical authorities tried to take jurisdiction over the Jewish minority away from organs of the State. Even in the Savoy Kingdom, however, and despite the shared anti-Jewish policy, the very late establishment of ghettos in midst of the 18th century and the restrictive measures that were adopted ended up becoming a part of the political gamesmanship in Torino's negotiations for a concordat with Rome.

This three-way relationship between the Church, the State, and the condition of the Jews is even more evident in the Italian domains of the Habsburgs. Here, the advocates of tolerance also used the Jewish question to oppose the Church of Rome: thus, the thesis of antisemitism as a political resource appears to be applicable in reverse, to the opposite pole of pro-Judaism. The Edict of Tolerance towards the Jews therefore played an important role in Joseph II's jurisdictional offensive and his political-religious project, inspired by the principle of a "true Christian tolerance". Enacted for Austria on January 2, 1782, the edict had already been introduced in the Italian dominions at the end of 1781: at Mantua, Trieste and in the counties of Gorizia and Gradisca, whose Jewish populations had recently been enlarged by immigration from the Venetian territories after the expulsions that took place there in 1777. The edict in favor of the Jews represented an important aspect of the Emperor's offensive against ecclesiastical power and influence, and was part of the more general religious reform he introduced in his States, fiercely and unsuccessfully opposed by Rome.

The connection between the Jewish question and the more general reforms of secularization, and the State's claim of its prerogative against ecclesiastical demands emerges with clarity from the lively debate that erupted over the case of the annulment of the marriage of a converted Jew. It was a story that captured European public opinion and which also resonated in Italy. In 1752, the Alsatian Jew Baruch Levi converted to Catholicism. Because his Jewish wife had refused to convert, or to follow him and continue living with him, he intended to remarry according to the provision of the so-called "Pauline privilege" in canonical law. This was a rule that permitted the annulment of a first marriage and the possibility of entering into a second one. In the case that followed, Levi's defenders based their requests first and foremost on the passage from St. Paul (I Cor. 7,15), which provided for dissolution of a marriage by a converted infidel, and secondly on the authority of canonists. The defense made particular reference to a bull by the then reigning pontiff, Benedict XIV, *Apostolici ministerii munus* of September 16, 1747, which reiterated the position that a Jewish marriage could be broken up in the case of conversion by one of the spouses and the refusal to convert on the part of the other. Representatives of the secular powers and the monarchy instead registered their clear opposition to the dissolution of a marriage believed to be absolutely legitimate and valid with a resolution of the Parliament of Paris. The secular politicians supported the thesis of the absolute indissolubility of a legitimate marriage, independent from the sacrament that blessed it, referring to modern arguments of natural law, respect for the laws of the State, and theories about the contractual nature of marriage.[10]

This conflict paradoxically pitted traditionalist and pro-Roman Catholics who were in favor of divorce, along with the convert Levi and his lawyers, against jurisdictionalist politicians who defended the indissolubility of marriage to the bitter end. This prolonged and reflected the centuries-old clash over the nature of matrimony and the right of control over the matter: a conflict that constituted one of the central issues of 18th-century reform theory and policy, and the most important effort to elaborate a new state doctrine governing marriages after the framework given by the Council of Trent.

There was also a strong echo of the Levi case in Habsburg Italy, where in 1785–86 the marriage laws for Jews had been brought into line with the new laws in force for Catholics since 1783. The new imperial matrimony legislation distinguished aspects of the civil contract from the sacrament, and also allowed divorce in specific cases. In 1783, the appendix to the volume *De tolerantia*, published in Pavia under the name of Count Thaddeus von Trauttmansdorff, but in reality, the work of Jansenist professors from Pavia, Pietro Tamburini, and Giuseppe Zola, refuted the protests of those – and the pope included was among these – who challenged the anti-divorce thesis by referring to the Pauline passage, and reiterated that the matrimonial bonds of Jews or non-Catholics could not be dissolved by the conversion of one of the spouses. Thus, while baptism could certainly erase sins it did not dissolve unions, something which would have openly trampled on theories of marriage as a civil contract.

Other Jewish divorce cases from the end of the century further demonstrate how the relationship between the absolute State and Jewish communities very frequently played out in conflicts related to decision-making powers around the subject of marriage.[11] These cases revolved around defining which of the two laws, Jewish or State, would be followed in these unions since, at least in Habsburg Italy, the marriage license of 1783 and the Civil Code of 1786 introduced the definition of matrimony as a civil contract, and placed it under secular and state jurisdiction. Here too individual Jews ended up as instruments, but also actors in a clash between jurisdictional competencies and spheres of power – the Church, the State, and the Jewish communities themselves – all of which claimed the right of control, as well as procedural and decision-making prerogatives over matters (marriages and divorces, which were permitted by Jewish law) in which legal-political factors and religious factors were intimately intertwined.

Jews and Reforms

The liberalizing reforms of Joseph II, who was moreover a firm Catholic, were inspired by the idea of a political organization in which the different confessions had to coexist for the purposes of the State, and the design of a state structure in which the different autonomous bodies, such as those constituted by the Jewish communities, had to be dissolved. These were concepts that anticipated, for one thing, the emancipation of the Jews, which the French Revolution would extend from the plane of civil rights to that of political rights and full citizenship. On the other hand, however, the reforms also anticipated the contradictions of emancipation and the paradoxes of Enlightenment, because the principle of absolute equality involved the risk of assimilation/erasure of diverse identities. This risk was especially present in the rules that most insisted on cultural integration, such as those of the Habsburgs: for example, the obligatory use of the language of the country instead of Hebrew, mandatory attendance of children at the normal elementary schools, or even a Christian school if there was none in the community, onomastic reform with the imposition of new names, the abolition of internal courts and weakening of community autonomy, and of course marriage reform. There was no lack of tension in these areas in the Christian schools attended by Jews, in resistance to the mandatory use of German and the reform of last names; there was even opposition, albeit limited, to the abolition of the ghetto in Trieste.

We must also take into account the religious aspiration behind these reforms, which pushed towards the so-called "regeneration of the Jews": that is, they responded to the need for the Jews' cultural and economic integration into Christian society, and were certainly not exempt from more or less explicit conversionist ends. This danger was quite clear, and was denounced in the world of German Jewry – for example, by Moses Mendelssohn – but it did not seem, at least according to what we know from the current state of research, to be of much concern to Italian Judaism. In Habsburg Trieste and Gorizia, in fact, Joseph II's legislation and principles for reforming education in a modern and secularized sense received broad support and wide application, and were also advocated by the Jewish Enlightenment, with which the two communities had come into contact.[12]

However, questions remain about the attitude of Italian Jews towards the reforms and, vice-versa, about that of Italian reformers and Enlightenment thinkers concerning the issue of the Jews. Regarding the first aspect, it seems beyond doubt that, outside of some resistance from the most conservative and traditionalist sectors, and tensions aroused by some of the undeniable limitations of Joseph's legislation, the reforms met with broad and general support among the Italian Jews. As we can also see from the relationships established by the communities of Northeast Italy with the exponents of the

Berlin *Haskalah*, the theories of the so-called Jewish Enlightenment pushed towards a rearrangement of the conflicts between tradition and modernity and in favor of a greater openness to secular culture and more intense relations with the Christian world. On the other hand, Italian Jews, unlike those of other European countries, were able to attend Christian universities, albeit in very few disciplines (for the most part in medicine), well before Joseph II's reforms and also in States that were not under Austrian rule, for example, at the University of Padua. This created a further point of contact for Jews with the external culture more than anywhere else; 162 Jews from various places earned doctorates at Padua between 1700 and 1794.

The cultural reawakening produced by Joseph II's new political-reformist conjuncture by is made clear by the increase of Jewish printing at Gorizia, in Italian and German, directed at the diffusion of Jewish-Enlightenment ideology, and at the same time, support for imperial legislation. In 1783, we find Elia Morpurgo of Gradisca, a very interesting figure who was an intellectual and a silk industrialist, at the center of this effort at reconciliation with modern culture. He promoted the establishment of normal schools for Jews as a first step towards more complete integration, and launched an important publishing initiative with printer Giacomo Tommasini, aimed at the publication and diffusion of works of ancient and modern Jewish literature as well as Jewish historical sources.[13] These positions were new and not always completely shared by all Jews: however, they reveal that in 18th-century Italian communities, there was an interest in the history and historiography of diaspora Judaism which, according to Yosef Hayim Yerushalmi's thesis, represented a novelty for Jewish culture after the 16th century that was antithetical to tradition.[14]

Jewish Culture and the Enlightenment. Benedetto Frizzi, Isacco Reggio and Beniamino Foà

Jewish intellectuals' new attention to sources and their own history put them in contact with the segment of contemporary Catholic culture that was more open to the philological study of biblical and Jewish texts and the irenic appreciation of the Jewish roots of Christianity, as well as with secular and Enlightenment culture. The previously mentioned Elia Morpurgo had contact and correspondence with a scholarly clergyman and Hebraist from Parma, Giovanni Bernardo De Rossi, a collector of Hebrew manuscripts and antique editions as well as the author of various writings on the Jews, among which was his *Dizionario storico degli autori ebrei e delle loro opere*, published at Parma in 1802.[15] In Livorno, a premier center for books in the 18th century, both for production as well as trade, the printing of Hebrew books gained great momentum.[16] In Modena, Mosè Beniamino Foà, the official "Ducal bookseller" quietly imported and advertised the writings of all the exponents of the French Enlightenment, even the most radical and prohibited, avoiding the censors and customs officers by mixing them in his catalogs among the works on Jewish matters.

Also active in this period was doctor and rabbi Benedetto Frizzi (Ben Zion Refael Ha-Cohen, 1756–1844) of Ostiano, at the time a citizen in the Mantuan territory. His vast work, and also his practical behaviors were inspired by the ideal of agreement between the Jewish religion and Enlightenment reason. Frizzi's claim of the rationality of the Mosaic teachings would translate into confidence that tradition and modern science could cooperate in the perfection of humanity, freeing it from deeply rooted prejudices and harmful superstitions, and opening the way towards the emancipation and integration of the Jews. He earned a degree in medicine at the prestigious University of Pavia; in 1789, he moved to Trieste, by invitation of the Habsburg government, where he practiced medicine, quickly earning a well-deserved good reputation. In 1816, he founded a Jewish hospital in the city which provided free assistance for the sick and destitute. Frizzi was an attentive observer, open to the scientific and cultural experiences of his time. His *Giornale medico e letterario di Trieste*, which was released in four volumes between 1790 and 1791, was a very important journal, and one of the first medical periodicals published in Italy. Its contents featured letters and articles on a variety of current medical topics – such as typhoid fever, dysentery, or even new illnesses – alongside philosophical, mathematical, or medical discussions and reviews of medical books. He was the author of numerous volumes of *Dissertazioni di polizia medica sul Pentateuco*, which constituted a meticulous medical and philosophical study of the Mosaic precepts. Frizzi called these a "true health code" and interpreted them as rules valid for the spiritual and moral elevation of a man, aimed at conserving and bettering the species. The *Dissertazioni* also presents, along with critical and physical notes and philosophical reflections, an effort to correct some errors introduced by the rabbis in matters of public health.

Between 1790 and 1792, he published the *Opusculi filosofici e medici* in four volumes at Trieste, the first of which contained eleven essays on some of the best known illnesses suffered by biblical personalities (the blindness of Isaac and of Jacob, the sterility of Rebecca, Sara and Rachel, etc.). Among his works on medical subjects, we should mention the *Dissertazione sulla lebbra degli ebrei* (Trieste 1795) – a disease (leprosy) traditionally associated with Jews – and *Osservazioni e riflessioni sulla scarlattina* (Trieste 1811).[17] In addition to writing about medical interests, Frizzi was also the author of works that dealt with the practices, customs, and beliefs of the Jewish people, and included criticism of those he considered to be in error along with advice for needed reforms: these, however, were not well received by his Jewish audience. The original forms in which the demands of the Enlightenment and the considerations of Jewish tradition are combined in his writings, and his effort to open the Italian communities to the works of the Enlightenment, Jewish or not, also emerge from another important text, the *Difesa contro gli attacchi fatti alla nazione ebrea nel libro intitolato della influenza del ghetto nello Stato* (Pavia 1784); here, he refutes the *Della influenza del ghetto nello Stato*, a book published in Venice in 1782 by the Mantuan

Count Giovanni Battista Gherardo D'Arco, which we will examine further on. Other works, such as *Dissertazione in cui si esaminano gli usi ed abusi degli Ebrei nei luoghi ed effetti sacri e si propone la maniera di renderli utili in società* (Milano 1789) and l'*Elogio funebre di S. M. l'augusto Giuseppe ii imperatore* (Trieste 1790), eloquently demonstrate his effort at integration into the culture of the majority society. This effort is also reflected in the fact that he was among the founding partners and a protagonist of the *Accademia di Minerva* of Trieste, formed as a reading salon in 1810.

The story of how he opposed the rules of his community in the name of State law, in the very delicate area of marriage, is also very interesting and significant. In 1798, Frizzi and Relle (or Rachele) Morschene requested authorization from the imperial authorities to enter into a purely civil marriage, in order to get around the prohibition that Jewish law imposed on a *Kohein*, that is, a descendant of the ancient Israelite priests – to which group Frizzi, in fact, belonged – against marrying a woman who had been divorced, or more accurately, repudiated according to Jewish custom. When consulted by officials, the rabbis of Trieste refused permission based on Jewish law. Frizzi engaged in a scholarly explanation, based on the Old Testament and Montesquieu, to demonstrate how the "true" and "pure" Mosaic law distinguished between repudiation and divorce, permitting the latter based on the mutual consent of the spouses. What is striking about this affair, beyond its outcome, which saw imperial officials line up in favor of the doctor-rabbi and against the Jewish authorities, is Frizzi's free behavior, his use of arguments with references to Montesquieu, and especially the individualism in interpreting the law in defiance of the rabbis and the community of Trieste, with the clear choice in favor of the laws of the State.[18] An ideological challenge charged with novelty was emerging, which united "pure" Mosaicism with rationalism and tried to modernize the Jewish tradition with Enlightenment philosophy. This was a very strong break with tradition, through the claim of a personal and literal reading of the biblical text subjected to the rationalist criticism of the spirit of the Enlightenment, which aligned with similar operations underway in the world of non-Jewish culture.

Another illustrious exponent of the Jewish Enlightenment in Italy was Isacco Samuel Reggio of Gorizia (1784–1855), a rabbi, Hebraist, biblical exegete, mathematician, and philosopher who represented the point of contact and transmission of the Enlightenment ideas elaborated by the German theorists of the *Haskalah*. In his works, he proposed the theoretical foundations of the Jewish Enlightenment and the need to integrate the Law and the tradition with the concepts and criteria of secular philosophical and scientific thought.[19] His contribution was instrumental in constructing a new figure of the rabbi with a renewed role in the context of a Judaism that was in the midst of emancipation, offering useful tools for interpreting the new era while remaining within the Jewish tradition. His support for the foundation of the Rabbinic College established at Padua in 1829 and for the expansion of its programs was fundamental, and thus instrumental in the rise of the figure of the 19th-century Italian rabbi. Among his most important works, *La legge e la filosofia* of 1827 should be mentioned, a religious-philosophical essay written to demonstrate that there was no conflict between Mosaic law and philosophy.

Benedetto Frizzi, Elia Morpurgo and Isacco Samuel Reggio were therefore protagonists of a cultural and philosophical current that tried to introduce the reformist works and ideas of the Jewish Enlightenment, particularly those of Germans such as Moses Mendelssohn and Naphtali Herz Wessely, into the Italian Jewish communities. They anticipated the attempt to reorganize Italian Jewish culture which experienced its major developments in the 1800s, and influenced the cultural setting of Italian Judaism of the 19th century.[20]

Bookseller and publisher Mosé Beniamino Foà (Reggio Emilia, 1729–1821) was also an important figure. Foà maintained a wide range of relationships: he worked with the Ducal librarian, Jesuit Francesco Antonio Zaccaria, who was a major exponent of hardline Catholic zealotry, but he also had relations with the Theatine Paolo Maria Paciaudi, reorganizer of the University of Parma, a palatine librarian and exponent of Catholic reformism, with the scholarly ecclesiastic Hebraist Giovanni Bernardo De Rossi and, finally, with the future "Jacobin" Giuseppe Compagnoni, who was author of a much discussed *Saggio sugli Ebrei e sui Greci* (Modena 1791), which Foà himself had published. Foà's experience confirms the closely intertwined relations between Jewish culture and non-Jewish culture in this phase. Foà also obtained full citizenship in Modena, which assured him significant advantages, since Modena and Reggio were the main centers for his bookselling business, which grew enormously after the renovation of the University, for which he was the official printer. Thus, by the early 1770s, he had become the printer, bookseller, and publisher for Modena's high culture: all the works of Girolamo Tiraboschi were published by his printing company. Immediately after the arrival of the French in October of 1796, Foà's print house published the *Giornale repubblicano di Pubblica Istruzione*, which supported the struggles of the most ardent pro-French republicans in Modena and Reggio. The numerous public recognitions Foà received culminated in his nomination to represent the Jewish community of Reggio Emilia at the Great Sanhedrin of Paris in 1806, which, by order of Napoleon, brought together notable figures and rabbis from France, Italy, and Alsace.[21]

The Problems of Acculturation. Isacco Lampronti

There is no doubt that that the culture of reforms and more generally the cultural changes underway in the 18th century also impacted the Jews and involved the world of Italian Jewry, pushing it in the direction of a more open relationship with secular culture, as well as towards more intense relations with the Christian world. These changes, however, also provoked internal problems, particularly regarding the observance of tradition and religious obedience. According to some historians, the growing internal tensions, which we will see better further on, and the new doctrines of emancipation and the Enlightenment provoked a crisis in the Jewish community's authority structures, and particularly the rabbis' authority.[22] According to others, though, the process of the relaxation of ritual practices, departure from traditional models, and imitation of non-Jewish practices had begun, at least in the world of German Jewry, even before the Jewish Enlightenment and the 18th century.[23] From the historiographical point of view, this early manifestation of the process of acculturation implies that it was not directly connected to an ideology or a precise intellectual system in the same way the Enlightenment was. Most of all, it means that the increasingly accentuated social and cultural interaction between Jews and Christians did not in any way call into question the solidity of the Jewish identity. Let us see if that was actually so.

In a phase like that of the 18th century, which carried on into the 19th century, characterized by the oscillation between two different and often opposing processes – the push towards emancipation, acculturation and assimilation on one hand, and the effort to maintain and defend a specific identity on the other – the question of the rabbis' behavior and the response they developed to confront the changes of the modern world turns out to be central.[24] Openness to these changes could, in fact, lead to a gradual weakening or even to the transgression of religious precepts. It could also set up a conflict, especially in the revolutionary age, between belonging and loyalty to the State and the nation and the effort to maintain a particular and independent identity.

This brings us to the historiographic question of whether we find ourselves faced with a crisis of religious observance and obedience in 18th-century Italy, and consequently a challenge to the traditional community structure and its authority. We can respond by referring to the reflections of another distinguished personality, Isacco Lampronti (1679–1756), who was active in Ferrara, where he was chief rabbi, a doctor, and led the city's rabbinic academy. As a theologian and philosopher, he wrote a famous *Talmudic* encyclopedia, *Pahad Izchak* ("*The Fear of Isaac*"), during the same time period that saw the publication of the Enlightenment era *Encyclopédie* by Diderot and d'Alembert. This work, in which he addressed, in alphabetical order, questions regarding ritual, religion, medicine, and science, was published in numerous volumes between 1750 and 1887, for the most part released posthumously. It is a work that is still consulted by scholars of Jewish law, rich in information about customs, social and cultural aspects of Jewish life in Ferrara.[25] In the early 18th century, there was still a strong community of 1500 people including Ashkenazi, Sephardim, and Italiani Jews with their related synagogues, which represented 6% of the total of about 25,000 inhabitants in the city.

It emerges from Lampronti's observations on the behaviors of his community that although the cultural barriers with Christians were low and very

permeable, and violations of community rules were frequent, heterodox behaviors, according to the rabbi, did not really indicate a decline in religious
observance, although that did exist, but rather a weakening of obedience
to rabbinic authority. The various episodes reported by Lampronti record
a high rate of law breaking by the Italiani and Ferrarese Jews, which the
learned rabbi attributed to, among other things, the diffusion of Kabbalistic
orientations in his century. Moreover, he considered wealthy coreligionists
to be more inclined to laxity in the matter of religious observance compared
to people in the lower classes, who he considered more devoted and obedient to religious authorities. But, notwithstanding his complaints about the
behavior of his fellow Jews, Lampronti greatly downplayed the impact of
religious disputes and relaxation of observance on the community, leading
many historians to also take a reductionist point of view. In fact, the image
of Ferrara's Jewish society Lampronti delineates seems to respond more to
a representation dictated by fears of modern culture and the trend towards
secularization than to reality. These were the same fears that the Catholic
clergy faced in those decades, with the same threats from modernity. Even
the references to the differences in behavior between the disobedient rich
and the obedient poor seem to echo similar and parallel complaints that
were heard in the hardline Catholic world, which denounced the cooling religiosity of the elites; their strategies for recovering support, and the Catholic re-conquest of society, relied on the devoted faith of the popular masses.
In contrast with Lampronti's optimistic interpretation, and demonstrating
that a decisive transformation was also in progress at Ferrara in 1797, while
the publication of the volumes of his main work was still underway, the internal malaise within the community would lead some groups, evidently less
connected to the tradition, to present radical proposals for the dissolution
of the Jewish *Università* to facilitate its social and civic integration.

As for relations between Jews and Christians, Lampronti notes very open
attitudes among the former, with a high rate of participation in and identification with the general culture and social interaction. In fact, while the
Jews adopted gentile practices, like hunting, or listening to Christian music, Christians purchased books related to Judaism from Jews, or sought
treatment by Jewish doctors. In the picture of the panorama of exchanges
that emerges from the rabbi's descriptions, we also find the phenomenon of
the considerable number of Jewish conversions, and therefore their apostasies. The definitive act of conversion constituted the culminating moment
in the interaction between Jews and Christians, through the former's abandonment of their religious and cultural diversity. Conversions occupied an
important role in Lampronti's encyclopedia, inasmuch as for the poorest
Jews the threat of changing religions was a powerful weapon of extortion
that could be aimed at the rabbinic authorities themselves to extract concessions or approval for illegal conduct. While this phenomenon naturally
worried the rabbis, it once again proved the extent to which the barriers
between Jews and Christians were easily crossed, mostly, but not only, by

the former for instrumental and opportunistic reasons. The frequent conversions also indicated a low level of tension between the two communities, and constituted an aspect of interaction which on closer inspection calls into question Lampronti's belief that the poorest classes were also the most devout. However, the apostasies, demonstrating the Jews' awareness that they had an easy and advantageous choice available, were also an indication of opposition to authority and a lessened perception of borders and barriers between Jews and Christians, as well as the dangers to which Jewish identity was exposed.

The picture drawn by Lampronti, and accepted by many historians as reliable, refers to a low level of separation and easily crossed boundaries, with a high degree of interaction between the two groups as well as levels of familiarity and trust. However, the conclusions that some authors draw from this text are less easily shared. The fact that the rabbi did not consider the climate of social and cultural exchange to be a danger for the preservation of Jewish identity and a signal of the community's breakdown – which the numerous episodes of conversion he cited could refute – and the fact that he ascribes deviant behaviors to a mere relaxation of obedience to the rabbinic authorities, do not seem to constitute proof of the community's resistance to the pressures of the times and the maintenance of its structural integrity.[26] Nor would it seem to disprove the thesis of the crisis that was sparked by the cultural transformations taking place.

In reality, the weakening of the authorities who led the community was of primary importance, and as we will see, at the end of the century it would become internally disruptive. The progressive breakdown of the traditional community system, and the growing economic, social, and cultural differentiation produced by modernity, which also emerge from Lampronti's annotations, triggered tensions in the ghettos, undermining their cohesion. The conflict between emancipation, integration, and assimilation in Christian society on one hand, and the maintenance of Jewish identity in its traditional form, on the other hand, while this embarrassed the rabbis, confronting them with new forms of disobedience and a crisis of observance, it necessarily implied a challenge to the traditional community structure and its authorities.

The Debate over the Jewish Question

What were the attitudes of non-Jewish culture, whether Catholic or secular, towards the Jews? Here, we are faced with a complex and contradictory situation. In reality, the 18th century is the century that not only inaugurates reforms aimed at emancipation, but also launches an early and heated discussion about the Jewish problem on different levels: economic, legal and theological. It is also worth noting that the advocates of emancipation, as well as its opponents, came from both within the Catholic religious world as well as from the secular culture.

Regarding the Catholic world, the approach to Judaism cannot be explained by liberal economic transformations or cultural changes brought about by rationalism, the Enlightenment and the ideas of tolerance. Rather, it must be seen in the context of the transformations within Catholicism itself, and the ideological-political and theological rift between different conflicting currents. The question of the role of the Jews in the economy of salvation and in the reform of the Church took on an important function in this intra-Catholic conflict, similar to what happened externally in the conflict between Church and State. This means that the Catholic world as a whole did not completely share the Church of Rome's intransigence towards the Jews. The Jewish question, then, was at the heart of an internal rift in this world.

The pro-Jansenist Catholic circles and the anti-Curia ecclesiastical reformers, who demanded the elimination of the "abuses" introduced by Rome and the Papacy through the re-establishment of pure original Christianity, had since the 1770s based their millennial and palingenetic expectations on a firm pro-Judaism and a clear recovery of the Jewish origins of Christianity. Therefore, the roots of philosemitism grew out of the conflicts between dissident groups and the official Churches. Of course, pro-Jewish Catholic positions were also aimed at the final conversion of the Jews from an eschatological and millennialist perspective.[27] However, despite their assimilationist goals – which in fact were shared by Joseph's reforms, and later by revolutionary emancipatory liberalism itself – these positions translated into mindsets and practices that were favorable to tolerance and rights for the Jews, and totally in conflict with those of the Roman Church hierarchy and traditionalist Catholicism. Indeed, these concepts caused a clear division within the Catholic world on the Jewish question, destined to extend through the following two centuries. Starting in the 1700s, completely symmetrically in fact, intransigent Catholicism would link the fight against the modern world and against the new culture, as well as its efforts for the Christian re-conquest of society, to much harsher positions towards the Jews. From the papacy of Benedict XIV to that of Pius VI, up through the popes of the 1800s, there was a legal, mental and behavioral hardening which is at the root of contemporary antisemitism. In the heart of the Catholic world, this rift over the Jewish question was destined to last for a long time to come. It would only begin to recede after the Vatican Council II and the declaration *Nostra aetate* of 1965.

Regarding the world of secular and reformist culture, which is generally considered – often wrongly – as favorable to the Jews *in toto*, here too there were ambiguities and internal divisions. The anti-Jewish positions of French Enlightenment thinkers are well known, starting with Voltaire. In Italy, the debate focused primarily on ways to make the Jews' presence useful to the State and profitable for its economic development more than on the need to recognize equality for Jews in civil rights. These utilitarian motivations, encouraged by the widespread mercantilist mentality of the time, are explained and argued in detail in the work of Giovanni Battista Gherardo D'Arco, a moderate representative of Habsburg reformism.[28] His book *Della influenza del ghetto nello Stato* (*On the Influence of the Ghetto in the State*), published in Venice in 1782, appeared in the wake of Joseph II's Edict of Tolerance, and was influenced by the perspective of his city, Mantua, which was home to an important Jewish community. His arguments are relevant because they would have broadly influenced positions on the Jews among Enlightenment intellectuals between the 18th and 19th centuries, with all their contradictions and ambiguity, until the publication of *Interdizione israelitiche* by Carlo Cattaneo in 1835, and also others.

D'Arco starts from the controversial and traditional denunciation of the exclusive monopoly that the Jews held when it came to commercial activities, seen as a threat and harmful to the state, especially on the economic level. This monopoly derived, in his opinion, from their "national character", from their spirit of cohesion and "unsociability" and their desire for separation from the rest of the State. These negative factors, however, were also identified as the consequence of the degraded condition in which the Jews had always been forced to live by the majority society. We are therefore still dealing with a perception that was based on a centuries-old tradition, filled with religious and social prejudices, and which was still quite widespread in the 1700s.

However, immediately afterwards, in support of the Emperor's new policy of tolerance, education, and "enlightening" of the Jewish nation, the author argued that this policy would cut the roots of the asocial egoism and love "of party and conspiracy" that made the Jews a State within a State, and a separate body against the State, by urging them to extend the their field of initiative to other spheres also useful to the economy, such as agriculture, crafts, and manufacturing. The idea – already formulated the year before by Prussian philosopher Christian Wilhem Dohm, and again in 1782 by French Jansenist Henri Grégoire, which had great success later on – was to encourage Jews to take up agriculture in order to get them out of trade and moneylending, and in this way to procure their moral "regeneration" and emancipation. D'Arco's support for the Emperor's doctrine of fraternity, equality, and the principles of tolerance was accompanied, therefore, by the revival of a series of traditional stereotypes, such as the view of usury, trade, greed and antisocial behavior as natural and innate characteristics of the Jews. This has led some historians to brand the book as unquestionably anti-Semitic; it is interesting to note that Catholic traditionalists, on the contrary, considered the text to be excessively pro-Jewish.[29]

Mantuan Jewish Enlightenment thinker Benedetto Frizzi responded to Count D'Arco's work with his own *Difesa contro gli attacchi fatti alla nazione ebrea nel libro intitolato della influenza del ghetto nello Stato*, published in Pavia in 1784. His refutation of D'Arco's ideas around the nefarious effects of Jewish commercial activity is accompanied by an insistence on their sociability, willingness for exchanges, and openness to the world of Christians.

One of Frizzi's sources was probably the writing of Simone Luzzatto, who in 1638, as we saw earlier, [30] had outlined the arguments for the residence of Jews in the Republic of Venice. However, Frizzi's polemical and apologetic insistence on the Jewish capacity for integration, demonstrated precisely by the many productive and useful economic activities they engaged in, somewhat paradoxically slips into acceptance of D'Arco's criticisms of the community's jurisdictional autonomy, [31] demonstrating that even within the Jewish world the concept of a closed community group was beginning to decline. Thus, another important and difficult issue was introduced into the controversy between D'Arco and Frizzi, both adherents of the new ideas, albeit in different ways. It was the wholly modern problem of the relationships between individuals and bodies, the particular and the universal, that was hidden behind the accusation directed at Jews of constituting a separate body, a State within the State. This was an idea that would have extraordinary fortune and diffusion in the following centuries, until the 1900s, [32] but which was already acutely perceived as a crucial question by the most attuned intellectuals, Jewish or not, even before the French Revolution exposed it in all its dramatic clarity.

Individuals and Bodies. The Beginning of the End of the Community

Another delicate issue emerges, in fact, from the debates of that era. In addition to the conflict that pitted the States against the communities, there was also conflict between the Jewish community itself and its individual members, as the story of Benedetto Frizzi demonstrates. At that time each Jewish *Università* was defined by the civil and religious authorities as a "body" (*Universitas Iudaeorum*). Likewise, in 1798, the Venetian government did not recognize individuals for taxation, but only the *Università* as a body.[33] The character that made the Jewish "nation" one of the constituent bodies of the State had in the past strengthened the powers and the authority of the community leaders, because of their administrative functions and role in mediation with the governments as well as in maintaining internal cohesion; now, it was thrown into crisis, externally and internally.

In fact, this character also constituted one of the strongest elements of political criticism aimed at the Jews by Enlightenment culture until the French Revolution: that is, the criticism and accusation of wanting to continue in their particular status as a corporate group and not be dissolved in the great Nation. The widespread concept and traditional term of a Jewish "nation" used by Simone Luzzatto in the 1600s was fiercely opposed by the political culture of the century of the Enlightenment, on the grounds that it indicated the kind of State within a State that they wanted to eliminate. This had to be done in the name of the equality of all citizens and the abolition of particular bodies, and the Jews were accused of instead wanting to maintain that status. This, in fact, was the issue that Giovanni Battista Gherardo

D'Arco also addressed at the end of the 18th century in his discussion, albeit favorable (but with certain conditions), of the emancipation of the Jews. As we have seen, in D'Arco's writing the communities were attacked on the political level precisely as separate bodies, perceived as threateningly standing against the State, in particular because of their administrative and jurisdictional autonomy. This perception was not too different from the one that generally concerned all the particularisms and autonomies in society that conflicted with the project of centralization of power and administrative unification being pursued by enlightened absolutism: starting, for example, with the trade guilds and brotherhoods. However, as we will see better ahead, in the specific case of the Jews, the universal principle of equality and the push for assimilation translated to the renunciation of a different identity and the right to that difference, which was in clear conflict with Enlightenment principles. In these same years, and once again in relation to the modernizing reforms of the State, an element which until then had been a natural fact – the community structure – came to be seen by the majority society as a negative element to be repudiated. This rejection, once it was also applied to the Jews, would give life to one of the most successful and durable anti-Jewish stereotypes: that of wanting to continue to exist as a separate group.

The accusations of separateness and lack of patriotism ("the body of Jews [...] regards with indifference a country where they possess nothing that can attach them here, [...] whose members always make common cause")[34] were made at precisely the time when the idea of granting the Jews rights of citizenship took shape. In response, even the most open representatives of the communities and the Jewish Enlightenment, such as the Morpurgos or Benedetto Frizzi, pushed not only towards confederative solutions and the centralized systems of the Italian communities – just as would happen in Revolutionary and Napoleonic France, albeit with difficulty – but especially in the direction of moving beyond any idea of an autonomous nation and a closed body, and towards greater attention to the individual. In 1787, the Morpurgo family, on the subject of the charges of usury, reminded the Habsburg government that "in this philosophical and enlightened century one does not attribute the defects of the individuals to a group and even less to an entire nation".[35]

The tendencies of the Jews who were closer to Enlightenment ideas, and more ready to welcome the new cultural climate and smooth over the closure of the group with a focus more on individuals than on the community, which as we saw in the marriage story of Benedetto Frizzi, often provoked serious internal conflicts, revealing the transformations and tensions that were also happening within the Jewish organization. The new ideas exalted differences, social contradictions and breaks of solidarity, and weakened the traditional vision of the sacredness of the community. A change of mentality was also taking place within the Jewish world, though slowly, regarding the relationship of individual/body. The divisions this provoked are reflected by the internal contradictions that emerge from many documents of the era. Clearly appearing in these documents are claims of the role, rights and also responsibilities of individuals, as opposed to the long-defended traditional system of the community, understood as an entity with a moral personality. In particular, this change extended to the level of taxation and criminal liability, so now it was claimed that the *Università* and its leaders no longer had to answer jointly, that is, personally, as was customary, for the failures of individual members, for example regarding the collection of taxes.

The body – as, for example, the Roman Jews asserted in the *Memoriale* of 1789 cited above,[36] which we will examine more closely ahead – did not have to assume legal responsibility for the free individuals who were its constituents: no more, at least, than a father towards his sons. The call to redefine the nomination and responsibilities of the community leaders, the criticisms aimed at the responsibilities and duties of the office of *fattore*, which was mandatory, the autonomy and fiscal separation, and the responsibility of the *Università in solidum* to the Roman Apostolic Camera; all of these meant questioning the *Università* as a moral and collective entity and constituent body, as well as its solidarity structure, in the name of the individualism and abstract equality of its members. All of this reveals to us a change in mindset that resonates with the new times.[37] But we will see this better further on.

In fact, before the question of the individual/community polarity became explosive in the revolutionary period, the unequal and solidarity-based, corporate style approach to the general overall structure of society dominated in the age of the Old Regime until the eve of the Revolution. The Jewish communities had full rights in this, belonging to a context of hyper-localism and widespread particularities, in which the gap between the project of strengthening the State and a general system of bodies, "nations" and "states" did not always imply antagonism and opposition to political centralization, as is generally believed, but often appeared complementary to the goals of the modern absolute States.[38] Until the end of the Old Regime, the omnipresent form of social organization and, at the same time, of self-representation in traditional society was that of a city made up of bodies and communities. Associative and collective forms of organization – legally recognized and endowed with autonomy and privileges in exchange for functions and services – were widespread, and extended well beyond the particular and better known case of the trade guilds to all sorts of organic communities, including Jewish ones. Within a vision of an extensively incorporated world, in which all social behaviors and relationships were mediated by these organizational structures, individuals did not exist other than within these communities.

Each Jewish *Università* was fully part of the social organization that was divided into bodies and communities, an organizing principle that only slowly began to enter into conflict with the modernizing State. Endowed with jurisdictional and administrative autonomy, regulated by *Capitoli*, authorized to nominate their own representatives and to enjoy monopolies or permanent concessions such as the provision of beds for soldiers in Rome, or managing the lending banks in Venice, they turned out to be independent and active social and political actors, able to enter into a dynamic relationship of continuous bargaining with the State and other bodies, manipulating the regulatory and relational context for their own ends. It was an activity of negotiation and mediation that could reshape spaces, control resources, and open significant gaps even within the restrictive and segregationist legal regime. On the other hand, from the point of view of the States, making concessions to the *Università* of the Jews meant containing and encroaching on the power of the trade guilds – as D'Arco had well understood when, for example, he proposed permitting Jews to engage in crafts businesses. Hannah Arendt has clearly outlined the importance and advantages of relations with the modern absolute State for the history of the Jews, emphasizing, however, the privileges obtained by single individuals at the expense of the rest of the people.[39] But that was not exactly the case. In reality, the Jews regularly engaged with the state authorities precisely as a body, extracting concessions and recognitions that, even when they were directed at individuals, extended to the group, enhancing the entire community and guaranteeing spaces of autonomy.

This tendency of the Jews in the diaspora to build vertical and direct alliances with the spheres of power has led historian Yosef Hayim Yerushalmi to highlight not only the non-passivity of the Jews but also their age old political tradition and rational political action, which had not been considered for a long time.[40] This is what happened, for example, in the case of Mosè Coen, a merchant-banker from Ferrara who was rewarded for the procurement and supply of grain to Rome and the Papal States during the serious famine of 1764, not only with commensurate personal compensation but also with declarations of public esteem and recognition from the secretary of State. Such recognitions, widely advertised and talked about by the recipient, served not only as evidence of the direct relationship that the most important Jews had with the government but were also used by the latter to negotiate on behalf of the entire group.[41] What's more, the *Università* reached the point of actually initiating legal actions against those very governing authorities; this happened in Ancona, Padua, and in Rome. Thus, there was a centuries-old Jewish political tradition of the "royal alliance", which would come to a definitive end with the "betrayal" and the trauma of the Shoah.[42] However, as we will see better, the moment that when the breaking of the pact of alliance with the central powers begins takes place in the revolutionary era, when the transformation of the Jews from subjects to citizens set up a conflict between individual identity and group identity.

On the other hand, still looking within the guild system, the documentary sources again allow us to ascertain how wide the gap was between legal restrictions and real practices, and the extent to which the rules themselves, which were not absolute systems of reference, were constantly changed by the authorities. For the Jews, just as for other subjects of States of the Old

Regime, the gaps in these normative systems allowed groups and individuals to bring their own strategies to bear, which in turn could modify and condition the forms of power. This is also evident when considering the Roman reality and that of the Papal States, that is, in the situation considered the most difficult and critical for the Jews, given the direct contact with the papacy. Prohibitions were routinely ignored, such as those on locating homes or storage units outside the ghetto, on employing Christian servants or workers, on not wearing the yellow sign, and even those on purchasing real estate and maintaining a partnership or co-ownership with Christians and converts. Obviously, this took place primarily among the wealthiest and most influential Jews, both before and after these measures were reiterated and hardened by the edict of Pius VI in 1775. Likewise, the prohibition on practicing liberal professions or trades that were not "the art of *stracceria*", prescribed by Paul IV's bull *Cum nimis absurdum* of 1555 and repeatedly confirmed afterwards, was also broadly circumvented well before emancipation. In any case, the Jews ably managed to exploit all sectors connected with the branch of used goods, which was an essential part of Old Regime society. The body of Jews thus entered into contact with the closest Christian guilds, mostly conflictual but not always losing, over the issue of professions, as well as the issue of geographic location in the urban spaces adjacent to the ghetto: such as the fish sellers, tanners, second-hand dealers, goldsmiths, and the butchers in Rome. These contentious relations, however, did not preclude personal relationships between members of the two groups.

The numerous legal disputes opened between the *Università* of the Jews and the Christian trade guilds clearly demonstrate how, despite the repeated attempts of Christian merchants to stop what were regular practices – such as, for example, the use of storage units and shops outside the ghetto by Jewish merchants – their demands were frequently dismissed. The Jews, however, just as frequently obtained licenses from the governing authorities not only for practicing the junk dealer trade (*rigattiere*) but also for all the other trades, excluding those having to do with food. The rich documentation we have about this conflict shows how the Jewish communities were used by state authorities to curtail the role or influence of the trade guilds, and to try to open up a more free market. It also reveals how the expansion of disputed economic spaces reached into the most important productive sectors, such as textile manufacturing. In addition to the well-known case of the silk industry in Padua, which was dominated by Jews until the Christian guilds won back the monopoly in 1779,[43] a government investigation in Rome in 1796 revealed that of 38 private wool "producers", seven of them were Jews.[44] Here too, the Christian merchants reacted violently. Not hesitating to resort to evoking ancient fears based on the connection of Jews and disease, they accused their competitors of working with and selling wool, covers, and mattresses that were infected because they came from the tuberculosis hospital, and thus of exposing the Christian population to disease. These accusations, though, did not achieve any substantial outcome. Similarly, the dispute that the druggists' and spice merchants' guilds was constantly engaged in against Jewish merchants of spices and medicinal substances, who they accused of poisoning Christians by manipulating the substances, went unheard by the authorities for a long time. Consequently, at least until the new anti-Jewish provisions adopted by Leo XII in 1824–25, Jewish commercial and productive activity outside the ghetto and partnerships with Christians remained a constant, even in Rome.[45]

So, participation in economic and productive activities and the assimilationist role of money led to a series of privileges and concessions that deviated from the prohibitions, including the traditional ban on owning or administering lands – as, for example, happened mid-century in the Mantovano – or even the prohibition on the ownership of real estate.[46] The evolution of *jus hazakah*, the right of perpetual residence that regulated the rental of homes in the ghettos, also moved towards the trend of individualization of ownership. It was a process – completely analogous with the contemporary transformation of other rights of use that were widespread in the Christian world – which would lead to the recognition of the full ownership of things and to total enfranchisement. Like other transformations, however, this produced further tensions in the communities.[47]

Integration with the local elites also happened through forms of recognition or relations that were not economic: from access to titles of nobility, especially for converts, but also for Jews themselves, to official honorifics and recognitions, membership in associations, such as Freemasonry (as happened in Livorno)[48] and participation in other expressions of elite sociability, such as frequenting theaters. A decline in endogamic marriages, that is, marriage contracts within a closed familial group, also contributed. Jews adopted some of the typical mechanisms used by gentiles for the conservation of status, such as establishing a trustee for real estate assets (*fidecommisso*), offering a further example of economic and social integration through money and assimilation of the behaviors of the majority society. Many deeds of this type were drawn up for wealthy Jews in Livorno from the end of the 17th century through the 18th century, although this was late with respect to a practice that had already begun to decline in the majority society, and had become the object of criticism.[49] A similar characteristic of assimilation with the external society involved the general practice of excluding female children from inheritance, subject to liquidation of the dowry, which was always substantial, while the male children inherited in equal parts.[50] This was a patrilineal practice that greatly conflicted with a fundamental element of the Jewish tradition, that is, the transmission of Jewish identity through the female, as well as the traditional, and anything but subordinate, role of women in families.

The *Università* of the Jews, therefore, moved flexibly within the corporate society of the Old Regime and followed its fate. Jews tried, with their own strategies, to insert themselves into the spaces of the system, and entered into a direct bargaining relationship both with state authorities and with other corporate groups; in any case, they asked to be treated as a body and claimed the exercise of certain rights they had acquired. On the other hand, however, at the end of the century and the beginning of the sunset of the traditional corporate organization, many Jews also began to reject this system, preferring a loosening of the boundaries and controls of the communities, and called for the recognition of individual rights, equal to other subjects and couched in a claim of the universality of the law. At this point, each member of the communities would have to play his own game alone, outside the material and psychological securities offered by the Jewish *Università*. As a result, the conflicts within the *Università* would be made more explosive but also clearer.

Notes

1 Wachtel, *Entre Moïse et Jésus*, 40.
2 Caffiero, *Battesimi forzati*; *Forced Baptisms*; *Legami pericolosi*.
3 Rovira Bonet, *Ristretto della vita*.
4 Caffiero, *Forced Baptisms*, 44–72.
5 Caffiero, *Legami pericolosi*, 331–61.
6 *Memoriale* of 1789.
7 The large changes induced in European Jewish communities starting from 1770 are a focus of the volume by Katz, *Out of the Ghetto*.
8 See Milano, *Storia degli ebrei in Italia*, which combines in a single "age of oppression" all of the 17th and 18th centuries. A similar assessment is found in De Felice, "Per una storia," 352. More recently, Israel, *Gli ebrei d'Europa*, 294–5 and 309 has also inserted Italian Judaism in the phase of demographic, economic, and cultural decay and impoverishment that the 18th century signaled for all of European Judaism. I do not share the thesis of the long decline of Italian Judaism.
9 Allegra, "L'antisemitismo come risorsa politica," 867–99.
10 Cristellon, "Borach Levi," 111–27, with a rich bibliography.
11 Dubin, "Les liaisons dangereuses," 1139–70; *The Port Jews of Habsburg Trieste*.
12 On Trieste and Gorizia, cfr. Ioly Zorattini, *Gli ebrei a Gorizia*; Dubin, *The Port Jews of Habsburg Trieste*; and more recently Gatti, *Tra demografia e storia sociale*.
13 Del Bianco Cotrozzi, "Tolleranza giuseppina," 715–25.
14 Regarding the debate relative to the evolution of Jewish historiography, see Chapter 6, p. 33 and note 60, with reference to the different theses of Yerushalmi and Bonfil.
15 Del Bianco Cotrozzi, "Un incontro fra letterati," 35–64.
16 Bregoli, "Hebrew Printing," 171–95; "L'editoria ebraica," 117–36.
17 Nissim, "Modernità di vedute," 279–91; Ceccone, "Frizzi, Benedetto," 579–81. Now see Brignani and Bertolotti, *Benedetto Frizzi*; Dubin, "Medicine as Enlightenment cure," 201–21. We still lack a complete biography on Frizzi.
18 Dubin, "Les liaisons dangereuses".
19 Luzzatto Voghera, *Il prezzo dell'eguaglianza*, 135–6.
20 Luzzatto Voghera, *Il prezzo dell'eguaglianza*, 134.
21 Balsamo, "Editoria e biblioteche," 505–31; "Gli ebrei nell'editoria," 49–65.
22 Katz, *Tradition and Crisis*.

23 For a picture of these positions, cfr. Malkiel, "Ebraismo, tradizione e società," 9–10.
24 AA.VV., "Rabbini e maestri".
25 Malkiel, "Ebraismo, tradizione e società," 9–42.
26 Malkiel, "Ebraismo, tradizione e società," 42.
27 Cfr. Caffiero, *La nuova era.*
28 Mori, "Lo Stato e gli ebrei mantovani," 224 ss.
29 Caffiero, "Tra Chiesa e Stato," 1113–4.
30 Cfr. here Ch. 6.
31 On the D'Arco-Frizzi controversy, cfr. Nissim, "Modernità di vedute," 282–3; Luzzatto Voghera, *Il prezzo dell'eguaglianza*, 45–8.
32 Regarding this accusation, cfr. Katz, *Out of the Ghetto*, 99.
33 Berengo, "Gli ebrei veneziani," 14. Simone Luzzatto also used the metaphor of the body in 1638: Luzzatto, "Discorso circa lo Stato degli Hebrei," 14 and 27.
34 *Efemeridi letterarie di Roma.*
35 Del Bianco Cotrozzi, "Tolleranza giuseppina," 726.
36 Pagina da definire
37 On the *Memoriale* from the Jews to the pope in 1789, see Caffiero, *Legami pericolosi*, 331–61.
38 On the role of bodies in the functioning of the State in the Old Regime even at the cusp of the Revolution, and on the substantial solidarity that linked the absolute State and the bodies, cfr. Revel, "Les corps et communautés," 225–42.
39 Arendt, *Le origini del totalitarismo*, especially Ch. 2.
40 Yerushalmi, *Servitori di re.*
41 Angelini, *Gli ebrei di Ferrara*, 170 and 311. The correspondence between Coen and the Secretary of State, Cardinal Torrigiani, is transcribed and used in the Roman *Memoriale* of 1789 written on behalf of the community.
42 Yerushalmi, *Servitori di re*, 60.
43 Castelbolognesi, "Gli ebrei di Padova," 149–56. Conflicts with the corporations are documented also for Piedmont, Venice and Rome: cfr. Segre, "Gli ebrei piemontesi," 73; Berengo, "Gli ebrei veneziani," 13–16.
44 Parisi, "Mercanti e lavoranti della lana," 77.
45 Caffiero, "Le botteghe degli ebrei," 273–92; *Legami pericolosi*, 296–330.
46 In 1767, the Coen family's Mantuan company rented the fief of Virgiliana, introducing agricultural innovations and increasing revenue. B. Frizzi, in his writing against D'Arco, also spoke of Jewish land ownership in the Mantovano and in Emilia: regarding Rome, various documents state that for all of the 1700s Jews owned real estate outside the ghetto "fraudulently".
47 Laras, "Intorno al 'ius cazacà'," 44–55.
48 Regarding adherence to Masonry as a rite of passage for Jews into modern society, cfr. Katz, *Jews and Freemasons in Europe.*
49 Frattarelli Fischer, "Proprietà e insediamento ebraici".
50 Allegra, "Modelli di conversione," 91; Bonazzoli, "Sulla struttura familiare," 144.

8 The Contradictions of the "Happy Regeneration" of the Jews

The 1789 of the Italian Jews

The clearest confirmation of the new atmosphere that was penetrating the ghettos came from the Roman community, which in 1789 addressed a bold and provocative *Memoriale* to the then reigning pontiff, Pius VI. This was a pope who had issued a very harsh edict against the Jews just after he was elected in 1775, in which he reiterated and reinforced the restrictive provisions imposed two centuries earlier by the bull *Cum nimis absurdum* of 1555. The decree was repeated in 1793, not by chance at the height of the revolutionary climate. Very sensitive political and ideological issues relative to the relationship between the popes and the Jews, as well as the latter's role in the majority society, were addressed for the first time through the detailed and reasoned writing of the *Memoriale*. These subjects were discussed from a completely new perspective, one which referred to the debate regarding the Jewish question taking place in Europe. The document is also important because through it we can observe how, in that fateful year of 1789, the language of modernity and the claims of rights and equality had already been appropriated by the Roman Jews, well before the revolutionary wave that would recognize the rights of citizenship and political and civil emancipation even for the Jewish world extended into Italy and Rome itself. Which is to say, appropriated by a community that historians have long considered – wrongly – among the most backwards in Italy, the victim of a process of economic decline and cultural poverty that, according to some, would accentuate between the 17th and 18th centuries, but which in reality can be verified only much later, in the 19th century. In fact, the *Memoriale*, through the rhetoric of its argumentation and the demands it makes in the name of rights, first and foremost suggests a relationship with the papal authorities that is freer and more unscrupulous than expected, at times even audacious and disrespectful; however, it is also the echo of a climate, internal and external to the community, that announces new times.[1]

The Roman Jews advanced their claims in the very heart of the Catholic world, which just a few years later would become the bulwark of reaction and opposition against the principles of the Revolution, and therefore also

DOI: 10.4324/9781003188445-12

against the Jews who had benefitted from those principles. Those claims, grounded in arguments of justice and equality, deserve to be highlighted for their scope. The lexicon of the Enlightenment and the Revolution had also entered the walls of the ghettos. The authors of the *Memoriale* invoked "beautiful, natural liberty, still common to the Brutes".[2] This was the claim of natural law, universal and equal for all men, that the new cultural climate applied to the Jews as well, and which they used by adopting daring words that evoked the contemporary and dangerous language of liberty and equality.

The new ideas had therefore penetrated the ghettos, in addition to the Catholic society of the Papal States and the other Italian States, preparing the Jewish world to fully enter the forms and language of the new politics and confront profound transformations. The keywords of Enlightenment rhetoric and culture – citizenship, justice, equality – also resonated within the "cloisters" of the Jews, not without conflicts internally and with the outside. These contradictions and paradoxes of the revolutionary age, and the subsequent emancipation of the Jews, will fully explode in tensions between universalism and diversity, assimilation and Jewish identity, with disruptive results for future decades.[3]

The new egalitarian ideas, which were hostile to any form of particularism, privilege, and autonomy, all of which were considered to be feudal remnants by the new political thinking, in parallel with the tensions and internal conflicts prompted by the transformations of modernity, threw the community system that governed the Jewish world in Italy into crisis at the end of the century.[4] In particular, the social, economic, and cultural differentiation within the ghetto produced tensions that damaged its unity and cohesion. In the community of Ancona in 1785, in a scenario of great conflict which was defined as a genuine "class struggle", the heads of poor Jewish families, protesting increases in rent and reduction of living spaces, opposed the wealthy Coen, Morpurgo, and Fermi families who monopolized the housing market.[5] For their part, the property owners accused the protesters of being "sick subversives", thus anticipating the extension of the social conflict to the political sphere that soon, in the revolutionary phase, would also take place in the ghettos.

For example, throughout the century in Rome criminal complaints were filed continuously, revealing a high degree of internal conflict and combativeness. Starting especially with the 1780s, there were persistent grievances presented to the Roman religious and civil authorities against the *fattori*. These mainly concerned matters of taxation, and were aimed at winning exemptions by external means from paying the taxes established by the heads of the community. On the opposite side, however, the *fattori* also turned to the same Christian authorities to punish members of the community that did not obey their orders. In Ferrara, in the second half of the 18th century, the *Massaria,* the institution of Jewish government, was often involved in internal disputes and arguments indicative of great disruption. As we saw earlier in the story of Benedetto Frizzi, the conflicts in Trieste were also quite significant.

Community office holders such as the *fattori* and *massari*, who already found themselves in the difficult position of being mediators/managers between the ghetto and the civil and ecclesiastic authorities, now became the owners of an oligarchic monopoly over increasingly contested leadership functions within their communities. They were seen as less and less credible and authoritative mediators with the state powers, and sometimes even as enemies, as demonstrated by the appeals sent by Jewish leaders to the Christian powers, who they regarded as an effective resource against disobedient and recalcitrant coreligionists. On the other hand, exemptions and privileges of not wearing the yellow sign, granted to only the most influential and wealthy families of notables like Coen in Ferrara, or Ascarelli in Rome, exposed wealthy and privileged Jews to the envy and malice of the others. The questioning of these old internal balances and a long-standing stability, and the impossibility of being able to channel the conflicts and tensions as in the past, can be seen in two related developments. First, there was the repeated issuance of sumptuary laws against the exhibition of wealth by the most affluent Jews, aimed at appeasing the hostility of the Christians as much as that of poor Jews themselves. Second, efforts were made to break up the monopolies of some of the Jewish confraternities that were held by a restricted elite.[6] These efforts illustrate how, similar to what took place in the Christian world, the confraternities were losing their traditional social-political function of calming tensions between groups and re-establishing social balance and unity.

In reality, the communities expressed internal hierarchies and conflicts that corresponded to now diversified interests and a loss of role. The community and corporate ideology was only theoretically that of equality, solidarity and fraternity, but it also effectively concealed, in addition to intergenerational conflicts, concrete hierarchical and well differentiated relationships, especially on the economic level. In the case of the Jewish communities, the asymmetrical relationships were underlined by the fact that the restricted leadership group of the *Università* was selected based on census criteria. Looking at the concentration of Jewish wealth in Venice, just six families held more than 57% of taxable assets in 1801; the data in Rome are similar, where in the 1780s, just five families possessed almost half of all the assets declared by the community. In Livorno at mid-century, twenty-eight families, who possessed half of all the real estate assets, hegemonized the government of the nation.[7] These are contradictions which the age of Revolution and emancipation will bring to an explosive head.

The gap between the egalitarian representation of the body's ideology and its actual hierarchical and oligarchical function resoundingly emerges with the crisis at the end of the century – turning the Jewish *Università* in almost every community into the scene of conflicts over the management of common affairs, especially in the council bodies. This reflected the devaluation and often the de-legitimization of the leadership's roles as social and political mediators, clearly confirming how the Jewish associative forms, like all the other bodies, also became occasions and places for sociability and a true political apprenticeship, which prepared the Jewish world to fully enter into the forms and languages of politics. There are numerous indicative cases: from the conflicts between rich and poor and those between the leadership and the people which cropped up in Casale in 1797 on the occasion of the new division of tax burdens, as well as in Venice, in the same year and for similar reasons; there is the complaint against the "despotic" government of the *massari* made the previous year in Livorno; and finally the unrest in Rome on the occasion of the *Purim* holiday, also in 1796, which expressed a strong popular and youth opposition to the *fattori*, who were once again forced to turn to the papal authorities against the rebels, in doing so only increasing the hostility towards themselves.[8]

In these episodes, the idea of the tyranny of a restricted group of notables who were almost "naturally" deputized to government thanks to their traditional social and economic role was contrasted with the vision of "democratic" representation, expressed by the community as a whole. In addition to social conflict, this opposition reveals a political language that appears in the arguments, the vocabulary, and the forms of debate that developed in the contemporary dominant society. Thus, the lexicon of revolutionary discourse, with terms such as democracy, virtue, citizenship, liberty, equality, and regeneration openly echoed within the demolished walls of the ghettos, exposing not only how the two cultures and societies were not strangers to each other but also the greater ability of the Italian communities – compared, for example, to those of the French in the East[9] – to make the idioms and images of the Enlightenment and of the Revolution their own, transferring them within their own tradition. It is a process of political acculturation that, for example, in Venice leads to democratization of the procedures and governing bodies of the community and conflict between the new individualism and traditional forms of government.[10] The coercive power of the community bodies to control the religious and civil behavior of individuals, for example through the traditional punishment of excommunication, no longer seems a natural fact but rather an anomaly to be eliminated: and the element which seems most noteworthy is that the pressure in this sense seems to come from below more than from the elite.

Jewish Citizens Confront the Revolution

The revolutionary period, with its radicalization of external as well as internal conflicts, also represents an important phase for understanding the different levels of Italian Jewish involvement in the new politics, and above all the cultural reactions set in motion in the face of this later and upsetting phase of modernity. For example, and as we will see better further ahead, these reactions corresponded to attempts to understand the new and disruptive events by placing them within well-known and reassuring traditional cultural and interpretive categories.

The three years of the republican period in Italy (1796–99) introduced great changes, and in particular sanctioned emancipation through the acquisition of full citizenship and political and civil rights. The process, however, was not without repercussions, both internal and external to the community. On one hand, as we have seen, the revolutionary period exacerbated internal conflicts, creating a crisis in the community system that had governed the Jewish world for centuries, a system which had already been weakened. Social rivalries and differences became more pronounced, while challenges to the oligarchies that monopolized community offices and control grew increasingly frequent. On the other hand, outside in Christian society, the rights acquired by the Jews and the equality they obtained led even the revolutionary ruling classes, though they were the authors of Jewish emancipation, to criticize the organizational autonomy of the communities, which were now seen as separate bodies that had to be dissolved into the new, united Nation. However, and most importantly, the acquisition of full citizenship by the Jews aroused the hostility and resistance of a large part of the small population and the Catholic clergy.

Emancipation and the elimination of the civil and political differences between Jews and Christians provoked negative and violent reactions among the latter. These reactions coalesced in a strong popular antisemitism, also the consequence of the link between Jews and Revolution postulated by the widespread Catholic apologetics and propaganda of the day. Rejection of the Jews' new legal and political status, and the need to mark their difference in one of the strongest symbols of equality and citizenship – the republican cockade worn on hats – led Romans, who were hostile to the Jews as much as they were to the French, to add a small crucifix to theirs, marking their difference from the Jews. It was a gesture that signified that "narcissism of small differences" upon which, according to Sigmund Freud's well-known definition, the expression of antisemitism has always been based.[11]

The supposed connection between Jews and the French not only reinforced the nascent stereotype of Jewish responsibility in the outbreak of the Revolution, which would last long into the following centuries, but it also triggered widespread acts of violence against them and attacks on the ghettos. There are numerous episodes to recall: the events of 1790 in Tuscany, when the popular reaction to the enlightened, economic and ecclesiastic reforms of Grand Duke Pietro Leopoldo also involved the Jews of Livorno and Florence, who suffered violence and looting; the assault on the ghetto of Rome, with the attempt to burn it down in 1793, immediately after the French representative, Bassville, was murdered at the hands of an enraged mob; the various attacks against the ghettos – at Fossano, Ancona, Chieri, Venice – which took place during the descent of the French into Italy. The anti-Jewish violence became even more ferocious when the French army withdrew from the peninsula. The communities, left defenseless, became

easy targets for fanaticism and the counter-revolutionary insurgency, en-
during genuine *pogroms* that culminated in the massacres of Senigallia and
Siena, carried out by bands of Sanfedists.[12]

These cases of assaults on the ghettos gave rise to local observances and
religious ceremonies that were modeled after the holiday of *Purim*, meant to
annually commemorate the danger escaped and recall the frequent "mirac-
ulous" interventions that had saved the communities in spite of everything.[13]
The establishment of revolutionary *Purims* demonstrates the way in which
new tragic events were made understandable and acceptable by translating
them into traditional and familiar language, images and culture, and linking
them with the events of the ancient biblical story of Ester. This story, as we
have seen, occupied a very important role in Jewish culture (and fascinated
non-Jews to no small extent as well). Local *Purims* were established this way
in Livorno, Fossano, Ancona, Chieri, Ferrara, Urbino, Pesaro, Senigallia,
Pitigliano, and Ivrea. These revolutionary *Purims*, so frequent and common
during the 1790s, not only express an explicit correspondence with a phase
of serious crisis and acute external dangers that seems to rekindle and rein-
vigorate traditional religious values through the revival of ritual. They also
reveal themselves as mechanisms for dispelling internal tensions and crises, which at least momentarily found channeling and control in the ritual
re-composition of the group's unity.

However, if the revolutionary period also exacerbated internal conflicts,
as we have seen, it has scarcely been noticed that – due to the rhetorical
exaltation of the myths of the Revolution – even within an overall Jewish
adherence to revolutionary principles, Jews did not always and not everywhere, side indiscriminately with the new regimes and new ideas, or harbor
pro-French sentiments, as much of historiography still maintains. Naturally, anti-revolutionary and anti-Jewish propaganda spread the belief in an
obvious alliance between the French and the Jews. This assertion of the
latter's natural seditiousness and anarchy served as a justification for the
violent popular reaction against them, and for invoking the joint intervention of State and Church, which were newly allied against the subversive
revolutionary danger.

In reality, even for this aspect regarding the adherence, or lack thereof,
to the principles of revolutionary government, the different normative situations in which the Jews found themselves influenced their behavior and
their choices, which were further conditioned by the more or less favorable
geopolitical contexts of the disparate local realities in which the Jews were
inserted. At Livorno, for example, where there had never been a ghetto,
and Jews were recognized as citizens with very broad civil and economic
rights acquired over a long time, the interests of the *massari* and many of the
wealthiest members of the community were hurt by the French occupation
and the British blockade of the city port, and they accordingly did not follow the new democratic ideas: only two notables adhered to the new regime,
while many others left the city.[14] This loyalty of Livorno's privileged Jews

to fate of the Old Regime affected public opinion, to the point that even the Catholic-reactionary camp, and therefore not suspect, denounced how only the "dregs of the Jewish people" purported to shake off the yoke of obedience owed to their leaders and "govern themselves in a kind of anarchy".[15] The same anti-French choice can also be found in other areas where Jews already enjoyed a situation that was not negative. At Trieste, where they had long benefitted from various and extensive privileges, the community armed the civic guard against the French, organized a revolt against the occupiers and celebrated the return of the Austrians. At Ferrara, where many criticisms had also been directed at the *massari's* authoritarian system of government, some Jews abstained from voting on the Cispadane Constitution of the Republic in 1797. Even in the ghettos of the Savoy Piedmont, which were quite repressive towards the Jews, there were no great echoes of revolutionary events and ideas, while the elders, in their moderation, did not hesitate to proclaim loyalty to the monarchy.

These facts once again confirm the differentiation which cut through various social groups and classes within the communities, leading to different reactions to the Revolution. The hostility between the poor and the rich, which even before the Revolution was evident in cases of conversion that took place as a result of reaction and protest, or in the frequent conflicts between the people and the leaders, also led to a socially differentiated perception of revolutionary events. This perception was therefore affected not only by the more or less favorable geopolitical situations where individual communities were based, which caused the effects of the introduction of the new regimes to vary widely, but, again, by internal relationships. Another widespread belief turns out to be problematic from this perspective; that is, the conception that adherence to the new ideas was, as in the Christian world, mainly the prerogative of the bourgeois elite rather than of the lower classes.[16]

In any case, beyond broad adherence to the new ideas, which there certainly was, and the perhaps better studied subject of the closer relationships established between Jews and Christians as a consequence of the Revolution, the historiographical problem of the relationship of Italian Jews to events such as the Revolution and then the Napoleonic Empire remains open. This means asking if it is necessarily true, as is asserted in reactionary propaganda, that all Jews *must* unquestionably be "Jacobins". But it also means asking which Jews fully adhered to the new regime, and what their reasons were for this choice, apart from the clear political and economic benefits that derived from emancipation. Furthermore, we must inquire into how they reconciled adherence to the new values and the religion of country with faithfulness to their tradition: a problem which, for example, became clear for members of the military given how difficult it was for them to follow the Jewish holiday calendar. Adhesion to the new regimes, in fact, did not only mean active involvement in general politics and an increasingly close and integrated contact with the non-Jewish world – aspects which, while not completely new, now assumed new forms. It also meant the development of further and broader openness to the modern world, and this could lead to a decline in the observance of religious precepts and ritual prescriptions, or even their transgression. It could also set up a conflict between belonging and loyalty to the new Nation and the effort to maintain a particular identity. In short, it could lead to assimilation.

According to current scholarship, in Italy we do not find rigid positions such as those of the Jews in Holland, who actually declared themselves to be against the right of citizenship, or like those of the Eastern French communities of Metz, Alsace, and Lorena. These communities were reluctant to be absorbed into the Nation and give up the autonomy and special privileges of the community organization, and they only came to accept the new ideas by translating them into the traditional language of biblical republicanism.[17] These differences and difficulties would seem to bear out the thesis of those who have argued that the Jews were more interested in obtaining economic rights and freedoms than political rights and equality.[18] However, it would be interesting to investigate if there was a parallel effort within Italian Judaism, similar to what had started among the Catholic democrats in these decades, aimed at reconciling Revolution and religion, and establishing the compatibility between religion and the modern obligations of citizenship; in short, whether a debate took shape in the Jewish world that reflected the ways in which emancipation was perceived, and how, in addition to its advantages, they were warned of its risks of assimilation and loss of identity. So, for example, the project that proposed dissolving the *Università* of the Jews at Ferrara in 1797 came from groups that mostly tended towards full civic and social integration and appeared to be less conditioned by religious tradition: significantly, however, the proposal was not adopted.[19] On the other hand, there were echoes of uneasiness in places, for example in Rome, where the observance of religious precepts such as rest on the Sabbath or dietary restrictions conflicted with the obligations and demands of participation in political and military life. Even the abolition of the ghettos could arouse opposition and disturbance, as happened in Trieste.

Other partial signs of conflict and widely varying positions towards the revolutionary innovations can be deduced from the discussions carried on within the conciliar bodies of the "Jewish citizens" regarding preservation of the tool of excommunication, traditionally imposed on tax evaders. The debate over this issue that took place at Venice, but also in other places, seems to have juxtaposed two forces. On one hand, there were the secularizing and modern political demands, such as from those who claimed, in the name of "democratic" virtue and honesty, that sanctions must not be religious in nature and that the community could no longer judge the behavior of individuals. On the other hand, the opposing positions of the notables, who wanted to keep religious censure, invoking the "need for a curb against the temptations of interest".[20] Once again, the opposition between the social fronts of the lower classes and the ruling class – which was destined to emerge victorious – not only marked the divergence of material interests, but also merged these motivations with political-religious choices that aligned the former with the innovators and supporters of change, and the latter with tradition.

With the demolition of the ghetto gates, the names that had until then formally marked the diversity and the separation of the Jews also fell. So, in Venice, the Jewish quarter was renamed *Contrada dell'Unione*, and the community leaders saw their titles changed to deputies of the Jewish citizens. In Ferrara, the old terminology was also erased: *Università degli ebrei*, *massari*, ghetto. On the other hand, the discourses inspired by brotherhood, philanthropy, and universal tolerance announced a "happy regeneration" for the Jews as well as for Christians. They delineated, in openly millennial tones that were not unfamiliar to either group, especially in those decades, a redefinition of religious membership within a common foundation and a tendency towards the dilution of theological and even ritual differences.[21] However, beyond the utopian and short-lived illusion of unity and brotherhood between Jews and Christians, there remains the problem of the extent to which the short democratic and emancipatory interlude contributed to the explosion of the community system. This system had already been in crisis for some time, under pressure from the new ideas because of its bias towards interests of the few and the anachronism of its governing bodies. At the end of the revolutionary period and the Napoleonic era, and despite the efforts at re-composition, this system would not be the same, and would never be the same again.

The Myth of Napoleon

The difficulties in combining innovation with tradition, and the ambiguities of an emancipation/equality that was granted implicitly at the cost of renouncing diversity and the autonomy of the community organization became much more pronounced during the phase of Napoleon's direct domination of Italy. This period also had a strong impact on the community fabric. The Constitutions of the various Italian Republics extended the rights of civil and political citizenship to the Jews, even though their decrees relative to the problem of religion and the freedom of worship differed. However, the Napoleonic rules, which were conditioned by the new regime imposed by the concordat stipulated with Rome and the pope in 1801, turn out to be much more ambiguous, and above all decisively aimed at assimilation. This is demonstrated, for example, by the Constitution of the Italian Republic, then the Kingdom of Italy, which only granted the private practice of worship, as well as by the subsequent restrictive legislation regarding Jewish economic activity and full civil equality issued with the decree of March 17, 1808 which was called "infamous", but which also contemplated broad exceptions regarding Italy.[22]

The elusive Napoleonic policy, significantly influenced by 18th-century anti-Jewish stereotypes, especially those regarding economic matters and the obsessively present subject of usury, was aimed at pushing in the direction of assimilation by granting an incomplete emancipation. This accentuated the tensions within the communities, which particularly manifested in connection with the sensational gathering in Paris, in February 1807, of a Great Sanhedrin of Jews from the Empire and the Kingdom of Italy. This was preceded the year before by a general assembly of 111 notables from the Empire, from which the government had requested precise positions on various delicate subjects, especially those of mixed marriages and usury. The Great Sanhedrin had a more religious character, as indicated by the title itself, which revived that of the ancient court of Israel, as well as the fact that rabbis predominated among the seventy-one members.

The existing conflict between the two components, rabbis and notables, also became evident among the Italians.[23] In addition to ratifying the State's supremacy in marriage law with a distinction between a religious ceremony and the civil one, which still had to precede the former, the Sanhedrin was called on by the Emperor to address the issue of loyalty to the government and its laws, based on the ambiguous philosophy of "regeneration" which was to guide and condition the process of emancipation. This process, in fact, was subordinate to a series of transformations begun by the Jews which had to be reflected on the level of behavior: for example, with the choice of liberal professions, the abandonment of moneylending, and the acquisition of estates that, through their connection to the land, also solidified bonds with the host country.

As is easily understandable, the questions Napoleon posed to the assembly reflected old fears, stereotypes, and prejudices towards the Jews and their relations with civil authorities, fears it was hoped would be resolved with simple legislative decrees. The Sanhedrin assumed a precise political function – that of imposing assimilation on their coreligionists by law, even at the expense of fundamental modifications to the traditional rules of Judaism, as happened, for example, with the dispensation from religious observances for soldiers. In addition, it gave rise to a new general organization for the Jews of the Empire, first because rabbinic authority in the management of the communities was subjected to the power of the top elite, members of the most visible and wealthy families, and second because a decentralized system was inaugurated, based on local religious councils – ten in Italy – that responded to the central one in Paris. The mediation of the local oversight entrusted to the Jewish leaders, rabbis, and notables permitted the most effective state control over the communities, and the possibility of measuring their degree of assimilation, upon which the granting of civil rights was contingent.[24] A significant number of Italians participated in the work, even though not all of the communities sent representatives: neither Livorno nor Rome sent delegates, nor did the majority of the communities of central Italy, while the most important representatives came from the

North of the peninsula, such as Abraham Cologna (1755–1832), a Mantuan rabbi.[25] Notwithstanding the brief duration of the new system, it was these figures who were more inclined to accepting the consequences of the concept of "regeneration" that would influence the process of Italian Judaism's transformation towards the religious and cultural forms that it assumed in the 1800s, assuring the rapid integration and acculturation of the Jewish population.[26]

The limits and ambiguities of the Napoleonic regulations sharpened the tensions between emancipation, assimilation, and Jewish identity that were already evident in the revolutionary phase, and clearly exposed how the universalism of rights and the differences between individuals and groups had not yet been reconciled, with disruptive results for the Jewish world both internally and externally. In addition to this, the Napoleonic regime triggered a complex symbolic process with important future consequences. On one hand, in fact, it created the myth of Napoleonic pro-Judaism, widespread among the Jews themselves; on the other hand, however, in the context of the eschatological speculation and prophetic-apocalyptic tensions nourished in the Catholic world by revolutionary and Napoleonic events, it triggered the explosion of the theme of an anti-Christian plot hatched by a coterie of Jews, Masons, and philosophers, an idea that would play a large role in the revival of antisemitism in the age of Restoration. This led to challenging any right of citizenship for the Jews unless they had first converted. On the political level, for the sovereigns of restored Europe, it also translated into the prospect of a dangerous and solid link between membership in the separate Jewish nation and revolutionary subversion.

Revenge

An event that is emblematic of the extraordinary level of conflict which the revolutionary period triggered between Jews who were partisans of the new regimes and the majority Christian society, which was substantially anti-French and anti-Republican, took place in Rome during the Roman Republic of 1798–99. There was a certain Gioacchino Savelli, *alias* Cimarra, a fish seller who was part of the important fish merchants' trade guild, who was particularly loathed by the Jews. This guild was a corporate group that, in addition to living and working at the gates of the ghetto, in Portico d'Ottavia, was also the organizer of the so-called *giudate*, street theater performances held during Carnival, which took aim at the Jews and their religion.[27] During the Neapolitan occupation between November 27 and December 12, 1798, which briefly interrupted the Republic that had been proclaimed in February of that year, Cimarra, who had previously left Rome, returned to the city under the protection of the Neapolitans and participated in the violent counter-revolutionary actions that took place over the next two weeks: the trees of liberty were burned, the bodies of republican heroes were disinterred and burned, and the Jews were harassed.

Following the return of the French at the beginning of 1799, and with them the restoration of the Republic, Cimarra's body was found in the Roman countryside. The crime was immediately ascribed to the Jews, who actually organized the transportation of the body back to Rome, exhibiting it to the public in a parade that crossed the whole city.

The spectacle of the corpse of the counter-revolutionary Cimarra, a fierce enemy of the ghetto, who was assassinated by wealthy Jewish "Jacobins" from the Ascarelli and Baraffael families and then paraded around the *Urbe* to the sound of tambourines in a sort of macabre victory celebration, might have been sweet revenge for the mistreated Jews. However, this took place just as the end of the Republic and the return of the papacy were approaching.[28] While Christians represented the event like a renewal of the crucifixion of Jesus, which replicated the derisive rites and mockery of the perfidious Jews, the Jews themselves viewed the jubilation and triumph organized around the corpse of their enemy, who was also an enemy of the Republic, as a sort of *Purim*, the celebration instituted by communities to commemorate and celebrate the escape from a grave danger. However, an episode which had displayed and ritually discharged strong accumulated tensions with the external world again led back to conflicts internally which were never completely pacified. In fact, the event deeply divided the Roman Jews, and provoked differing and contrasting reactions. For example, the community leaders and the rabbi, who opposed both the mutilation of the body by the people and their parading of the corpse in the ghetto, sought to avoid further unrest with a decidedly more political option, which was perhaps also due to the fear of the imminent end of the Republic. Thus, the event reveals contrasts and firm internal differences which passed from the ethical and religious plane to that of political choices and the ability to look ahead to the imminent, harsh future of restoration.

Rome 1825. The Anti-Jewish Turn of the Restoration

In 1800 and in 1814–15, the two restorations of the Old Regime governments and papal power led to a radical overturning of the Jews' legal situation almost everywhere on the peninsula, erasing the conquest of civil and political emancipation that had recognized their full citizenship and equality in revolutionary and Napoleonic Europe. And so the gates of the ghettos were closed again. The attitude of the pontiffs particularly influenced the new changes, starting with yet another strict turn in papal policy towards the Jews, which remained a point of reference for at least part of the restored States. This turn was already underway during the pontificate of Pius VII, even before the better known anti-Jewish rigidity of Leo XII. The signs of radical change in the situation of the Jews in Italy can be followed on three levels, connected to each other and constantly intertwining: the first is the hostility of the Catholic population, which was widespread and growing in the wake of the Revolution and Napoleon, events which had been favorable to the Jews; the second involves repressive measures first initiated by the papal government, but then also followed by various other governments; the third element is the revival of Catholic apologetics and propaganda, and the much more general political significance that anti-Judaism was assuming in this phase.[29] Naturally, the desire for conversion and related activities were always present. If the connection between renewed anti-Jewish hostility and the recent events of the French Revolution stands out clearly on all three of these fronts, it also confirms the persistent and repeated close relationship over time between every phase of Catholic re-conquest, ideological reorganization and counterattack by the papacy, and the reigniting of anti-Jewish propaganda, precisely as happened with the phase in progress.

During the pontificate of Leo XII, an anti-modern and zealous pope whose reign saw a strong surge of anti-Jewish policy, the religious and the economic motivations of anti-Judaism were greatly strengthened. The repressive line towards the Jews that was rigorously renewed during the Restoration reflected the papacy's general policy of strenuous opposition to cultural pluralism and the civil rights brought about by the new European culture. Anti-Judaism was just one facet of the Church's confrontational relationship with the modern world that emerged from the Revolution.

The year 1825 in particular represents a central date both for the Catholic world and for the religious and polemical motivations of anti-Judaism. In the first place, it was the year when the first Jubilee of the 1800s was celebrated, after a pause of half a century and the recent religious and political upheavals; it was also to be the last one held in papal Rome. Prepared with particular care by Leo XII, the event was charged with deep symbolic significance relating to the triumph of the Church and the papacy against unbelief, and the "satanic" enemies produced by the modern world and recent political events. However, in connection with the Jubilee, which was meant to celebrate the reorganization of the united and combative Catholic world, the year 1825 is also when the pontiff imagined and even planned a new ghetto for Rome to be built in another part of the city, to which the Jews would be forcibly relocated in order to confine them with greater severity. The "dire consequences" of the freedom they had enjoyed in the preceding decades were explicitly recalled, just as was the urgent need to close the shops located outside the ghetto, though they had existed for a very long time, and to "drive them from the center of the city".[30]

The existence of a very close relationship between these two events, the Jubilee and the hardening of anti-Jewish policy, and the fact that both were aimed at the reaffirmation of the leadership role of religion and the papacy in society and European politics as much as they were at the exaltation of the sacred function of Rome, is demonstrated by the flourishing of violent anti-Jewish publishing, often derived from preaching, which in the mid-1820s accompanied these two developments and referred to them explicitly. In fact, Leo XII, when he was still Annibale Della Genga, a powerful cardinal vicar during the papacy of Pius VII, was the one who decided to reintroduce forced preaching to the Jews. This preaching had been discontinued for several decades due to revolutionary politics ("for the past disgusting events") and had not taken place since then.[31]

In that same year of 1825, a violent booklet entitled *Degli Ebrei nel loro rapporto colle nazioni cristiane* was published; it went through four editions between 1825 and 1826, and numerous subsequent re-printings. It was authored by a Dominican, the Frenchman Ferdinand Jabalot, who was Procurator General of the Order. This booklet represents a cornerstone of and the point of reference for Italian Catholic anti-Judaism for all of the 1800s.[32] All of the traditional anti-Semitic stereotypes were reiterated in it, from then on openly taken up and increasingly strengthened by the reactionary Catholicism of the 19th century: deicide, the greed for enrichment directed at ruining Christians, the ambitions for world domination, the damage caused to morals and customs, the hatred of the Christian religion that extended to the worst barbarianism ("wash your hands in the blood of Christians, set the churches on fire, stomp on the consecrated host, crucify the faithful in hatred of Jesus Christ, kidnap children and slaughter them, violate the virgins who are sacred to God, and abuse the baptized").[33]

Above all, the booklet heavily attacked the moderately pro-Jewish positions of those Catholics who, though also aiming for the conversion of the Jews, had nevertheless supported the emancipationist policies of the secular governments, and saw the so-called Jewish "return" to the true religion, to Catholic Christianity, as a guarantee of the reform and transformation of Christianity itself towards the purity of its origins. It is not by chance that the two most important works of pro-Jewish Catholic millenarianism, those of Manuel de Lacunza and Bernard Lambert, were officially condemned and placed in the *Indice* in these same years, respectively, in September 1824 and March 1825. It is therefore worth taking note of this radical split in the Catholic world towards the Jews, a fracture that was ripe with future developments, and which calls into question the current idea of a homogenous Catholicism that is substantially united on the Jewish question.

However, Jabalot lashed out at the "self-appointed philosophers" who invoked the laws of nature and the principles of good policy in favor of the Jews and human rights and touted the advantages that society would gain from their emancipation, and he attacked the exponents of masonic philanthropy, who were also committed to protection of the Jews. In this way, the idea of a Jewish-philosophical-Masonic conspiracy was made explicit, and would become a fundamental element of reactionary Catholicism for all of the 19th century and part of the 20th. The Dominican also criticizes the argument made by 18th-century philosophers and reformers such as Giovanni Battista Gherardo D'Arco, later taken up by liberals like Carlo Cattaneo in the 19th century, according to which emancipation of the Jews would be sufficient in order to achieve reform of their customs and their assimilation into the majority society, in other words, their "regeneration". Jabalot instead interpreted the miserable condition of the Jews simply as the consequence of divine punishment and curse. Hence, political emancipation could never have come before, much less brought about a change in the customs of the Jews and made them citizens like the others, regenerating them, if it was not preceded by conversion.

Jabalot's explanation for why Jews as such could not be granted the right of citizenship was their "natural" and age-old propensity for manifesting their hatred for Christians in open revolt, political turbulence, and in alliances with the enemies of the State which hosted them. Perhaps, European rulers believed – the Dominican asked rhetorically – "that such a people could ever be a people of obedient and peaceful citizens with affection for the country in which they were born, and for the fellow citizens with whom they live?".[34] The Jews considered themselves foreigners, even slaves, in the countries where they lived, and aspired only to overturning their slavery into dominion. However, continued Jabalot, their constant enrichment at the expense of Christians and insatiable greed for goods were no more than the basis for achieving power and world rule. The antisocial character of the Jews, the fact that they considered themselves a separate nation apart, and their dangerous and subversive form as a State within a State necessarily placed them, therefore, outside the sphere of civil and political rights.

As we have seen, Jewish membership in a separate "nation" was the most widespread accusation in the context of anti-Jewish prejudice, one also shared by the secular circles of the Enlightenment. The accusation was destined to gain force later, when the idea of nation and country begin to clash with the collective identity of the Jews.[35] Thus, concluded Jabalot, reiterating the argument that saw emancipation as preceding "regeneration", the sole path to emancipation for the Jews was the total abandonment of their identity and their total integration within the various European countries, which itself could only take place through conversion: "Ceasing to belong to their nation and incorporating themselves to ours, professing our religion, and they would immediately enjoy the rights of nationals".[36] Thus, "regeneration", understood as conversion and total assimilation, had to take place first, and only afterwards could civil and political emancipation be granted. It should be recalled that Jabalot's writing was taken up almost verbatim many years later by the anonymous, violent anti-Jewish pamphlet entitled *Che cosa sono gli ebrei? Lettera d'un cittadino romano al Sig. Salvadori*, published in Rome in 1873, written in opposition to allowing the membership of the Jewish nation to join the Italian Nation. This reprise of the Dominican's traditionalist and backwards arguments is a sign of the importance and the continuity of reactionary Catholic theories on the subject of nation, especially since the anonymous pamphlet came out in precisely the year that a famous controversy broke out over the question of if a Jew, even an assimilated Jew, could become a Minister of the Kingdom of Italy.[37]

During the Restoration, the status of the Jews became less and less secure, even on the level of professions and trades. Economic freedom, which
seemed to have been acquired long ago in many localities, even before the
events of the revolution, began to be strained again. It was obvious that the
permanent residence of Jews in areas without a ghetto, which became possible after emancipation, would no longer be tolerated, especially in Rome
and the Papal States. This radical rearrangement of the Jewish businesses
and shops that were part of the fabric of the territory upended a framework that had been acquired over the years of tolerance and permission
during the time of the Republic and the Napoleonic Empire. It also included
an injunction requiring all Jews who for purposes of trade had moved to
Rome "from outside the State", and vice-versa from Rome to the provinces,
to return to their place of origin. Therefore, the Jews had to return to the
ghettos, abandoning any unauthorized residences in places that had been
forbidden to them in the past.[38]

An effective demonstration of the degree to which the climate was changing
was the lengthy legal case brought against the family of wealthy merchants,
Ascarelli, which ended up being examined by the court of the Inquisition
itself. The new situation could not help but also affect this important Roman
family, who along with some other family members were now established residents at the port of Civitavecchia for almost fifty years. The machine of popular antisemitism was set back in motion, especially among the merchants,
who at the time were trying to rid themselves of Jewish competition by taking
advantage of the new regulations and the government's turn.[39] In a near repetition of what happened to the Jews of the Papal States after the Bull of 1555,
which had required all of them to take up residence in the Ghetto of Rome
or Ancona, in May 1826 Angelo Ascarelli, the new head of the family nucleus
based in Civitavecchia, was ordered to leave the port city and to re-enter the
ghetto of Rome within two years. The Ascarelli family tried to resist, presenting petitions and briefs that insisted on the usefulness of their trade for the
entire Papal State, and especially their decades of loyal fidelity to the pope,
which they had maintained throughout all of the recent political events.

But the climate had changed, and on the other hand, the events of the
Revolution were too recent for the papal government to not recall the active
role that the Ascarelli family had played in the years of the Revolution and
the expulsion of the pope. Why, then, did the family insist so much on its
loyalty to the pontiff and how it remained substantially outside the Republic
of 1798–99? This was probably in an attempt to obfuscate a very unpleas-
ant and inconvenient memory for its members: that of the spectacle of the
corpse of the counter-revolutionary insurgent Cimarra, a fierce enemy of
the ghetto and the Jews, who the heads of the two wealthy Roman families
of Ascarelli and Baraffael had assassinated to punish him for his persecutions, and whose corpse was exhibited in a triumphant procession that had
crossed the whole city. Now, the Ascarelli family of Civitavecchia could not
escape paying dearly for the consequences.[40]

Notes

1 For a detailed analysis of the *Memoriale* addressed to the pope in 1789 cfr. Caffiero, *Legami pericolosi*, 331–61.
2 *Memoriale, All'Illustrissima Congregazione.*
3 Regarding the process of emancipation as long, complex and articulated, see Sorkin, *Jewish emancipation.*
4 Concerning the crisis of the community structures in the 18th century in Europe and the diffusion of more secular attitudes and greater attention on the individual, see Israel, *Gli ebrei d'Europa*, 311–9. For Italy, cfr. Maternini Zotta, *L'ente comunitario ebraico.*
5 Sori, "Una 'comunità crepuscolare'," 198–9.
6 There is an example in Sermoneta, "Una vertenza tra i circoncisori," especially 219–26.
7 These data come from Berengo, "Gli ebrei veneziani," 25; Milano, *Il ghetto di Roma*, 167 and 170; Frattarelli Fischer, "Proprietà e insediamento ebraici," 888.
8 For these episodes, cfr. Segre, "Gli ebrei piemontesi," 80; Berengo, "Gli ebrei veneziani," 26; Sonnino, "Gli ebrei a Livorno," 37; Caffiero, *Legami pericolosi*, 369–75.
9 Schechter, "Translating the 'Marseillaise'," 108–35.
10 Ottolenghi, "Il governo democratico di Venezia," 96. The example of Venice is also invoked in Livorno: cfr. Sonnino, "Gli ebrei a Livorno," 37.
11 Freud, "Psicologia delle masse," 290. But see also the fifth paragraph of "Das Unbehagen in der Kultur", in *Gesammelte Werke XIV*, 421 ss.
12 Salvadori, *1799.*
13 Roth, "Some Revolutionary Purims," 451–82. Regarding the Roman episode see Milano, *Il ghetto di Roma*, 253–4.
14 Sonnino, "Gli ebrei a Livorno," 30 and 38–9.
15 Sonnino, "Gli ebrei a Livorno," 38.
16 According to the thesis in De Felice, "Per una storia del problema ebraico," 352–5.
17 Popkin, "Les Caraïtes," 135; cfr. also Schechter, "Translating the 'Marseillaise'," 108–35.
18 This thesis, already expressed by Arendt, *Le origini del totalitarismo*, has recently been taken up by Schwarzfuchs, "Les nations juives de France," 135.
19 Angelini, *Gli ebrei di Ferrara*, 265–73.
20 Ottolenghi, "Il governo democratico di Venezia," 99; Berengo, "Gli ebrei veneziani," 26. An analogous episode and similar social and political factions at Casale: Segre, "Gli ebrei piemontesi," 80.
21 Caffiero, *La nuova era*, 116–29.
22 Poliakov, *Storia dell'antisemitismo*, 267 ss; Caffiero, "Spazi urbani e scene rituali," 113–5.
23 On the Grand Sanhedrin, cfr. the contributions in Blumenkranz and Soboul, *Le Grand Sanhédrin*; Schwarzfuchs, *Napoleon, the Jews*; Sofia, "Il tema del confronto," 103–24.
24 For the new consistorial system in Italy, cfr. Milano, *Storia degli ebrei*, 350–1; and especially Schwarzfuchs, "Les communautés italiennes," 109–72.
25 Bernardini, *La sfida dell'eguaglianza.*
26 Luzzatto Voghera, *Il prezzo dell'eguaglianza*, 119–20, with a list of the Italian representatives.
27 Caffiero, *Legami pericolosi*, 362–9.
28 Damascelli, "Cimarra e gli ebrei," 35–60. Not by chance, during the Restoration the Ascarelli family was subject to major restrictions that hurt their economic activities: cfr. further ahead, 213–4; Caffiero, "Gli ebrei tra Rivoluzione".

29 Regarding the virulence of Catholic anti-Jewish publishing during the Restoration, cfr. Caffiero, *Religione e modernità*, 251–71.
30 Caffiero, *Religione e modernità*, 256–9.
31 The resumption of forced preaching, which since its origins (1584) had been entrusted to the Dominicans, took place on February 20, 1823; the locations were the Oratorio della Confraternita della Santissima Trinità dei Pellegrini or the Oratorio di Santa Maria del Pianto. On forced preaching see Caffiero, *Legami pericolosi*, 269–95.
32 Jabalot, *Degli Ebrei nel loro rapporto.*
33 Jabalot, *Degli Ebrei nel loro rapporto*, 20–1.
34 Jabalot, *Degli Ebrei nel loro rapporto*, 21.
35 For the importance of this theme in the post-unity phase, see Caviglia, *L'identità salvata*. Cfr. also Luzzatto Voghera, *Il prezzo dell'eguaglianza*; Toscano, *Ebraismo e Antisemitismo*. On the complexity of the relationship between liberalism and antisemitism, now see Green and Levis Sullam, *Jews, Liberalism, Antisemitism*.
36 Jabalot, *Degli Ebrei nel loro rapporto*, 25.
37 Caviglia, *L'identità salvata*, 60 ss.
38 There were eight ghettos in the State: Rome, Ancona, Ferrara, Cento, Lugo, Urbino, Pesaro, and Senigallia.
39 Regarding the numerous requests for expulsion presented to the Holy Office in the first decades of the 1800s by various localities in the pontifical State, for motives that were essentially, but not exclusively, economic, cfr. Kertzer, *Antisemitismo popolare*.
40 Caffiero, "Gli ebrei tra Rivoluzione," 21–37.

Conclusion

Anti-Judaism and Antisemitism. The Modern Roots of Antisemitism

We have seen how the civil and political emancipation of the Jews sanctioned by the French Revolution inflamed Catholic anti-Judaism. In the context of a widespread belief in the clear connection between the emancipation of the Jews, Masonry, Revolution, and ultimately processes of de-Christianization, anti-Judaism became a primary component of 19th-century intransigentism. While the myth of a Jewish conspiracy against the Christian world regained energy and momentum throughout the 1800s and into this century, anti-Judaism turned out to be one of the main "insignia of counter-revolutionary restoration"[1] and a concrete medium of the struggle against modernity.

The question of the relationship between the traditional anti-Judaism that was active in the modern age and the antisemitism of the 19th–20th century remains to be addressed.[2] Current and until now predominant definitions interpret anti-Judaism as a Christian aversion towards post-Biblical rabbinical Judaism. It is seen mainly as an ideology inspired by purely religious motives, linked to the Jews' failure to recognize Jesus as the Messiah and their role in his death. The term antisemitism, on the other hand, refers to the more recent phenomenon born at the end of the 1800s, along with its innovative and unprecedented secular and racial contents. However, these definitions are not entirely exact, and are somewhat problematic.

There is a widespread insistence in today's media and public opinion that anti-Judaism, or anti-Jewishness, is not comparable to antisemitism, emphasizing the distinction between the religious mentality and the secular mentality, and widening the conceptual and chronological polarity between the terms. This distinction serves to absolve the first term on the grounds that it is more moderate and less violent, and can be changed, for example by baptism of the Jews. Most importantly, this view presents anti-Judaism as being separate from the racist and biological element that characterizes antisemitism. This clear distinction is accepted by many authors who do not consider 15th–16th-century Spain, with its Statute on purity of blood, to be a historical precedent that can be invoked with respect to the anti-Semitic and racial laws of the 20th century. In a recently reprinted essay, however, Yosef Hayim Yerushalmi, an author often cited in this work, proposes an

DOI: 10.4324/9781003188445-13

analogical and phenomenological link between the Iberian model and the German model, demonstrating that the creation of suitable terms for a phenomenon – such as race, racism, or antisemitism – is not necessary for the phenomenon to exist.[3]

On one hand, the innate component of Jewishness to which early modern Spanish treatises refer is explicitly biological, not religious. On the other hand, secularism, secularization, and anti-Christianity could not have been the decisive factors for the early modern racial antisemitism, since these phenomena did not exist in 16th-century Spain. Nor should we accept the claim made by some authors that the Statutes of *limpieza de sangre* were not directed against the Jews, but only against converted Jews. This would make it necessary to distinguish between religious persecution of the Jews and ethnic discrimination aimed at "new Christians". However, this objection may be easily dismissed.

In Spain, baptism did not make converted Jews the equals of their Christian counterparts, as is stated by theological doctrine. In fact, the stamp of Jewishness and its immutable inheritance of biology, blood, and behaviors were seen as remaining after baptism, even across many generations – for some contemporary Spanish treatises as far back as twenty. This makes it clear that the opposition of religion versus biology cannot be the justification for the opposition of anti-Judaism versus antisemitism. Why, then, do we insist on this distinction?

In fact, the only argument that offers a way to face the difficulties and discomforts of the next century's tragic events, culminating in the Shoah, is this still widely embraced denial of the existence of racial antisemitism from the 16th century until at least the 1800–1900s. In the modern era, this allows for a clear distinction between the Catholic anti-Judaism that is related to centuries-old Christian religious canons and the new political and racial ideology represented by Nazi and Fascist antisemitism. As such, it is a comforting and reassuring thesis for Catholic authors who tend to base the distinction between religious anti-Judaism and racist antisemitism on both chronology (first anti-Judaism, then antisemitism) and on of degree and severity (with anti-Judaism being more moderate, and antisemitism more radical and violent).

In reality, the whole discussion about the relationship between anti-Judaism and antisemitism rests on the ambiguity of the anti-Jewish theological system itself, which reflects the ambivalence of historical relations between Jews and Christians. The theological system judged Jews to be a people of the letter and not of the spirit regarding interpretation of the Scripture[4] in addition to being guilty of deicide and justly punished by God with their dispersion across the world. However, according to Augustine, the Jews were also the witnesses to the truth of Christianity, as was clearly demonstrated by their perennial condition of degradation and subordination. Most importantly, the Jewish people were considered necessary for the final redemption, according to a theology of history which saw the mass conversion of the Jews as the sign of the end times and the second coming of Christ.

Thus, the Augustinian vision set up a dual view of the Jews: "perfidious" deniers, but also needed witnesses to the Christian faith, a group to be discriminated against, but also to be protected and helped to survive until their final conversion. This summarizes Christian anti-Judaism from the Middle Ages up to the Age of Emancipation, with the entire set of stereotypes, prejudices, and incriminations that went along with it. This formulation also contains the origins of accusations against Jews of ritual murder, of profaning the Eucharist, and of hating and exploiting Christians. It also served as the basis for stereotypes of Jews making pacts with the devil, practicing magic and witchcraft, and using blasphemous and heretical books, such as the *Talmud*, and the insidious stereotype of Jews preferring usury as an occupation.

However, the history of prejudice is not a constant. The 16th and 18th centuries corresponded to two decisive phases regarding Catholic policy and ideology towards the Jews, even before the developments of the 19th and 20th centuries. The first important turning point took place in the 1500s with the "invention" of the ghetto; the second turning point instead came at the end of the 18th century, with a difficult Jewish emancipation.

The 16th century was no mere reworking of traditional theological paradigms towards Jews; it was instead a genuine escalation and innovation that framed the terms of the question in a completely new way. First of all, the anti-Judaism of the Catholic Counter Reformation was closely linked to the fight against Protestant "heresy". Indeed, the newly-formed Roman Inquisition surreptitiously inserted the Jews into the category of "heretics", even though they could not legally be considered heretics since they were not baptized. Although the segregationist option chosen by the Roman Church was not as severe as the Spanish and Portuguese expulsion of the Jews from their Kingdoms, it was nevertheless steeped in the same conversionist mentality. Furthermore, Italian Catholicism ended up endorsing the Iberian principle of purity of blood even though it did not formally adopt or approve it. In fact, Italian Catholic thought went so far as to relocate the metaphorical impurity of the Jews from the theological and religious realm to the medical and biological level, connecting it to the diseases that were supposedly spread by Jews: leprosy, plague, syphilis, tuberculosis.

The ghetto itself, however, with its ambiguous function of exclusion and protection, served as an instrument of conversion and signaled the need to keep Christians and Jews separate in order to prevent the physical and spiritual contamination. Between the 16th and 18th centuries, Jews were considered to be servants, and therefore could not be granted rights, including citizenship. They were seen as "objects" that could be denounced, imprisoned, and "offered" to the Christian faith, and they could be required to change their names, allegiances, and identities through forced baptisms. Over time this mental and ideological arsenal of perceptions consolidated and reinforced the habits, attitudes, social behaviors, and practices which lay at the historical roots of 19th–20th-century religious and secular antisemitism, generating practices of exclusion and persecution of Jews *just for being Jews.*

The other significant turning point in relations between Jews and Christians came at the end of the 1700s, during the decades of political and civil emancipation. Here, the contradictions reach their peak. On one hand, emancipation assumed the Universalist and abstract logic of the equality of rights for all citizens, including the Jews. For the Jews, however, this equality came at the cost of their particular diversity, in the name of a call for complete assimilation and renunciation of their identity, and therefore of a right. On the other hand, intransigent and reactionary Catholic ideology was opposed to emancipation, and denied the principle of equality based precisely on its recognition and assumption of Jewish difference, which was described as threatening and unyielding unless the Jews converted. However, even in this context, there was not a pure repetition and replication of the schemes of traditional and purely religious anti-Judaism. After the French Revolution, anti-Judaism in the 1800s took on new historical and political features that were much different from the past, linked to the rejection and fear of modernity and the political and social transformations it introduced.

It is clear that the call for special discriminatory laws repeated by polemicist Ferdinand Jabalot and reactionary Catholicism's rejection of emancipation were not simply reiterations of a traditional anti-Jewish vision. The context in which these measures were invoked was completely changed; in fact, these measures were in direct conflict, not just theological but also political, with the system of universal human rights and the concept of the State and sovereignty introduced by the Revolution. Furthermore, it was not only the contents of anti-Judaism that changed. The language of Catholic anti-Judaism itself was also transformed, especially in the 20th century, when the appeal to "a healthy antisemitism" was joined by terms such as "race", "bloodline", and "nation". These terms were applied to the Jews as innate and unalterable characteristics and as indications of their inherently foreign nature within the various national states. To what extent, then, did this reactionary Catholic anti-Judaism, which can unquestionably be labeled antisemitism, influence and condition the nationalistic and secular antisemitism of the 19th and the 20th centuries? Respected historians David Kertzer and Giovanni Miccoli have no doubts about the continuity and contiguity between Catholic anti-Judaism and antisemitism: the former would pave the way for and fuel the latter.

Notes

1 The expression is from Miccoli, "La Santa Sede," 286. On the attitudes and themes of Catholic anti-Judaism between the 19th and 20th centuries now, see *Antisemitismo e cattolicesimo.*

2 Here, I refer back to observations I made in Caffiero, "Antigiudaismo, antisemitismo"; *Storia degli ebrei*. On anti-Judaism and antisemitism as interrelated phenomena, see Katz, *From Prejudice to Destruction*; Kertzer, *Antisemitismo popolare*; Yerushalmi, *Assimilazione e antisemitismo*; Miccoli, *Antisemitismo e cattolicesimo*; Caffiero, *Storia degli ebrei*, 215–9. There is a different position in Nirenberg, *Anti-Judaism*, which clearly distinguishes the two concepts. See also the discussion in Caffiero, "Antigiudaismo, antiebraismo, antisemitismo", 427–34. The English translation fails to account for the term "anti-Jewishness" (*antiebraismo*), which is used in Italian more frequently than "anti-Judaism", but is not used in English.

3 Yerushalmi, *Assimilazione e antisemitismo*.

4 Cfr. at least this formulation of the concept, which can be found in many places in the New Testament and Christian theology, "He has made us competent as ministers of a new covenant – not of the letter but of the Spirit", 2 Corinthians 3: 4–6 NIV.

Bibliography

Print Sources

Bullarum Diplomatum et Privilegiorum Sanctorum Romanorum Pontificum (1860). Taurinensis editio..., Sebastiani Franco et Henrico Dalmazzo editoribus, 25 vols., Augustae Taurinorum, 1857–1872, 6, 498–500.

Caffiero, Marina, ed. *Rubare le anime. Diario di Anna del Monte ebrea romana.* Rome: Viella, 2008.

Cattaneo, Carlo. *Le interdizioni israelitiche*, edited by Luigi Ambrosoli. Turin: Einaudi, 1962 (originally published in 1835).

Cebà, Ansaldo. *Lettere d'Ansaldo Cebà scritte a Sarra Copia e dedicate a Marcantonio Doria.* Genova: for Giuseppe Pavoni, 1623.

Copio Sullam, Sara. *Manifesto di Sarra Copia Sullam Hebrea.* Venezia: Giovanni Alberti, 1621.

Corcos, Tranquillo Vita. *Discorso accademico del Rabbi Tranquillo Vita Corcos fatto recitare dalli giovani della sua Accademia in occasione della festività degli Ebrei per l'historia d'Ester, e Mordacheo nell'anno 5470 dalla creazione del mondo.* Rome: in the Stamperia di Gio. Francesco Chracas at S. Marco al Corso, 1710.

Corcos. *Spiegazione ovvero Riflessione sopra l'uso delle Pergamene scritte con Caratteri Hebraici, Nelle quali si mostra non esser' in esse cosa alcuna Superstiziosa, ma esser' appoggiato ad Instituti Universali della Nazione il praticarle come Religiose, e piene di Sacre Cognizioni, Opera, e studio di T. V. C. al Reverendissimo Padre Maestro Giuseppe Maria Tabaglia Commissario Generale della Sac. Inquisizione.* Rimini: nella Stamperia del Salimbeni, 1713.

D'Arco, Giovanni Battista. *Dell'influenza del ghetto nello Stato.* Venezia: G. Storti, 1782.

Efemeridi letterarie di Roma. Rome: nella Stamperia di Giovanni Zempel, 1782.

Frizzi, Benedetto. *Difesa contro gli attacchi fatti alla nazione ebrea nel libro intitolato della influenza del ghetto nello Stato.* Pavia: Stamperia del monastero di San Salvatore, 1784.

Jabalot, Ferdinand. *Degli Ebrei nel loro rapporto colle nazioni cristiane del Reverendissimo Padre Ferdinando Jabalot Pro-procuratore Generale dell'Ordine de' PP. Predicatori. Estratto dal tomo terzo del Giornale ecclesiastico di Roma.* Rome: at Vincenzo Poggioli, 1825.

Luzzatto, Simone. "Discorso circa lo Stato degli Hebrei et in particolar dimoranti nell'inclita città di Venezia di Simone Luzzatto rabbino hebreo (1638)".

In *Luzzatto, Scritti politici e filosofici di un ebreo scettico della Venezia del Settecento*, edited by Giuseppe Veltri, 3–106. Milano: Bompiani, 2013.

Medici, Paolo Sebastiano. *Riti, e costumi degli ebrei confutati dal dottore Paolo Medici sacerdote fiorentino.* Florence: nella nuova stamperia di Pietro Gaetano Viviani da Santa Maria in Campo, 1736.

Memoriale (1789), *All'Illustrissima Congregazione particolare deputata dalla Santità di N. S. Pio PP. VI... Memoriale con Sommario*, per Mezzanini in Roma.

Modena, Leon. *Novo Dittionario hebraico et italiano, cioè Dichiaratione di tutte le voci Hebraiche più difficili delle scritture Hebree nella volgar lingua italiana....* Venice: Giacomo Sarzina, 1612 (reprinted 1640).

Modena. *Historia de' Riti Hebraici, vita ed osservanze de gl'Hebrei di questi tempi di Leon Modena da lui corretta e riformata.* Venice: Giovanni Calleoni, 1638 (first published in Paris, 1637); edition edited by Adolfo Ottolenghi in *La Rassegna Mensile di Israel*, no. 7, 7–8 (1932): 204–34; 9 (1932): 385–509, 560–77.

Precetti da hesser imparati dalle donne hebree composto per Rabbi Biniamin d'Harodono in lingua Todesca Tradotto ora di nuovo dalla detta lingua nella Volgare per Rabbi Giacob Halpron Hebreo, appresso Giacomo Sarzina, in Venetia 1616.

Rossi Artom, Elena et al., ed. *Vita di Jehudà. Autobiografia di Leon Modena rabbino veneziano del XVII secolo.* Torino: Silvio Zamorani, 2000.

Rovira, Francesco Bonet. *Ristretto della vita e martirio di S. Simone fanciullo di Trento....* Rome: nella Stamperia di Giovanni Bartolomicchi, 1775.

Secondary Sources

AA.VV. "Rabbini e maestri nell'ebraismo italiano." *Zakhor. Rivista di storia degli ebrei d'Italia*, 8 (2005).

Abulafia, David. "Le comunità di Sicilia dagli arabi all'espulsione (1493)." In *Storia d'Italia*, Annali 11, *Gli ebrei in Italia*, 1: *Dall'alto Medioevo all'età dei ghetti*, edited by Corrado Vivanti, 45–82. Torino: Einaudi, 1996.

Al Kalak, Matteo "Convertire e sostenere. Archeologia ed esordi dell'Opera pia dei catecumeni di Modena." In *Le radici storiche dell'antisemitismo*, edited by Marina Caffiero, 71–105. Roma: Viella, 2009.

Allegra, Luciano "Modelli di conversione." *Quaderni storici*, 78, 3 (1991): 901–15.

Allegra. "L'antisemitismo come risorsa politica. Battesimi forzati e ghetti nel Piemonte del Settecento." *Quaderni storici* 84 (1993): 867–99, now in Allegra, *Identità in bilico*. Torino: Silvio Zamorani, 1996.

Allegra. *Identità in bilico. Il ghetto ebraico di Torino nel Settecento.* Torino: Silvio Zamorani, 1996.

Allegra. "La madre ebrea nell'Italia moderna: alle origini di uno stereotipo." In *Storia della maternità*, edited by Marina D'Amelia, 53–75. Roma-Bari: Laterza, 1997.

Andreoni, Luca. "'Detestare la sua perfidia'. La Casa dei catecumeni di Ancona e la conversione degli ebrei nell'Ottocento." *Studia picena* 72 (2007): 155–210.

Andreoni. "'Perché non si abbia più a tribulare'. Gli ebrei della Marca fra spazi economici e conflitti giudiziari intorno alla metà del xvi secolo." In *Gli ebrei nello Stato della Chiesa. Insediamenti e mobilità (secoli xiv–xviii)*, edited by Marina Caffiero and Anna Esposito, 109–47. Padua: Esedra Editrice, 2012.

Andreoni. *Una nazione in commercio. Ebrei di Ancona, traffici adriatici e pratiche mercantili in età moderna.* Milano: Franco Angeli, 2019.

Angelini, Werher. *Gli ebrei di Ferrara nel Settecento. I Coen e altri mercanti nel rapporto con le pubbliche autorità*. Urbino: Argalìa editore, 1973.

Arendt, Hannah. *Le origini del totalitarismo*. Milano: Feltrinelli, 1967 (originally published 1951).

Bachi, Roberto. "La demografia dell'ebraismo italiano prima dell'emancipazione." *La Rassegna Mensile di Israel* 12, 7–8–9 (1938): 256–320.

Bachi, Roberto, and Sergio Della Pergola, "Gli ebrei italiani nel quadro della demografia della diaspora." *Quaderni storici* 19, 55 (1984): 155–91.

Balsamo, Luigi. "Editoria e biblioteche della seconda metà del Settecento negli Stati estensi." In "Reggio e i territori estensi dall'antico regime all'età napoleonica," in *Atti del Convegno di studi (Reggio Emilia, 18–19–20 marzo 1977), vol. 2*, edited by Marino Berengo and Sergio Romagnoli, 505–31. Parma: Pratiche, 1979.

Balsamo. "Gli ebrei nell'editoria e nel commercio librario in Italia nel '600 e '700." In "Italia Judaica. Gli ebrei in Italia dalla segregazione alla prima emancipazione," in *Atti del iii Convegno internazionale (Tel Aviv, 15–20 giugno 1986)*, 49–65. Rome: Pubblicazioni degli Archivi di Stato Ministero per i Beni Culturali e Ambientali, 1989.

Barbierato, Federico. *Nella stanza dei circoli. "Clavicula Salomonis" e libri di magia a Venezia nei secoli xvii e xviii*. Milan: Sylvestre Bonnard, 2002.

Bartolucci, Guido. "Venezia nel pensiero politico ebraico rinascimentale: un testo ritrovato di David de Pomis." *Rinascimento. Rivista dell'Istituto Nazionale di Studi sul Rinascimento*, second series 44 (2005): 225–47.

Bassani, Giorgio. *Il giardino dei Finzi Contini*. Torino: Einaudi, 1962.

Bastos Mateus, Susana, and James W. Nelson Novoa. "De Lamego para a Toscana: o périplo do médico Pedro Furtado, cristão-novo português." *Cadernos de Estudos Sefarditas* 5 (2005): 313–38.

Belligni, Eleonora. *Renata di Francia (1510–1575). Un'eresia di corte*. Torino: UTET, 2012.

Benocci, Carla, and Enrico Guidoni, eds. "Il Ghetto." In *Atlante storico delle città italiane, vol. 2*, 9–30. Rome: Bonsignori, 1993.

Berengo, Marino. "Gli ebrei veneziani alla fine del Settecento, in Italia Judaica. Gli ebrei dalla segregazione alla prima emancipazione." In *Atti del iii Convegno internazionale (Tel Aviv, 15–20 giugno 1986)*, 9–30. Rome: Ministero per i Beni Culturali e Ambientali, Pubblicazioni degli Archivi di Stato, 1989.

Bernardini, Paul. *La sfida dell'eguaglianza. Gli ebrei a Mantova nell'età della rivoluzione francese*. Rome: Bulzoni, 1996.

Blumenkranz, Bernhard. *Il cappello a punta. L'ebreo medievale nello specchio dell'arte cristiana*, edited by Chiara Frugoni. Roma-Bari: Laterza, 2003.

Blumenkranz, Bernhard, and Albert Soboul, eds. *Le Grand Sanhédrin de Napoléon*. Toulouse: E. Privat, 1979.

Boccato, Carla. "Un episodio nella vita di Sara Copio Sullam: Il Manifesto sull'immortalità dell'anima." *La Rassegna Mensile di Israel* 39, 11 (1973): 633–46.

Boesch Gajano, Sofia, and Michele Luzzati. "Introduction to Ebrei in Italia." *Quaderni storici* 18, 54 (1983): 779–82.

Bonazzoli, Viviana. "Ebrei italiani, portoghesi e levantini sulla piazza commerciale di Ancona intorno alla metà del Cinquecento." In *Gli ebrei a Venezia. Secoli xiv–xviii*, edited by Gaetano Cozzi, 727–70. Milano: Edizioni di Comunità, 1987.

Bonazzoli. "Sulla struttura familiare delle aziende ebraiche nella Ancona del '700." In *La presenza ebraica nelle Marche. Secoli xiii–xx*, edited by Sergio Anselmi and

Viviana Bonazzoli, 139–54. Quaderni monografici di "Proposte e Ricerche" 14, 1993.

Bonazzoli. "Una identità ricostruita. I portoghesi ad Ancona dal 1530 al 1547." *Zakhor. Rivista di storia degli ebrei d'Italia* 5 (2001–02): 9–38.

Bonfil, Roberto. "How Golden Was the Age of the Renaissance in Jewish Historiography?" *History and Theory* 27, 4 (1988): 78–102.

Bonfil. "La lettura nelle comunità ebraiche dell'Europa occidentale in età medievale." In *Storia della lettura nel mondo occidentale*, edited by Guglielmo Cavallo and Roger Chartier, 155–97. Rome: Laterza, 1995.

Bonfil. "Lo spazio culturale degli ebrei d'Italia fra Rinascimento ed Età barocca." In *Storia d'Italia*, Annali 11, *Gli ebrei in Italia*, i: *Dall'alto Medioevo all'età dei ghetti*, edited by Corrado Vivanti, 412–73. Torino: Einaudi, 1996.

Bonfil, Roberto, and David Malkiel, eds. *The Lion Shall Roar. Leon Modena and His World*. Jerusalem: The Hebrew University Magnes Press, 2003.

Bregoli, Francesca. "Hebrew Printing in Eighteenth-Century Livorno: From Government Control to a Free Market." In *The Hebrew Book in Early Modern Italy*, edited by Joseph R. Hacker and Adam Shear, 171–95. Philadelphia: University of Pennsylvania Press, 2011.

Bregoli. "L'editoria ebraica a Livorno nel '700, tra Toscana granducale e Nord Africa." In *Editori, tipografi e Lumi. La stampa a Livorno tra il 1644 e il 1830*, 117–36. Livorno: Benvenuti & Cavaciocchi, 2012.

Bregoli. *Mediterranean Enlightenment: Livornese Jews, Tuscan Culture, and Eighteenth-Century Reform*. Stanford, CA: Stanford University Press, 2014.

Brignani, Marida, and Maurizio Bertolotti, eds. *Benedetto Frizzi: un illuminista ebreo nell'età dell'emancipazione*. Firenze: Giuntina, 2009.

Busetto, Giorgio. "Copio Sullam, Sara." In *Dizionario biografico degli italiani*, 28, 582–4. Rome: Istituto dell'Enciclopedia Italiana, 1983.

Caffiero, Marina. *La nuova era. Miti e profezie dell'Italia in Rivoluzione*. Genoa: Marietti, 1991.

Caffiero. "Tra Chiesa e Stato, Gli ebrei italiani dall'età dei Lumi agli anni della Rivoluzione." In *Storia d'Italia*, Annali 11, *Gli ebrei in Italia*, ii: *Dall'emancipazione a oggi*, edited by Corrado Vivanti, 1089–132. Torino: Einaudi, 1997.

Caffiero. "La maestà del papa. Trasformazioni dei rituali del potere a Roma nella seconda età moderna." In *Religione e modernità in Italia (secoli xvii–xix)*, 67–95. Pisa-Roma: IEPI, 2000.

Caffiero. "Le botteghe degli ebrei. Lavoro e comportamenti economici a Roma in un censimento del 1827." In *Religione e modernità in Italia (secoli xvii–xix)*, 273–92. Pisa-Roma: IEPI, 2000.

Caffiero. *Religione e modernità in Italia (secoli xvii–xix)*. Pisa-Roma: IEPI, 2000.

Caffiero. *Battesimi forzati. Storie di ebrei, cristiani e convertiti nella Roma dei papi*. Rome: Viella, 2004 (3rd ed. Viella, 2009).

Caffiero, ed. *Rubare le anime. Diario di Anna del Monte ebrea romana*. Rome: Viella, 2008.

Caffiero. "Non farsi rapire l'anima." In *Rubare le anime. Diario di Anna del Monte ebrea romana*, 7–55. Rome: Viella, 2008.

Caffiero. "Introduzione." In *Le radici storiche dell'antisemitismo*, edited by Marina Caffiero, 9–18. Rome: Viella, 2009.

Caffiero. "Antigiudaismo, antisemitismo." In *Dizionario storico dell'inquisizione*, i, edited by Adriano Prosperi et al., 65–8. Pisa: Edizioni della Normale, 2010.

Caffiero. "Le doti della conversione. Ebree e neofite a Roma in età moderna." *Geschichte und Region/Storia e regione* 19, 1 (2010): 72–91.

Caffiero. "Ebrei." In *Italia napoleonica. Dizionario critico*, edited by Luigi Mascilli Migliorini, 113–5. Torino: UTET, 2011.

Caffiero. *Forced Baptisms. Histories of Jews, Christians, and Converts in Papal Rome.* Berkeley: University of California Press, 2011.

Caffiero. "Introduzione." In "Ebrei. Scambi e conflitti tra xv e xx secolo." Monograph edition of *Roma moderna e contemporanea* 19, 1 (2011): 3–9.

Caffiero. "Spazi urbani e scene rituali dell'ebraismo romano in età moderna." In *Judei de Urbe. Roma e i suoi ebrei: una storia secolare*, edited by Marina Caffiero and Anna Esposito, 3–22. Rome: Ministero per i Beni e le Attività Culturali-Direzione Generale per gli Archivi, 2011.

Caffiero. *Legami pericolosi. Ebrei e cristiani tra libri proibiti, eresia e stregoneria.* Torino: Einaudi, 2012.

Caffiero. "Gli ebrei tra Rivoluzione e Restaurazione. Insediamento e cacciata degli Ascarelli da Civitavecchia." *Dimensioni e problemi della ricerca storica* 1 (2013): 21–37.

Caffiero. *Storia degli ebrei nell'Italia moderna. Dal Rinascimento alla Restaurazione.* Rome: Carocci, 2014.

Caffiero. "Amor platonico tra conversione e immortalità. Le lettere d'Ansaldo Cebà a Sara Copio Sullam." In *Lettere d'amore*, edited by Manola Ida Venzo, 97–126. Rome: Viella, 2015.

Caffiero. "Il rabbino, il convertito e la superstizione ebraica. La polemica a distanza tra Corcos e Medici." In *Prescritto e proscritto. Religione e società nell'Italia moderna (secc. xvi–xix)*, edited by Andrea Cicerchia, Guido Dall'Olio and Matteo Duni, 127–50. Rome: Carocci, 2015.

Caffiero. "Le disgrazie della conversione. Un memoriale inedito di Giulio Morosini sul ripudio della moglie ebrea e la restituzione della dote (1676)." *Itinerari di ricerca storica* 30, 2 new series (2016): 127–38.

Caffiero. "Antigiudaismo, antiebraismo, antisemitismo. A proposito di una discussione recente." *Rivista di storia del cristianesimo* 14, 2 (2017): 427–34.

Caffiero. *Il grande mediatore. Tranquillo Vita Corcos, un rabbino nella Roma dei papi.* Rome: Carocci, 2019.

Caffiero. "Tra due fuochi. Ebrei, Inquisizione e Case dei catecumeni." In *L'Inquisizione e gli ebrei. Nuove ricerche*, edited by Marina Caffiero with the collaboration of Giuseppina Minchella, 83–110. Rome: Edizioni di Storia e Letteratura, 2021.

Caffiero, ed. *L'Inquisizione e gli ebrei. Nuove ricerche.* Rome: Edizioni di Storia e Letteratura, 2021.

Calabi, Donatella. "Il ghetto e la città." In *La città degli ebrei*, edited by Donatella Calabi, et al., 125–203. Venice: Albrizzi editore, 1991.

Calabi. "Gli stranieri e la città." In *Storia di Venezia. Dalle origini alla caduta della Serenissima, v, Il Rinascimento società ed economia*, edited by Alberto Tenenti and Ugo Tucci, 913–46. Rome: Istituto della Enciclopedia italiana, 1996.

Calabi, Donatella et al., eds. *La città degli ebrei. Il Ghetto di Venezia: architettura e urbanistica.* Venice: Marsilio, 1996.

Calimani, Riccardo. *Storia del ghetto di Venezia.* Milan: Mondadori, 1995.

Campanini, Antonella. "L'identità coatta. La Casa dei catecumeni a Bologna." In *Verso l'epilogo di una convivenza: gli ebrei a Bologna nel xvi secolo*, edited by Maria Grazia Muzzarelli, 155–76. Florence: Giuntina, 1996.

Canonici, Claudio. "La presenza ebraica nel Patrimonio di San Pietro fra xvi e xviii secolo: fonti e problemi." In *Gli ebrei nello Stato della Chiesa. Insediamenti e mobilità (secoli xiv–xviii)*, edited by Marina Caffiero and Anna Esposito, 89–108. Padua: Esedra Editrice, 2012.

Capriotti, Giuseppe. *Lo scorpione nel petto. Iconografia antiebraica tra xv e xvi secolo alla periferia dello Stato Pontificio.* Rome: Gangemi, 2014.

Castelbolognesi, Gustavo. "Gli ebrei di Padova e l'industria della seta fra il 1779 e il 1803." *La Rassegna Mensile di Israel* 5, 3 (1930–31): 149–56.

Cavarocchi, Francesca. *La comunità ebraica di Mantova fra prima emancipazione e unità d'Italia.* Florence: Giuntina, 2002.

Cavarocchi-Arbib, Marina. "Rivisitando la biblica Esther: implicazioni sottese all'immagine femminile ebraica nell'Italia del Seicento." In *Le donne delle minoranze*, edited by Claire E. Honess and Verina R. Jones, 143–57. Turin: Claudiana, 1999.

Caviglia, Stefano. *L'identità salvata. Gli ebrei di Roma tra fede e nazione. 1870–1938.* Roma-Bari: Laterza, 1996.

Ceccone, Cristina. "Frizzi, Benedetto." In *Dizionario biografico degli italiani* 50, 579–81. Rome: Istituto dell'Enciclopedia Italiana, 1998.

Chajes, Jefferey H. *Posseduti ed esorcisti nel mondo ebraico.* Turin: Bollati Boringhieri, 2010 (originally published 2003).

Cioni, Alfredo. "Bomberg, Daniel." In *Dizionario biografico degli italiani* 11, 382–7. Rome: Istituto dell'Enciclopedia Italiana, 1969.

Cioni. "Bragadin, Alvise." In *Dizionario biografico degli italiani* 13, 659–61. Rome: Istituto dell'Enciclopedia Italiana, 1971.

Colletta, Claudia. *La comunità tollerata. Aspetti di vita materiale del ghetto di Pesaro dal 1631 al 1860.* Pesaro: Società pesarese di studi storici, 2006.

Cooperman, Bernard Dov. "Portuguese Conversos in Ancona: Jewish Political Activity in Early Modern Italy." In *Iberia and Beyond: Hispanic Jewry Between Cultures*, edited by Bernard Dov Cooperman, 297–352. Newark-London: Associated University Press, 1998.

Cozzi, Gaetano, ed. *Gli ebrei a Venezia. Secoli xiv–xviii.* Milan: Edizioni di Comunità, 1987.

Cristellon, Cecilia. "Borach Levi, la censura e la giurisdizione sul matrimonio degli ebrei (secc. XVI–XVIII)." In *L'Inquisizione e gli ebrei. Nuove ricerche*, edited by Marina Caffiero, 111–27. Rome: Edizioni di Storia e Letteratura, 2021.

Curtin, Philip D. *Cross-Cultural Trade in World History.* Cambridge: Cambridge University Press, 1984.

Da Fonseca-Wollheim, Corinna. "Acque del Parnaso, acque del battesimo: fede e fama nell'opera di Sara Copio Sullam." In *Le donne delle minoranze*, edited by Claire E. Honess and Verina R. Jones, 159–70. Turin: Claudiana, 1999.

Damascelli, Andrea. "Cimarra e gli ebrei nella Repubblica romana del 1798–1799." *Archivi e Cultura*, 23–24 (1990–91): 35–60.

Dan, Joseph, ed. *The Christian Kabbalah: Jewish Mystical Books and their Christian Interpreters.* Cambridge, MA: Harvard College Library, 1998.

De Felice, Renzo. "Per una storia del problema ebraico in Italia alla fine del xviii secolo e all'inizio del xix. La prima emancipazione (1792–1814)." In *Italia giacobina*, 317–96. Naples: Edizioni Scientifiche Italiane, 1965.

Dedieu, Jean-Pierre. "Conversos, Spagna." In *Dizionario storico dell'inquisizione, i*, edited by Adriano Prosperi et al., 406–8. Pisa: Edizioni della Normale, 2010.

Del Bianco Cotrozzi, Maddalena. "Tolleranza giuseppina ed illuminismo ebraico: il caso delle unite principesche contee di Gorizia e Gradisca." *Nuova Rivista storica* 73 (1989): 689–726.

Del Bianco Cotrozzi. "Un incontro fra letterati alla fine del Settecento: il carteggio di Elia Morpurgo con Giovanni Bernardo De Rossi." *Annali di Storia Isontina* 4 (1991): 35–64.

Della Pergola, Sergio. "La popolazione ebraica in Italia nel contesto ebraico globale." In *Storia d'Italia*, Annali 11, *Gli ebrei in Italia*, ii: *Dall'emancipazione a oggi*, edited by Corrado Vivanti, 897–936. Turin: Einaudi, 1997.

Di Castro, Daniela, ed. *Gli ebrei romani e la cerimonia di insediamento dei pontefici* (Catalog from the exhibit "Et ecce gaudium"). Rome: Araldo De Luca Editore, 2010.

Di Leone Leoni, Aron. "Alcuni esempi di quotidiana imprenditorialità tra Ferrara, Ancona e Venezia nel xvi secolo." *Zakhor. Rivista di storia degli ebrei d'Italia* 4 (2000): 57–114.

Di Leone Leoni. "Per una storia della Nazione Portoghese ad Ancona e a Pesaro." *L'identità dissimulata. Giudaizzanti iberici nell'Europa cristiana dell'età moderna*, edited by Pier Cesare Ioly Zorattini, 27–97. Florence: Olschki, 2000.

Di Leone Leoni. *La nazione ebraica spagnola e portoghese a Ferrara (1492–1559)*. Florence: Olschki, 2 vols., 2011.

Di Leone Leoni. "Sedaqua." In *Dizionario storico dell'inquisizione, iii*, edited by Adriano Prosperi et al., 1405. Pisa: Edizioni della Normale, 2011.

Di Nepi, Serena. "Dall'astrologia agli Astrologo: ebrei e superstizioni nella Roma della Controriforma." In *Le radici storiche dell'antisemitismo. Nuove fonti e ricerche*, edited by Marina Caffiero, 41–70. Rome: Viella, 2009.

Di Nepi. *Sopravvivere al ghetto. Per una storia sociale della comunità ebraica nella Roma del Cinquecento*. Rome: Viella, 2013.

Di Sivo, Michele. "Giudicare gli ebrei: i tribunali penali romani nei secoli xvi–xviii." In *Judei de Urbe. Roma e i suoi ebrei: una storia secolare*, edited by Marina Caffiero and Anna Esposito, 81–102. Rome: Ministero per i Beni e le Attività Culturali-Direzione Generale per gli Archivi, 2011.

Dubin, Lois C. "Les liaisons dangereuses. Mariage juif et État moderne à Trieste au xviiie siècle." *Annales H.S.S.* 5 (1994): 1139–70.

Dubin. *The Port Jews of Habsburg Trieste. Absolutist Politics and Enlightenment Culture*. Stanford, CA: Stanford University Press, 1999.

Dubin. "Medicine as Enlightenment Cure: Benedetto Frizzi, Physician to Eighteenth-Century Italian Jewish Society." *Jewish History* 26, 1–2 (May 2012): 201–21.

Dweck, Yaacob. *The Scandal of Kabbalah: Leon Modena, Jewish Mysticism, Early Modern Venice*. Princeton: Princeton University Press, 2011.

Ernst, Germana. ""Dalla Bolla "Coeli et terrae" all' "Inscrutabilis". L'astrologia tra natura, religione e politica nell'età della Controriforma." In *Religione, ragione e natura. Ricerche su Tommaso Campanella e il tardo Rinascimento*, 255–79. Milan: Franco Angeli, 1991.

Esposito, Anna. "Normativa statutaria e ebrei." In *La storia degli ebrei nell'Italia medievale: tra filologia e metodologia*, edited by Maria Grazia Muzzarelli and Giacomo Todeschini, 98–101. Bologna: Istituto per i beni artistici, culturali e naturali della Regione Emilia-Romagna, 1990.

Esposito. *Un'altra Roma. Minoranze nazionali e comunità ebraiche tra Medioevo e Rinascimento*. Rome: Il Calamo, 1995.

Esposito. "Matrimonio, convivenza, divorzio: i rapporti coniugali nella comunità ebraica di Roma tra Quattro e Cinquecento." *Zakhor. Rivista di storia degli ebrei d'Italia* 3 (1999): 109–12.

Esposito. "Credito, ebrei, monte di pietà a Roma tra Quattro e Cinquecento." *Roma moderna e contemporanea* 10, 3 (2002): 113–36.

Esposito. "The Sephardic Communities in Rome in the Early Sixteenth Century." *Imago temporis. Medium Aevum* 1 (2007): 171–80.

Esposito. "Gli ebrei di Roma prima del ghetto: nuovi spunti." In *Monaci, ebrei, santi. Studi per Sofia Boesch Gajano*, edited by Antonio Volpato, 384–91. Rome: Viella, 2008.

Esposito. "Conflitti interni alla comunità ebraica di Roma tra Quattro e Cinquecento." In *Judei de Urbe. Roma e i suoi ebrei: una storia secolare*, edited by Marina Caffiero and Anna Esposito, 69–80. Rome: Ministero per i Beni e le Attività Culturali-Direzione Generale per gli Archivi, 2011.

Esposito, Anna, and Micaela Procaccia. "La 'schola Sicolorum de Urbe': la fine della storia?" In *Italia Judaica. Gli ebrei in Sicilia sino all'espulsione del 1492*, Atti del v Convegno internazionale (Palermo, 15–19 giugno 1992), 412–22. Rome: Ministero per i Beni Culturali e Ambientali, Ufficio centrale per i Beni Archivistici, 1995.

Esposito and Procaccia. "Un astrologo e i suoi prognostici. Bonnet de Lattes a Roma alla fine del Quattrocento." *Materia Giudaica* 7, 1 (2002): 92–106.

Esposito and Procaccia. "Ebrei in giudizio: centro e periferia dello Stato pontificio nella documentazione processuale (secc. xv–xvi)." In *Ebrei. Scambi e conflitti tra xv e xx secolo*, edited by Marina Caffiero. A monograph edition of *Roma moderna e contemporanea* 19, 1 (2011): 11–28.

Favero, Giovanni, and Francesca Trivellato. "Gli abitanti del ghetto di Venezia in età moderna: dati e ipotesi." *Zakhor. Rivista di storia degli ebrei d'Italia* 8 (2004): 9–50.

Ferrara, Piera Micol. "La struttura architettonica del "serraglio" degli ebrei romani (secc. xvi–xix)." In *Ebrei. Scambi e conflitti tra xv e xx secolo*, edited by Marina Caffiero. A monograph edition of *Roma moderna e contemporanea* 19, 1 (2011): 83–102.

Filippini, Jean-Pierre. "La nazione ebrea di Livorno." In *Storia d'Italia*, Annali 11, *Gli ebrei in Italia, ii: Dall'emancipazione a oggi*, edited by Corrado Vivanti, 1045–66. Turin: Einaudi, 1997.

Foa, Anna. "Il nuovo e il vecchio: l'insorgere della sifilide (1494–1530)." *Quaderni storici* 19, 55 (1984): 11–34.

Foa. "Un vescovo marrano: il processo a Pedro de Aranda." *Quaderni storici* 33, 99 (1998): 533–51.

Fortis, Umberto. *La "bella ebrea". Sara Copio Sullam poetessa nel ghetto di Venezia del '600*. Turin: Silvio Zamorani, 2003.

Foucault, Michel. *Storia della follia nell'età classica*. Milan: Rizzoli, 1973 (originally published 1961).

Frattarelli Fischer, Lucia. "Proprietà e insediamento ebraici a Livorno dalla fine del Cinquecento alla seconda metà del Settecento." *Quaderni storici* 18, 54, 3 (1983): 893–4.

Frattarelli Fischer. "Gli ebrei, il principe e l'Inquisizione." In *L'Inquisizione e gli ebrei in Italia*, edited by Michele Luzzati, 217–31. Roma-Bari: Laterza, 1994.

Frattarelli Fischer. "Ebrei a Pisa e Livorno nel Sei e Settecento tra Inquisizioni e garanzie granducali." In *Le inquisizioni cristiane e gli ebrei*, 253–95. Rome: Accademia Nazionale dei Lincei, 2003.

Frattarelli Fischer. "Reti toscane e reti internazionali degli ebrei di Livorno nel Seicento." *Zakhor. Rivista di storia degli ebrei d'Italia* 6 (2003): 93–116.

Frattarelli Fischer. *Vivere fuori dal ghetto. Ebrei a Pisa e Livorno (secoli xvi–xviii)*. Turin: Silvio Zamorani, 2008.

Freud, Sigmund. "Psicologia delle masse e analisi dell'Io." In *Opere* 9, edited by E. Q. Panaitescu. Torino: Boringhieri, 1997 (originally published in 1921: Massenpsychologie und Ich-Analyse.

Freud. "Das Unbehagen in der Kultur." In *Gesammelte Werke XIV* (Eng. tr. Civilization and Its Discontents), 421 et seq. 1929.

Galasso, Cristina. *Alle origini di una comunità. Ebree ed ebrei a Livorno nel Seicento*. Florence: Olschki, 2002.

Galasso. "'La moglie duplicata'. Bigamia e levirato nella comunità ebraica di Livorno (secolo xvii)." In *Trasgressioni. Seduzione, concubinato, adulterio, bigamia (xiv–xviii secolo)*, edited by Silvana Seidel Menchi and Diego Quaglioni, 417–41. Bologna: il Mulino, 2004.

Garin, Eugenio. "L'umanesimo italiano e la cultura ebraica." In *Storia d'Italia*, Annali 11, *Gli ebrei in Italia, i: Dall'alto Medioevo all'età dei ghetti*, edited by Corrado Vivanti, 361–83. Turin: Einaudi, 1996.

Gasperoni, Michaël. "I banchieri ebrei nel Ducato di Urbino tra Cinque e Seicento." In *Gli ebrei nello Stato della Chiesa. Insediamenti e mobilità (secoli xiv–xviii)*, edited by Marina Caffiero and Anna Esposito, 149–61. Padua: Esedra Editrice, 2012.

Gatti, Carlo. *Tra demografia e storia sociale. Gli ebrei di Trieste nel Settecento*. Trieste: Edizioni dell'Università di Trieste, 2008.

Goetschel, Roland. *La Cabbalà*. Florence: Giuntina, 1995.

Graizbord David L. *Souls in Dispute. Converso Identities in Iberia and the Jewish diaspora, 1580–1700*. Philadelphia: University of Pennsylvania Press, 2004.

Green, Abigail, and Simon Levis Sullam, eds. *Jews, Liberalism, Antisemitism. A Global History*. London: Palgrave Macmillan, 2020.

Groppi, Angela, ed. *Gli abitanti del ghetto di Roma. La Descriptio Hebreorum del 1733*. Rome: Viella, 2014.

Grünebaum-Ballin, Paul. *Joseph Naci duc de Naxos*. Paris-La Haye: Mouton, 1968.

Guetta, Alessandro. "Qabbalah e razionalismo nell'opera di Mošeh Hayyim Luzzatto." In *Ramhal. Pensiero ebraico e kabbalah tra Padova ed Eretz Israel*, edited by Gadi Luzzatto Voghera and Mauro Perani, 39–86. Padua: Esedra Editrice, 2010.

Harris, Alan Charles. "La demografia del ghetto in Italia (1516–1797 circa)." *La Rassegna Mensile di Israel* 33, 2–3 (1967): 1–16.

Idel, Moshe. "The Magical and Neoplatonic Interpretation of the Kabbalah in the Renaissance." In *Jewish Thought in the Sixteenth Century*, edited by Bernard Dov Cooperman, 186–242. Cambridge, MA: Harvard University Press, 1983.

Idel. "Major currents in Italian Kabbalah between 1560–1666." In *Italia Judaica. Gli ebrei in Italia tra Rinascimento ed età barocca*, Atti del ii convegno internazionale (Genova, 10–15 giugno 1984), 242–62. Rome: Ministero per i Beni Culturali e Ambientali, Pubblicazioni degli Archivi di Stato, 1986.

Idel. *Golem. Jewish Magical and Mystical Traditions on the Artificial Anthropoid*. Albany: State University of New York Press, 1990.

Idel. *Kabbalah in Italy, 1280–1510: A Survey.* New Haven, CT – London: Yale University Press, 2011.

Ioly Zorattini, Pier Cesare, ed. *Gli ebrei a Gorizia e a Trieste tra "ancien régime" ed emancipazione.* Udine: Del Bianco, 1984.

Ioly Zorattini. *Processi del S. Uffizio di Venezia contro ebrei e giudaizzanti, iv (1571–1580).* Florence: Olschki, 1985.

Ioly Zorattini, ed. *L'identità dissimulata. Giudaizzanti iberici nell'Europa cristiana dell'età moderna.* Florence: Olschki, 2000.

Ioly Zorattini. "Ancora sui giudaizzanti portoghesi di Ancona (1556): condanna e riconciliazione." *Zakhor. Rivista di storia degli ebrei d'Italia* 5 (2001–02): 39–51.

Ioly Zorattini. "Gracia Nasci alias Beatriz Mendes De Luna, la Señora." *Archivio Veneto*, 6, 6 (2013): 113–34.

Ioly Zorattini, Pier Cesare, and Arnaldo Morelli. "Modena, Leon." In *Dizionario biografico degli italiani*, 75, 193–200. Rome: Istituto dell'Enciclopedia Italiana, 2011.

Ioly Zorattini, Pietro. *I nomi degli altri. Conversioni a Venezia.* Florence: Olschki, 2008.

Israel, Jonathan I. *Gli ebrei d'Europa nell'età moderna (1550–1750).* Bologna: il Mulino, 1991 (originally published 1985).

Jacobs, Martin. "Joseph ha-Kohen, Paolo Giovio and Sixteenth-Century Historiography." In *Cultural Intermediaries: Jewish Intellectuals in Early Modern Italy*, edited by David B. Ruderman and Giuseppe Veltri, 67–85. Philadelphia: University of Pennsylvania Press, 2004.

Kaplan, Yosef. *Les nouveaux-juifs d'Amsterdam. Essais sur l'histoire sociale et intellectuelle du judaïsme séfarade au xviie siècle.* Paris: Chandeigne, 1999.

Katz, Jacob. *Jews and Freemasons in Europe. 1723–1934.* Cambridge, MA: Harvard University Press, 1970.

Katz. *Out of the Ghetto. The Social Background of Jewish Emancipation, 1770–1780.* Cambridge, MA: Harvard University Press, 1973.

Katz. *From Prejudice to Destruction: Anti-Semitism, 1700–1933.* Cambridge, MA: Harvard University Press, 1980.

Katz. *Tradition and Crisis: Jewish Society at the End of the Middle Ages.* New York: New York University Press, 1993.

Kertzer, David I. *Prigioniero del papa Re.* Milan: Rizzoli, 2005 (originally published 1997).

Kertzer. *Antisemitismo popolare e Inquisizione negli Stati pontifici, 1815–1858, with an introduction by Marina Caffiero.* Rome: Unione Internazionale degli Istituti di Archeologia Storia e Storia dell'Arte in Roma, 2006.

Laguna, Andres. *Avventure di uno schiavo dei Turchi*, edited by Cesare Acutis. Milan: Il Saggiatore, 1983.

Laras, Giuseppe. "Intorno al 'ius cazacà' nella storia del ghetto di Ancona." *Quaderni storici delle Marche* 3 (1968): 44–55.

Lattes, Andrea Yaakov. "Il Maggid di Ramhal: alcune osservazioni sul fenomeno delle rivelazioni mistiche diffuso in Italia." In *Ramhal: Pensiero ebraico e kabbalah tra Padova ed Eretz Israel*, edited by Gadi Luzzatto Voghera and Mauro Perani, 209–18. Padua: Esedra editrice, 2010.

Lavenia, Vincenzo. "'Tenere i malefici per cosa vera'. Esorcismi e censura nell'Italia moderna." In *Dal torchio alle fiamme. Inquisizione e censura: nuovi contributi dalla più antica Biblioteca Provinciale d'Italia*, edited by V. Bonani, 129–71. Salerno: Biblioteca Provinciale di Salerno, 2005.

Lavenia. "La lunga possessione. Il caso del monastero di Santa Grata di Bergamo, 1577–1625." In *"Non lasciar vivere la malefica". Le streghe nei trattati e nei processi (secoli xiv–xvii)*, edited by Dinora Corsi and Matteo Duni, 213–42. Florence: Firenze University Press, 2008.

Lirosi, Alessia "Monacare le ebree. Il monastero romano della Ss. Annunziata ai Pantani. Una ricerca in corso." *Rivista di Storia del Cristianesimo* 1 (2013): 147–80.

Lirosi. "'Ritener dette donne con tal temperamento'. Case pie e monasteri per il recupero delle ex prostitute a Roma nel Cinque e Seicento." *Analecta Augustiniana* 76 (2013): 153–208.

Livi, Livio. *Gli ebrei alla luce della statistica*. Florence: Vallecchi, 2 vols., 1920.

Luzzati, Michele. *Il ghetto ebraico. Storia di un popolo rinchiuso*. Florence: Giunti, 1987.

Luzzati. "Ruolo e funzione dei banchi ebraici dell'Italia centro-settentrionale nei secoli xv e xvi." In *Banchi pubblici, banchi privati e monti di pietà nell'Europa preindustriale. Amministrazione, tecniche operative e ruoli economici*, Atti della Società Ligure di Storia Patria, n.s. 31(cv), 1 and 2 (1991): 733–50.

Luzzati. "Banchi e insediamenti ebraici nell'Italia centro-settentrionale fra tardo Medioevo e inizi dell'Età moderna." In *Storia d'Italia*, Annali 11, *Gli ebrei in Italia, i: Dall'alto Medioevo all'età dei ghetti*, edited by Corrado Vivanti, 173–235. Turin: Einaudi, 1996.

Luzzati. *Ebrei ed ebraismo a Pisa. Un millennio di ininterrotta presenza*. Pisa: ETS, 2005.

Luzzatto Voghera, Gadi. *Il prezzo dell'eguaglianza. Il dibattito sull'emancipazione degli ebrei in Italia (1781–1848)*. Milan: Franco Angeli, 1998.

Luzzatto Voghera, Gadi, and Mauro Perani, eds. *Ramhal. Pensiero ebraico e kabbalah tra Padova ed Eretz Israel*. Padua: Esedra Editrice, 2010.

Maifreda, Germano. *I denari dell'Inquisitore. Affari e giustizia di fede nell'Italia moderna*. Turin: Einaudi, 2014.

Malkiel, David. "Ebraismo, tradizione e società: Isacco Lampronti e l'identità ebraica di Ferrara del xviii secolo." *Zakhor. Rivista di storia degli ebrei d'Italia* 8 (2005): 9–42.

Marcocci, Giuseppe. *I custodi dell'ortodossia. Inquisizione e Chiesa nel Portogallo del Cinquecento*. Rome: Edizioni di storia e letteratura, 2004.

Marcocci. "Itinerari marrani. I portoghesi a Livorno nei secoli dell'età moderna." In *Livorno 1606–1806. Luogo di incontro di popoli e culture*, edited by Adriano Prosperi, 405–17. Turin-London-Venice-New York: Umberto Allemandi & Co., 2009.

Marconcini, Samuela. "La Pia Casa dei catecumeni di Firenze." In *Le radici storiche dell'antisemitismo*, edited by Marina Caffiero, 107–27. Rome: Viella, 2009.

Marconcini. *Per amor del cielo. Farsi cristiani a Firenze tra Seicento e Settecento*. Florence: Firenze University Press, 2016.

Maternini Zotta, Maria Fausta. *L'ente comunitario ebraico. La legislazione degli ultimi due secoli*. Milan: Giuffrè, 1983.

Melasecchi, Olga, and Amedeo Spagnoletti, eds. *Antique Roman Ketubot: The marriage Contracts of the Jewish Community of Rome*, Catalog from the exhibit. Rome: Campisano Editore, 2018.

Meyrink, Gustav. *Il Golem*. Milan: Bompiani, 1966 (originally published 1914).

Miccoli, Giovanni. "La Santa Sede nella ii guerra mondiale: il problema dei "silenzi" di Pio xii." In *Tra mito della cristianità e secolarizzazione. Studi sul rapporto chiesa-società nell'Italia contemporanea*. Casale Monferrato: Marietti, 1985.

Miccoli. *Antisemitismo e cattolicesimo*. Brescia: Morcelliana, 2013.

Milano, Attilio. "I Capitoli di Daniel da Pisa e la comunità di Roma." *La Rassegna Mensile di Israel* 10, 9–10 (1935–36): 324–38, 409–26.

Milano. *Il ghetto di Roma. Illustrazioni storiche*. Rome: Staderini editore, 1964.

Milano. *Storia degli ebrei in Italia*. Turin: Einaudi, 1992 (originally published 1963).

Moretti, Massimo. "'Glauci coloris'. Gli ebrei nell'iconografia sacra di età moderna." In *Ebrei. Scambi e conflitti tra xv e xx secolo*, edited by Marina Caffiero. A monograph edition of *Roma moderna e contemporanea* 19, 1 (2011): 29–64.

Mori, Simona. "Lo Stato e gli ebrei mantovani nell'età delle riforme." In *La questione ebraica dall'Illuminismo all'Impero (1700–1815)*, edited by Paolo Alatri and Silvia Grassi, 209–34. Naples: Edizioni Scientifiche Italiane, 1994.

Mutini, Claudio. "Cebà, Ansaldo." In *Dizionario biografico degli italiani*, 23, 184–6. Rome: Istituto dell'Enciclopedia Italiana, 1979.

Muzzarelli, Maria Grazia. "Beatrice de Luna, vedova Mendes, alias Donna Grazia Nasi: un'ebrea influente (1510–1569 ca.)." In *Rinascimento al femminile*, edited by Ottavia Niccoli, 83–116. Roma-Bari: Laterza, 1991.

Naylor Pearson, Michael. *The Portuguese in India*. Cambridge: Cambridge University Press, 1987.

Nirenberg, David. *Anti-Judaism. The Western Tradition*. New York-London: Norton & Company, 2013.

Nissim, David. "Modernità di vedute in un nostro illuminista: Benedetto Frizzi e le sue opere." *La Rassegna Mensile di Israel*, 34, 5 (1968): 279–91.

Novoa, James W. Nelson. "Portugal in Rome: Glimpses of the Portuguese New Christians Representation in Rome through the Archivio di Stato di Roma." *Giornale di storia* 3 (2010): 1–14.

Novoa, James W. Nelson, and Susana Bastos Mateus. "The Case of New Christians in Lamego as an Example of Resistance against the Portuguese Inquisition in Sixteenth Century Portugal." *Hispania Judaica Bulletin* 6 (2008): 83–103.

Ottolenghi, Adolfo. "Il governo democratico di Venezia e l'abolizione del Ghetto." *La Rassegna Mensile di Israel* 5, 2 (1930–31): 88–104.

Paiva, José Pedro, with Giuseppe Marcocci. *História da Inquisição Portuguesa, 1536–1821*. Lisbon: Esfera dos Livros, 2013.

Parente, Fausto. "La Chiesa e il 'Talmud'. L'atteggiamento della Chiesa e del mondo cristiano nei confronti del "Talmud" e degli altri scritti rabbinici, con particolare riguardo all'Italia tra xv e xvi secolo." In *Storia d'Italia*, Annali 11, *Gli ebrei in Italia, i: Dall'alto Medioevo all'età dei ghetti*, edited by Corrado Vivanti, 580–91. Turin: Einaudi, 1996.

Parente. "The Index, The Holy Office, the Condemnation of the Talmud and the Publication of Clement VIII's Index." In *Church, Censorship and Culture in Early Modern Italy*, edited by Gigliola Fragnito, 164–94. Cambridge: Cambridge University Press, 2001.

Parente. "L'Église et le Talmud." In *Les Juifs et l'Église romaine à l'époque moderne (xve-xviiie siècle)*, 233–394. Paris: Honoré Champion, 2007.

Parente. "Cabbala." In *Dizionario storico dell'inquisizione, i*, edited by Adriano Prosperi *et al.*, 239–40. Pisa: Edizioni della Normale, 2010.

Parisi, Emanuela. "Mercanti e lavoranti della lana a Roma alla fine del Settecento. Conflitti, mobilità sociale e trasformazioni tecniche." *Dimensioni e problemi della ricerca storica* 1 (1994): 56–81.

Poliakov, Leon. *Storia dell'antisemitismo, iii: Da Voltaire a Wagner.* Florence: La Nuova Italia, 1976.

Popkin, Richard. "Les Caraïtes et l'emancipations des juifs." *Dix-huitième siècle* 13 (1981): 137–47.

Procaccia, Claudio. "Banchieri ebrei a Roma. Il credito su pegno in età moderna." In *Iudei de Urbe. Roma e i suoi ebrei: una storia secolare*, edited by Marina Caffiero and Anna Esposito, 155–79. Rome: Ministero per i Beni e le Attività Culturali-Direzione Generale per gli Archivi, 2011.

Procaccia, Micaela. "L''ape ingegnosa'. Debora Ascarelli, poetessa romana." *Rivista di Storia del Cristianesimo* 4, 2 (2007): 355–67.

Pullan, Brian. *The Jews of Europe and the Inquisition of Venice (1550–1670).* Oxford: Basil Blackwell, 1983.

Ravid, Benjamin. "A Tale of Three Cities and their Raison d'Etat. Ancona, Venice, Livorno and the Competition for Jewish Merchants in the Sixteenth Century." In *Jews, Christians and Muslims in the Mediterranean World after 1492*, edited by Alisa Meyuhas Ginio, 138–62. London: Cass, 1992.

Ravid. "From Yellow to Red. On the Distinguishing Head Covering of the Jews of Venice." *Jewish History* 6, 1–2 (1992): 179–210.

Ravid. "The Venetian Government and the Jews." In *The Jews of Early Modern Venice*, edited by Robert C. Davis, and Benjamin Ravid, 3–30. Baltimore, MD – London: The Johns Hopkins University Press, 2001.

Ravid. "'Cum nimis absurdum' and the Ancona Auto-da-Fé revisited: Their Impact on Venice and Some Wider Reflections." *Jewish History* 26 (2012): 85–100.

Révah, Israel Salvador. "Les marranes portugais et l'Inquisition au xvi siècle." In *Études Portugaises*, 185–232. Paris: Fundação Calouste Gulbenkian-Centro Cultural Português, 1975.

Revel, Jacques. "Les corps et communautés." In *The French Revolution and the Creation of Modern Political Culture, i, The Political Culture of the Old Regime*, edited by Keith Michael Baker, 225–42. Oxford – New York: Pergamon Press, 1987.

Ricci, Saverio. *Il sommo inquisitore. Giulio Antonio Santori tra autobiografia e storia (1532–1602).* Rome: Salerno Editrice, 2002.

Rocciolo, Domenico. "Documenti sui catecumeni e neofiti a Roma nel Seicento e Settecento." *Ricerche per la storia religiosa di Roma* 10 (1998): 391–452.

Romani, Marina, ed. *Storia economica e storia degli ebrei. Istituzioni, capitale sociale e stereotipi (secc. XV–XVIII).* Milan: Franco Angeli, 2017.

Romeo, Giovanni. *Inquisitori, esorcisti e streghe nell'Italia della Controriforma.* Florence: Sansoni, 1990.

Romeo. *Esorcisti, confessori e sessualità femminile nell'Italia della Controriforma.* Florence: Le Lettere, 1998.

Roth, Cecil. "Some Revolutionary Purims (1799–1801)." *Hebrew Union College Annual* 10, (1935): 451–82.

Roth. *The House of Nasi: the Duke of Naxos*, Philadelphia, PA: Jewish Publication Society in America, 1948.

Roth. *Storia dei Marrani. L'odissea degli "ebrei invisibili" dall'Inquisizione ai nostri giorni.* Milan: Serra e Riva, 1991 (originally published 1932).

Rozen, Minna. *A History of the Jewish Community in Istanbul. The Formative Years, 1543–1566.* Leiden – Boston, MA: Brill, 2002.

Ruderman, David B., ed. *Essential Papers on Jewish Culture in Renaissance and Baroque Italy.* New York: Columbia University Press, 1992.

Rudt de Collenberg, Wipertus Hugo. "Le baptême de juifs de Rome de 1614 à 1798 selon les registres de la 'Casa dei Catecumeni'." *Archivum historiae pontificiae* 24 (1986): 91–231; 25 (1987): 105–261; 26 (1988): 119–294.

Ruspio, Federica. *La Nazione portoghese. Ebrei ponentini e nuovi cristiani a Venezia.* Turin: Silvio Zamorani, 2007.

Russell-Wood, Anthony John R. *The Portuguese Empire. 1415–1808: A World on the Move.* Baltimore, MD – London: The Johns Hopkins University Press, 1998.

Salvadori, Roberto G. *1799: gli ebrei italiani nella bufera antigiacobina.* Florence: Giuntina, 1999.

Schechter, Roland. "Translating the 'Marseillaise': Biblical Republicanism and the Emancipation of Jews in Revolutionary France." *Past and Present* 143 (1994): 108–35.

Scholem, Gershom. *Kabbalah.* New York: Meridian, 1974.

Scholem. *La Kabbalah e il suo simbolismo.* Turin: Einaudi, 1980 (originally published 1965).

Scholem. *Le grandi correnti della mistica ebraica.* Turin: Einaudi, 1993 (originally published 1941).

Schwarzfuchs, Simon "Les communautés italiennes et le Consistoire centrale (1808–1815). Un inventaire de leur correspondence." *Michael: On the History of the Jews in the Diaspora,* 1 (1972): 109–62.

Schwarzfuchs. *Napoleon, the Jews and the Sanhedrin.* London – Boston, MA – Henley: Routledge & Kegan Paul, 1979.

Schwarzfuchs. "Les nations juives de France." *Dix-huitième siècle,* Juifs et Judaïsme, 13 (1981): 127–36.

Secret, François. *Les kabbalistes chrétiens de la Renaissance.* Paris: Dunod, 1964.

Segre, Renata, ed. *The Jews in Piedmont (1297–1798).* Jerusalem: The Israel Academy of Sciences and Humanities and Tel Aviv University, 3 vols., 1986–90.

Segre. "Gli ebrei piemontesi nell'età dell'assolutismo." In *Italia Judaica. Gli ebrei dalla segregazione alla prima emancipazione,* Atti del iii Convegno internazionale (Tel Aviv, 15–20 giugno 1986), 67–80. Rome: Ministero per i Beni Culturali e Ambientali, Pubblicazioni degli Archivi di Stato, 1989.

Segre. "La Controriforma: espulsioni, conversioni, isolamento." In *Storia d'Italia,* Annali 11, *Gli ebrei in Italia, i: Dall'alto Medioevo all'età dei ghetti,* edited by Corrado Vivanti, 745–7. Turin: Einaudi, 1996.

Segre. "La formazione di una comunità marrana: i portoghesi a Ferrara." In *Storia d'Italia,* Annali 11, *Gli ebrei in Italia, i: Dall'alto Medioevo all'età dei ghetti,* edited by Corrado Vivanti, 779–841. Turin: Einaudi, 1996.

Sermoneta, Giuseppe. "Una vertenza tra i circoncisori e la confraternita dei compari nella Roma ebraica del primo Ottocento." *Annuario di studi ebraici* 11 (1988): 215–70.

Sestieri, Lea. *David Reubenì. Un ebreo d'Arabia in missione segreta nell'Europa.* Genoa: Marietti, 1991.

Settimi, Pia. *La donna e le sue regole. Ebraismo e condizione femminile tra xvi e xvii secolo.* Rome: Vecchiarelli, 2009.

Siegmund, Stefanie. "La vita nei ghetti." In *Storia d'Italia*, Annali 11, *Gli ebrei in Italia, i: Dall'alto Medioevo all'età dei ghetti*, edited by Corrado Vivanti, 845–92. Turin: Einaudi, 1996.

Siegmund. *The Medici State and the Ghetto of Florence: The Construction of an Early Modern Jewish Community*. Stanford, CA: Stanford University Press, 2005.

Silvera, Miriam, ed. *Momenti di storia della medicina ebraica*. Rome: Carocci, 2012.

Simonsohn, Shlomo. *The Jews in the Duchy of Mantua*. Jerusalem: Kiryath Sepher, 2 vols., 1962–64.

Simonsohn. *The Jews in the Duchy of Milan (1397–1768)*. Jerusalem: Israel National Academy of Sciences, 4 vols., 1982–86.

Simonsohn. *The Apostolic See and the Jews. Documents 1522–1538*. Toronto: Pontifical Institute of Mediaeval Studies, 1990.

Simonsohn. "La condizione giuridica degli ebrei nell'Italia centrale e settentrionale (secoli xii–xiv)." In *Storia d'Italia*, Annali 11, *Gli ebrei in Italia, i: Dall'alto Medioevo all'età dei ghetti*, edited by Corrado Vivanti, 97–120. Turin: Einaudi, 1996.

Sofia, Francesca. "Il tema del confronto e dell'inclusione. Il Sinedrio napoleonico." In *Le religioni e il mondo moderno, ii: Ebraismo*, edited by Giovanni Filoramo and David Bidussa, 103–24. Turin: Einaudi, 2008.

Sonnino, Guido. "Gli ebrei a Livorno nell'ultimo decennio del secolo xviii." *La Rassegna Mensile di Israel* 12, 1–2 (1937–38): 22–55.

Sori, Ercole. "Una 'comunità crepuscolare': Ancona tra Otto e Novecento." In *La presenza ebraica nelle Marche. Secoli xiii-xx*, edited by Sergio Anselmi and Viviana Bonazzoli. A monographic edition of *Proposte e Ricerche* 14 (1993): 198–9.

Sorkin, David. *Jewish Emancipation: A History Across Five Centuries*. Princeton, NJ: Princeton University Press, 2019.

Stefani, Piero. *L'Antigiudaismo. Storia di un'idea*. Roma-Bari: Laterza, 2004.

Stow, Kenneth. "Prossimità o distanza: etnicità, sefarditi e assenza di conflitti etnici nella Roma del sedicesimo secolo." In *Oltre il 1492*. A monograph edition of *La Rassegna Mensile d'Israel* 58, 1–2 (1992): 61–74.

Stuczynski, Claude B. "Marranesimo." In *Dizionario storico dell'inquisizione, ii*, edited by Adriano Prosperi et al., 989–97. Pisa: Edizioni della Normale, 2010.

Subrahmanyam, Sanjay. *The Portuguese Empire in Asia, 1500–1700: A Political and Economic History*. London – New York: Longman, 1993 (2nd ed. Chichester: Wiley-Blackwell, 2012).

Subrahmanyam. *From Tagus to the Ganges: Explorations in Connected History*. New York – Oxford: Oxford University Press, 2 vols., 2004.

Subrahmanyam. *Three Ways to be Alien. Travails and Encounters in the Early Modern World*. Waltham, MA: Brandeis University Press, 2011.

Subrahmanyam. *Mondi connessi. La storia oltre l'eurocentrismo (secoli xvi–xviii)*, edited by Giuseppe Marcocci. Rome: Carocci, 2014.

Tamani, Giuliano, ed. "Gershom Soncino/Hieronymus Soncino." In *L'attività editoriale di Gershom Soncino, 1502–1527*, Atti del convegno (Soncino, 17 settembre 1995), 1–7. Soncino: Edizioni dei Soncino, 1997.

Toaff, Ariel. *Gli ebrei a Perugia*. Perugia: Deputazione di storia patria per l'Umbria, 1975.

Toaff. "Ebrei spagnoli e marrani nell'Italia ebraica del '500. Una presenza contestata." In *Oltre il 1492*, A monograph edition of *La Rassegna Mensile di Israel*, 58, 1–2 (1992): 47–60.

Toaff. *The Jews in Umbria*. The Hague: Brill, 3 vols., 1994.

Toaff. "Gli insediamenti askenaziti nell'Italia settentrionale." In *Storia d'Italia*, Annali 11, *Gli ebrei in Italia, i: Dall'alto Medioevo all'età dei ghetti*, edited by Corrado Vivanti, 159–65. Turin: Einaudi, 1996.

Toaff, Renzo. *La Nazione ebrea a Livorno e a Pisa (1591–1700)*. Florence: Olschki, 1990.

Todeschini, Giacomo. *Visibilmente crudeli. Malviventi, persone sospette e gente qualunque dal Medioevo all'età moderna*. Bologna: il Mulino, 2007.

Todeschini. *La banca e il ghetto. Una storia italiana (secoli XIV-XVI)*. Roma – Bari: Laterza, 2016.

Todeschini. *Gli ebrei nell'Italia medievale*. Rome: Carocci, 2018.

Tollet, Daniel, ed. *Les Églises et le Talmud. Ce que les chrétiens savaient du judaïsme (xvie-xixe siècles)*. Paris: PUPS, 2006.

Tommasino, Pier Mattia. *L'Alcorano di Macometto. Storia di un libro del Cinquecento europeo*. Bologna: il Mulino, 2013.

Toscano, Mario. *Ebraismo e Antisemitismo in Italia. Dal 1848 alla Guerra dei sei giorni*. Milan: Franco Angeli, 2003.

Trachtenberg, Joshua. *The Devil and the Jews: The Medieval Conception of the Jew and Its Relation to Modern Anti-Semitism*. New Haven, CT: Yale University Press, 1943 (reprinted New York: Harper & Row, 1966).

Trachtenberg. *Jewish Magic and Superstition. A Study in Folk Religion*. Philadelphia: University of Pennsylvania Press, 2008 (originally published 1939).

Trivellato, Francesca. *The Familiarity of Strangers. The Sephardic Diaspora, Livorno, and Cross-Cultural Trade in the Early Modern Period*. New Haven, CT: Yale University Press, 2009.

Trivellato. *The Promise and Peril of Credit: What a Forgotten Legend About Jews and Finance Tells Us About the Making of European Commercial Society*. Princeton, NJ: Princeton University Press, 2019.

Urbani, Rossana. "Nuovi documenti sulla formazione della 'nazione' ebrea nel genovesato durante il xvii secolo." In *Italia Judaica, Gli ebrei in Italia tra Rinascimento ed età barocca*, Atti del ii Convegno internazionale (Genova, 10–15 giugno 1984), 193–209. Rome: Ministero per i Beni Culturali e Ambientali, Pubblicazioni degli Archivi di Stato, 1986.

Veronese, Alessandra. "La presenza ebraica nel ducato di Urbino nel Quattrocento." In *Italia Judaica. Gli ebrei nello Stato pontificio fino al Ghetto (1555)*, Atti del vi Convegno internazionale (Tel Aviv, 18–22 giugno 1995), 251–8. Rome: Ministero per i Beni Culturali e Ambientali, Pubblicazioni degli Archivi di Stato, 1998.

Veronese. *Gli ebrei nel Medioevo*. Rome: Jouvence, 2010.

Veltri, Giuseppe. *Filosofo e rabbino nella Venezia del Seicento. Studi su Simone Luzzatto con documenti inediti dall'Archivio di Stato di Venezia*. Rome: Aracne, 2015.

Wachtel, Nathan. *La fede del ricordo. Ritratti e itinerari di marrani in America (xvi–xx secolo)*. Turin: Einaudi, 2003 (originally published 2001).

Wachtel. *Entre Moïse et Jésus. Études marranes (xve-xxie siècle)*. Paris: CNRS Éditions, 2013.

Weinstein, Roni. *Marriage Rituals Italian Style: A Historical Anthropological Perspective on Early Modern Italian Jews*. Leiden – Boston, MA: Brill, 2004.

Weinstein. *Kabbalah and Jewish Modernity*. Oxford: The Littman Library of Jewish Civilization in association with Liverpool University Press, 2016.

Yates, Frances Amelia. *Cabbala e occultismo nell'età elisabettiana*. Torino: Einaudi, 1982 (originally published 1979).

Yerushalmi, Yosef Hayim. "Clio and the Jews: Reflections on the Jewish Historiography in the Sixteenth Century." *Proceedings of the American Academy for Jewish Research* 46–47 (1979–80): 607–38.

Yerushalmi. *Dalla corte al ghetto. La vita, le opere, le peregrinazioni del marrano Cardoso nell'Europa del Seicento.* Milan: Garzanti, 1991 (originally published 1971).

Yerushalmi. *Assimilazione e antisemitismo razziale: i modelli iberico e tedesco.* Florence: Giuntina, 2010 (originally published 1998).

Yerushalmi. *Zakhor. Storia ebraica e memoria ebraica.* Florence: Giuntina, 2011 (originally published 1982).

Yerushalmi. *"Servitori di re e non servitori di servitori". Alcuni aspetti della storia politica degli ebrei.* Florence: Giuntina, 2013 (originally published 2005).

Zazzu, Guido Nathan. *Sepharad addio. 1492: i profughi ebrei dalla Spagna al "ghetto" di Genova.* Genoa: Marietti, 1991.

Zemon Davis, Natalie. "Fama e riservatezza: la "Vita" di Leone Modena come autobiografia della prima età moderna." *Quaderni storici* 64, 22, 1 (1987): 39–60.

Zemon Davis. "Glikl bas Yehudah Leib. Discutere con Dio." In *Donne ai margini. Tre vite del xvii secolo, edited by Natalie Zemon Davis,* 7–66. Roma-Bari: Laterza, 1996.

Index

Note: *Italic* page numbers refer to figures and page numbers followed by "n" denote endnotes.